WORKING CAPITAL MANAGEMENT

Working Capital Management

Theory and Practice

Dr. P. Periasamy

Author

First Edition : 2005
Reprint : 2007, 2009, 2010
Second Revised Edition : 2012
Reprint : 2016, 2019
Reprint : 2022

Published by : Mrs. Meena Pandey for **Himalaya Publishing House Pvt. Ltd.,**
"Ramdoot", Dr. Bhalerao Marg, Girgaon, Mumbai - 400 004.
Phone: 022-23860170, 23863863; **Fax:** 022-23877178
E-mail: himpub@bharatmail.co.in; **Website:** www.himpub.com

Branch Offices :

New Delhi : "Pooja Apartments", 4-B, Murari Lal Street, Ansari Road, Darya Ganj, New Delhi - 110 002. Phone: 011-23270392, 23278631; Fax: 011-23256286

Nagpur : Kundanlal Chandak Industrial Estate, Ghat Road, Nagpur - 440 018. Phone: 0712-2721215, 2721216

Bengaluru : Plot No. 91-33, 2nd Main Road, Seshadripuram, Behind Nataraja Theatre, Bengaluru - 560 020. Phone: 080-41138821; Mobile: 09379847017, 09379847005

Hyderabad : No. 3-4-184, Lingampally, Besides Raghavendra Swamy Matham, Kachiguda, Hyderabad - 500 027. Phone: 040-27560041, 27550139

Chennai : New No. 48/2, Old No. 28/2, Ground Floor, Sarangapani Street, T. Nagar, Chennai - 600 017. Mobile: 09380460419

Pune : "Laksha" Apartment, First Floor, No. 527, Mehunpura, Shaniwarpeth (Near Prabhat Theatre), Pune - 411 030. Phone: 020-24496323, 24496333; Mobile: 09370579333

Lucknow : House No. 731, Shekhupura Colony, Near B.D. Convent School, Aliganj, Lucknow - 226 022. Phone: 0522-4012353; Mobile: 09307501549

Ahmedabad : 114, "SHAIL", 1st Floor, Opp. Madhu Sudan House, C.G. Road, Navrang Pura, Ahmedabad - 380 009. Phone: 079-26560126; Mobile: 09377088847

Cuttack : Plot No 5F-755/4, Sector-9, CDA Market Nagar, Cuttack - 753 014, Odisha. Mobile: 09338746007

Kolkata : 108/4, Beliaghata Main Road, Near ID Hospital, Opp. SBI Bank, Kolkata - 700 010. Phone: 033-32449649; Mobile: 07439040301

Printed at : Infinity Imaging System, New Delhi. On behalf of HPH.

PREFACE TO THE FIRST EDITION

A Study of working capital is of major importance of internal and external analysis because of its relationship with the current day to day operations. The present text of working capital management has been designed as per the syllabi of working capital management paper of most of the MBA; MIB (International Business) and other professional courses of different Universities. The basic purpose of this book is to assist the reader to develop through understanding the concepts, principles, techniques and theories underlying working capital management in a systematic way.

The book is highly useful for teachers, executives and students of Management, Commerce, International Business, Banking and Public Administration.

I am very much thankful to Shri D.P. Pandey, Shri Niraj Pandey and Shri K. Sivadasan, Area Manager of Himalaya Publishing House, Mumbai for bring out this book in a very short span of time.

I express my sincere gratitude to my wife Mrs. P. Fatima Mary, my daughters P. Nancy and P. Roscy for having put with the inconveniences caused during preparation of this book.

Dr. P. Periasamy

CONTENTS

Chapter *Pages*

Chapter

WORKING CAPITAL MANAGEMENT— Nature and Scope

Introduction

A study of working capital is of major importance of internal and external analysis because of its relationship with the current day to day operations of business. Funds, collected from different sources are invested in the business for the acquisition of assets. These assets are employed for earning revenue. The basic problem facing the finance manager of an enterprise is to trade off between conflicting but equally important goals of liquidity and profitability. The greater the liquid resources of the firm, the lesser will be its profitability and vice verse. The firm has to maintain the working capital at such level as may ensure satisfying earnings to the enterprise without jeopardizing its liquid position. Thus, working capital management is concerned with the problems that arise in attempting to discuss in details various tools and techniques which can be gainfully employed to solve the problem of determining optimum level of working capital.

Definition

In order to maintain flow of revenue from operations, every firm needs certain amount of current assets. For example, funds required either to pay for expenses or to meet obligations for service received or goods purchased etc by a firm. These funds are known as working capital.

Working capital is defined as the "excess of current assets over current liabilities and provisions". That is, the amount of surplus of current assets which remain after deducting current liabilities from total current assets which is equal to the amount invested in working capital consisting of work-is-progress, raw materials and component stocks, consumable items amounts owing by customers and cash at the or bank in hand.

According to shubin define working capital is the amount of funds necessary for the cost of operating the enterprise. Working capital in a going concern is a revolving fund, it consist of cash receipts from sales which are used to cover the cost of operation.

According to Hoagland define working capital is descriptive of that capital which is not fixed. But the more common use of working capital is to consider it as the difference between the book value of the current assets and the current liabilities.

In Accounting working capital is the different between the inflow and outflow of funds. In other words, it is the net cash inflow. Working capital is also known as Circulating Capital, Fluctuating Capital and Revolving Capital. The magnitude and composition keep on changing continuously in the course of business.

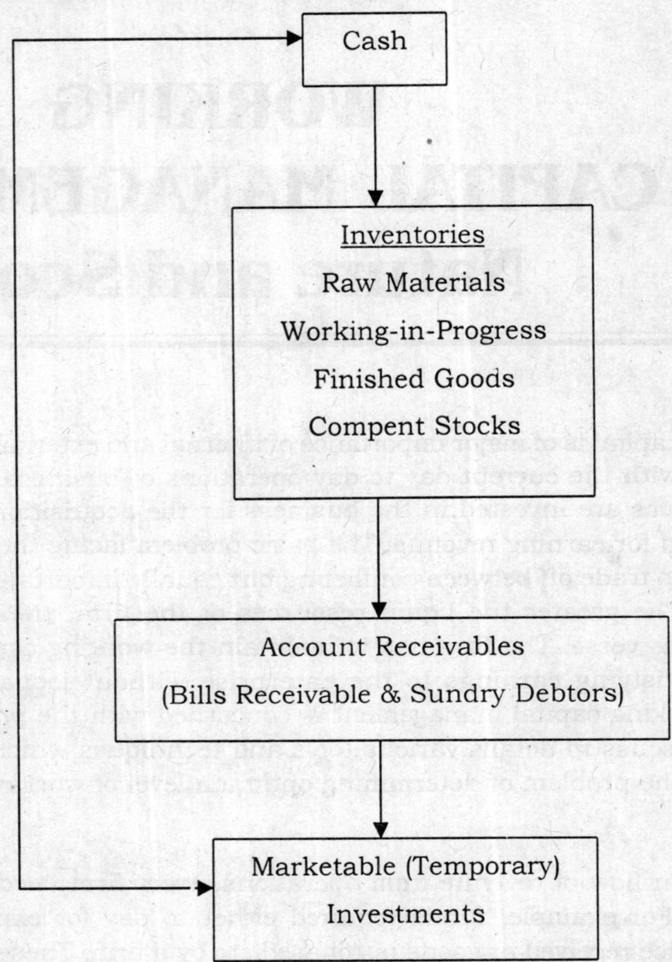

Fig. 1.1 : Circulating of Current Assets.

From the above chart, we can observed that circulating capital indicates the current assets of a company that are changed in the ordinary course of business from one from to another *i.e.*, from cash to inventories, inventories to accounts receivable, account receivables to marketable investment and marketable investments into cash. It can be explain it into the following ways also :

Cash Realized from

Stage : I – Closing stock of raw materials → converted into work-in-progress → converted into finished goods → sold in the market.

Stage : II – Closing stock of work-in-progress → converted into finished goods → sold in the market.

Stage : III – Closing stock of finished goods → sold in the market.

Stage : IV – Credit sales → Accounts Receivables (Bills Receivable and Sundry Debtors) → collection from book debts (Debtors).

Stage : V – Marketable (Temporary) Investments → Sold in the market.

Stage : VI – Cash in hand and Cash at bank.

Components of Working Capital

In a narrow sense, the term working capital refers to the net working capital. Net working capital is the excess of current assets over current liabilities. It can be expressed as :

Net Working Capital = Current Assets – Current Liabilities

Current assets refer to those assets which in the ordinary course of business can be, or will be, turned in to cash with in one year without under going a diminution in value and without disruping the operations of the firm. On the other hand, current liabilities are those liabilities which are intended at their inception to be paid in the ordinary course of business, with in a year, out of the current assets or earnings of the concern.

The components of current assets and current liabilities are listed below :

Current Assets	*Current Liabilities*
Sundry Debtors	Sundry Creditors
Bills Receivable	Bills Payable
Cash and Bank Balances	Advance Payments
Short Term Investments	Short term Borrowings
Inventories :	Bank Overdraft
Raw Materials and Components	Dividend Payable
Work-in-progress	Accured or Outstanding Expenses
Finished goods	Provision for taxation
Accured or Outstanding Income	Dividends Unclaimed Acceptances
Marketable Securities	
Loan and advances extended for a short period of time.	

Charactertics of Current Assets

Important charactertics of current assets are:

(1) Shorter life period

(2) Swift transformation into other assets form

(3) Easily convertible into cash

(4) Nature of repetitive and frequent

(5) Substantial portion of total investment

(6) Depends upon the changes in the level of business activities

(7) Indicator of the nature of financial planning

(8) Reveals the creditworthiness of the firm

(9) Current asset is identified as working capital

Need for Working Capital

Working Capital is significant because of:

(1) Adequate working capital is required to continue uninterrupted business operations

(2) It is essential to run the day to day business activities

(3) Greater volume of working capital required to invest in current assets for the success of sales activities

(4) To ensure the maximizing the wealth of the firm

(5) To enable to increase the rate of return on investment

(6) To meet the short-term obligations of a business enterprise

(7) To increase the operational efficiency of a firm

(8) To utilize the maximum available resources

(9) To earn considerable profits

Operating Cycle

The term operating cycle otherwise known as "Cash Cycle". In order to earn sufficient profits, a firm has to depend on its sales activities apart from others. We know that sales are not always converted into cash immediately, *i.e.*, there is a time—lag between the sale of a product and the realization of cash. The continuing flow from cash to suppliers, to investors, to account receivable and back in cash. The time gap is technically termed as operating cycle. In other words, the duration of time required to complete the following sequence of events, in case of a manufacturing firm, is called the operating cycle.

(1) Conversion of cash into raw materials

(2) Conversion of raw materials into work-in-progress

(3) Conversion of work-in-progress into finished goods

(4) Conversion of finished goods into accounts receivable and

(5) Conversion of accounts receivable into cash.

This cycle will be repeated again and again. The operation cycle of manufacturing business can be shown as in the following chart:

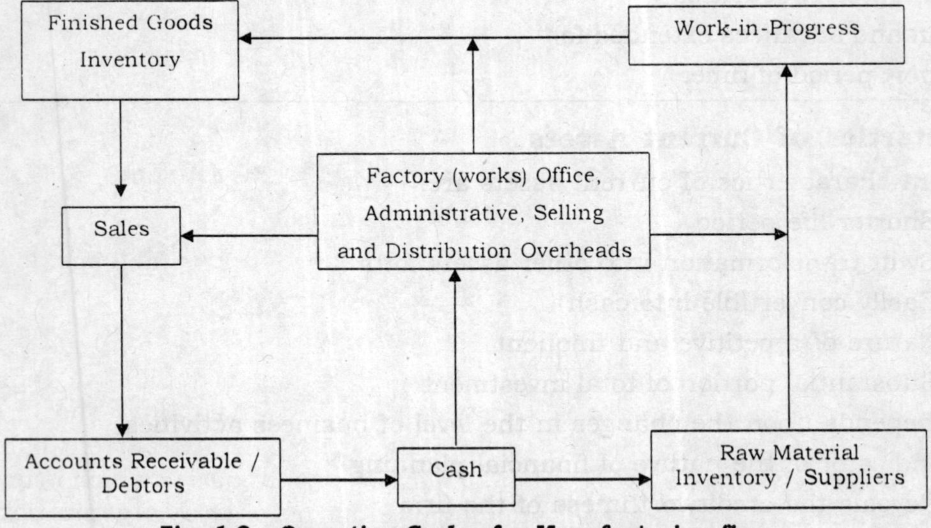

Fig. 1.2 : Operating Cycle of a Manufacturing firm.

From the above chart, we can observed that the firm's liquidity of a manufacturing firm depends an operating cycle involved into the conversion process from raw materials into finished goods and then sales into cash.

In the case of non-manufacturing firm, the operating cycle will include the length of time required to convert:

(a) Cash into inventories;

(b) Inventories into accounts receivable;

(c) Accounts receivable into cash.

In the case of service and financial concerns may not have any inventory at all. Thus, the operating cycle include the length of time taken for direct conversion of cash into debtors and then into cash.

Types of Working Capital

The Working Capital admits the following broad classifications :

I. Gross Working Capital

II. Net Working Capital

(a) Positive Net Working Capital

(b) Negative Net Working Capital

III. Permanent Working Capital

IV. Temporary Working Capital

V. Balance Sheet Working Capital

VI. Cash Working Capital

I. Gross Working Capital : The term Gross Working Capital refers to the total of all current assets. In other words, the firm's investments in total current or circulating assets. Current assets are the assets which can be converted into cash with in the accounting year. It represents short term securities, sundry debtors, bills receivable, stock (inventories) etc. The Gross concept of working capital is very suited to company organization where ownership is separated from management and control.

Advantages of Gross Working Capital : Gross Working Capital is the amount of funds invested in the various components of current assets. This concept has the following advantages :

(1) It provides the amount of working capital at the right time.

(2) It enables a firm to realize the greatest return on its investment.

(3) It helps in the fixing of various financial responsibility.

(4) It helps to the top executives to make plan and control funds and to maximize the return on investment.

(5) It enables a firm to operate its business more efficiently.

II. Net Working Capital : The net concept of working capital is qualitative, indicating the firm's ability to meet its operating expenses and current liability. The term Net Working Capital refers to the difference between current assets and current liabilities. Alternatively, it can be defined as the portion of a firm's current assets which is financed with long term funds. This concept is commonly used for proprietary organization such as sole trader and partnership firms. Net working capital can be grouped into "Positive Net Working Capital and Negative Net Working Capital". Net Working Capital can be expressed as:

Net Working Capital	=	Current Assets – Current Liabilities
Current Assets	=	Cash + Marketable Securities + Accounting Receivables + Notes and Bills Receivables + Inventories
Current Liabilities	=	Accounts Payable + Notes and Bills + Outstanding Expenses + Short Term Loans

"Positive net working capital" will arise when the excess of current assets over the current liabilities. On the other hand, where the current liabilities and provisions exceed current assets, the difference is referred to as "negative working capital" and is disastrous for the company.

Difference between Net Working Capital and Gross Working Capital

Net Working Capital	*Gross Working Capital*
(1) Net working capital is the concept of qualitative nature.	(1) Gross concept of working capital is quantitative nature.
(2) It is indicating the firm's ability to meet its operating expenses and current liability.	(2) It is pointing out the total amount available for financing the current assets.
(3) It expressed as current assets minus current liability.	(3) It indicating the total sum of current assets.
(4) It is a concept very popular in accounting system.	(4) It is a concept very popular in financial management circles.
(5) Net concept suitable for sole Trader and partnership firms.	(5) Gross concept suitable for companies.
(6) It is useful to find out the true financial financial position of a company.	(6) It can not reveal the true financial position of a company.
(7) Increase in bank loan can not increase working capital. Retained profits, sale of fixed assets will increase net working capital.	(7) Every increase in borrowing will increase the gross working capital. Under net concept, no change in working capital.

III. Permanent Working Capital : The minimum amount of current assets which are kept by a firm over the entire year to ensure uninterrupted course of operation. The minimum level of current asset is referred to as permanent working capital. It is also termed as Regular Working Capital or Core Working Capital or Fixed Working Capital. It may be noted that this amount of fixed working capital various from year to year, depending upon the changes in production and sales as a result of seasonal changes.

Charactertics of Permanent Working Capital : Permanent Working Capital has the following charactertics :

(1) Continue to exist for a longer period of time is the business activities.

(2) Constantly changes in the business from one asset to another.

(3) Required to meet permanent obligations along with other fixed assets.

(4) Grows the size or volume of business operations.

(5) Classified on the basis of the time factor.

(6) Minimum level of working capital always required to be maintained.

(7) Depends on the nature of operating cycle of the firm.

IV. Temporary Working Capital : Any amount over and above the permanent level of working is Temporary or Fluctuating or Variable Working Capital. In other worlds, it represents additional current assets required to meet fluctuations during the operating year. As it fluctuates according to the level of operation, it is termed as Fluctuating Working Capital. For example, due to seasonal variation/fluctuation, investment in inventories will fluctuate or fall. Practically, temporary working capital is required to meet the liquidity requirements for short term obligations.

Charactertics of Temporary Working Capital : The following are the charactertics of temporary working capital:

(1) It is an extra working capital needed to changing production and sales activities.

(2) It is created to meet liquidity requirements.

(3) Temporary working capital is fluctuating during the operating period.

(4) It fluctuates according to the level of operations.

(5) It is needed for shorter period.

The difference between the nature of permanent and temporary working capital can better be represented with the help of following diagram:

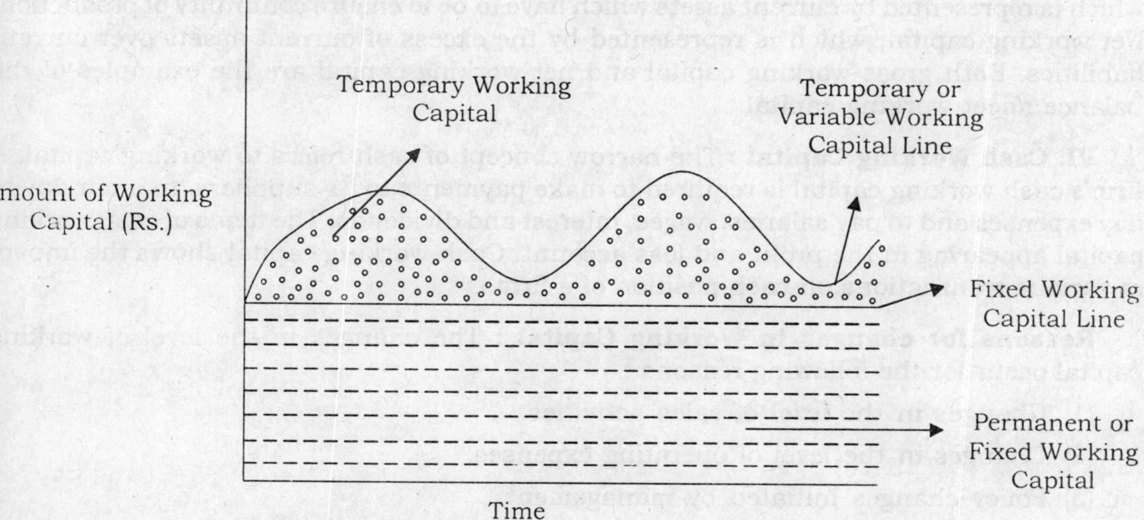

Fig. 1.3(A) : Permanent and Temporary working capital.

It is quiet clear from the figure A, that permanent working capital level is constant, while temporary working capital is fluctuating *i.e.*, sometimes increasing or sometimes decreasing according to the situation.

For a growing/expanding firm, the permanent working capital line may not be horizontal when the firm's requirement for permanent working capital increasing or decreasing over the period. In other words, the permanent working capital is increasing over a activity. Thus, the difference between the permanent and temporary working capital can be projected in figure B :

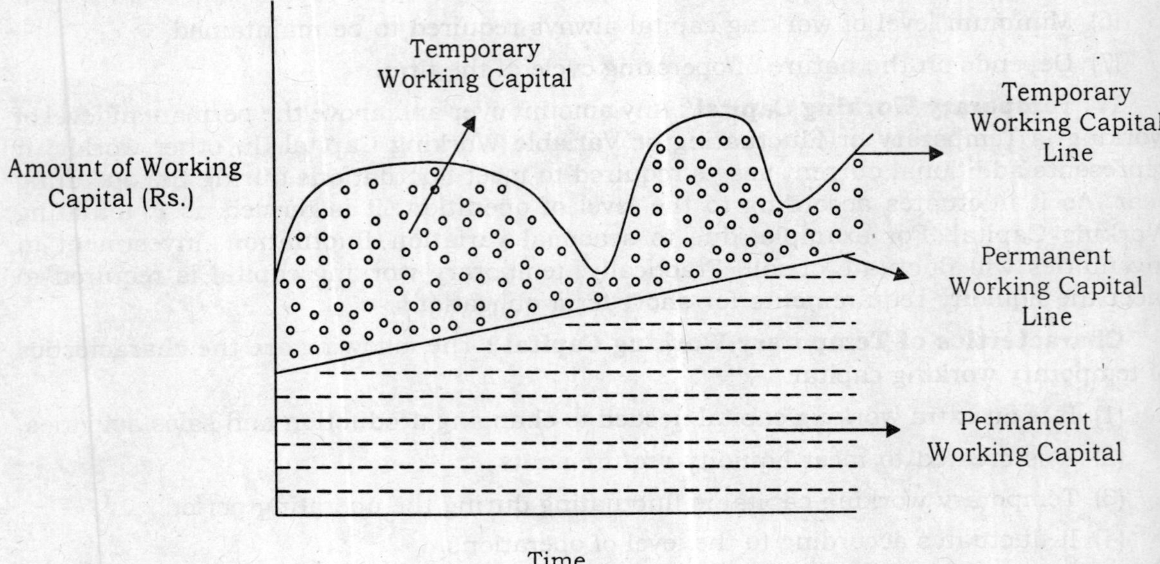

Fig. 1.3(B) : B. Permanent and Temporary Working Capital.

V. Balance Sheet Working Capital : The balance sheet working capital is one which is calculated from the items appearing in the Balance sheet. Gross working capital which is represented by current assets which have to be to ensure continuity of production Net working capital, which is represented by the excess of current assets over current liabilities. Both gross working capital and net working capital are the examples of the balance sheet working capital.

VI. Cash Working Capital : The narrow concept of cash refers to working capital. A firm's cash working capital is required to make payments to its suppliers, to incur day to day expenses and to pay salaries, wages, interest and dividends. The items of cash working capital appearing in the profit and loss account. Cash working capital shows the impact of various transactions on cash position of a firm.

Reasons for changes in Working Capital : The changes in the level of working capital occur for the following reasons :

(1) Changes in the level of sales activities.

(2) Changes in the level of operating expenses.

(3) Policy changes initiated by management.

(4) Technological changes.

(5) Cyclical changes in the economy.

(6) Changes in operating cycle.

(7) Source of change is seasonality in sales activity.

(8) Changes in the fixing the level of inventory and receivables.

Dangers of Excess Working Capital

The success and otherwise of a business depends on the adequacy of the said capital maintaining a desired level. Both excessive or inadequate working capital poses a serious problem to a company which may even lead to its doom. Excessive working capital means idle funds which earn no profits for the firm. Inadequate working capital impairs firm's profitability and liquidity. When working capital is excessive, a firm faces the following problems :

(1) It leads to unnecessary purchase and accumulation of inventories.

(2) Excessive working capital results in imbalance between liquidity and profitability

(3) It is an indication of defective credit policy

(4) A company may not be tempted to overtrade and lose heavily.

(5) Excessive working capital leads to operational inefficiency because large volume of funds not being used productively.

(6) This makes management complacent which degenerates into managerial inefficiency.

(7) High liquidity may induce a firm to under take great production which may not have a matching demand.

Dangers of Inadequate Working Capital

When working capital is inadequate, a firm faces the following problems.

(1) Inadequate working capital causes stagnates growth and expansion

(2) It may not able to utilize production facilities fully

(3) It becomes difficult to take advantages of profitable business opportunities

(4) It may not able to efficiently utilized fixed assets. This leads to low profitability

(5) A firm may not able to take advantages of cash discount facilities.

(6) Inadequate working capital causes paucity of funds. This leads to damage credit—worthiness of the firm

(7) It may not able to meet short term obligation

(8) Inadequate working capital causes unable to pay its dividends and interest

(9) A firm may not able to meet its day to day commitments. This leads to firm loses its reputation.

(10) Inadequate working capital would positively lead liquidation of firm

Determination of Working Capital

The total working capital requirement is determined by a wide variety of factors. It should be, however, noted that these factors affect different enterprises differently. The following is the description of the factors which generally influence the working capital requirements of the firms.

A. Internal Factors:

(1) Nature of Enterprise.

(2) Size of Business.

(3) Manufacturing Cycle.
(4) Firm's Credit Policy.
(5) Access to Money Market.
(6) Expansion and Growth of Business.
(7) Profit Margin and Dividend Policy.
(8) Depreciation Policy.
(9) Operating Efficiency of Firm.
(10) Co-ordination Activities of Firm.

B. External Factors:

(1) Business Cycle Fluctuations.
(2) Technological Development.
(3) Seasonal Fluctuations.
(4) Environment Factor.
(5) Taxation Policy.

A. Internal Factors

(1) Nature of Enterprise: The working capital requirements of a firm basically influenced by the nature of its firm. For example, trading and financial firms require a large amount of investment in working capital but a significantly smaller amount of investment in fixed assets. But in the case of manufacturing concern have to invest substantially in working capital and a normal amount in fixed assets. In contrast public utilities have a very limited need for working capital, while a merchandising department depends generally on inventory and receivable need a large amount of working capital. Needs for working capital are thus determined by the nature of an enterprise or business.

(2) Size of Business: The size of the firm is also an important factor to requirements of working capital. Because a smaller firm needs smaller amount of working capital on the basis of its production activities and *vise versa* in the opposite case.

(3) Manufacturing Cycle: Time span required for conversion of raw materials into finished goods is to block period. The period in reality extends a little before and after the work-in-progress. This cycle determine the need of working capital.

(4) Firm's Credit Policy: The level of working capital is also determined by credit policy which relates to sales and purchases. The credit policy influences the requirement of working capital in two ways *(a)* Through credit terms granted by the firm to its customers/buyers of goods; *(b)* Credit terms available to the firm from its creditors.

(5) Access to Money Market: Working capital requirements of a firms are conditioned by the firm's access to different sources of money market. Thus, firm with readily available credit from banks and trade credit facilities at liberal terms will be able to get by with less working capital than a firm without such facilities.

(6) Expansion and Growth of Business: It is obvious that, as business expands, it will require more working capital interms of sales or fixed assets. In the case of growth and expansion, there will be an all round increase in investment. That is to say, with the increase in fixed assets for increasing sales the requirement of working capital will be expanded not only for financing increased volume of raw materials but also to finance maintenance of inventory stock and grant credit to customers.

(7) Profit Margin and Dividend Policy: Magnitude of working capital in a firm depend upon its profit margin and dividend policy. As a matter of fact, a high net profit margin reduces the working capital requirements of the firm because it contribute towards working capital pool. Similarly, distribution of high proportion of profits in the form of cash dividend result in a drain on cash resources and thus reduces company's working capital to that extend. Where the management follows constructive dividend policy and retain larger portion of the net profits, the company's working capital position is strengthened.

(8) Depreciation Policy: The depreciation policy influences the level of working capital by affecting tax liability and retained earnings of the enterprise. Since depreciation is tax deductible expense item, this will affect the firm's tax liability and retained earning and thus strengthen the firm's working capital position.

(9) Operating Efficiency of Firm: The operating efficiency of management is also an important determinant of the level of working capital management can contribute to a sound working capital position through operating efficiency. Efficiency of operations accelerates the pace of the cash cycle and improves the working capital turnover.

(10) Co-ordination Activities of Firm: In addition, absence of co-ordination in production and distribution policies in a company results in a high demand for working capital. Where production and distribution activities are co-ordinated, pressure on working capital will be minimized.

B. External Factors

(1) Business Cycle Fluctuations: This is another factor which determines the need level. Barring exceptional cases, there are variations in the demand for goods/services handled by any organization. Economic boom/recession have their influence on the transactions and consequently on the quantum of working capital required.

(2) Technological Development: Changes in technologies may lead to improvements in processing raw materials, minimizing wastages, greater productivity, more speed of production. All these improvements may enable the firm to reduce investments in inventory. Thus changes in technology affect the requirements of working capital. If the firm decides to go for automation, thus world reduce the requirements for working capital. If the firm adopts a labour intensive process, the requirement for working capital will be larger.

(3) Seasonal Fluctuations: Seasonal fluctuations in sales affect the level of variable working capital. Often the demand for products may be of a seasonal nature. Yet inventories have got to be purchased during certain seasons only. The size of working capital in one period may therefore, be bigger than that in another.

(4) Environment Factors: Political stability in its wake bring in stability in money market and trade world, things mostly go smooth. Risk ventures are possible with enhanced need for working capital finance. Similarly, availability of local infrastural facilities, road, transport, storage and market etc. influence business and working capital need as well.

(5) Taxation Policy: Taxes must be paid out of profits. Tax liability is unavoidable and adequate provision should be made for it in working capital planning. If the tax liability increases, it will impose an additional strain on working capital. The finance manager must do tax planning in order to avail the benefits of all sorts of tax concessions and incentives.

Assessment of Working Capital Requirements

The term working capital as already point out, usually means the excess of current assets over current liabilities. In reality such excess of current assets over current liability may be either more or less than the working capital requirement of the company. Assessing the requirements of working capital to be employed during the immediate future period of operations. The working capital requirements can be determined by the following three techniques :

(1) Percentage of Sales Method.

(2) Estimation of Components of Working Capital Method.

(3) Operating Cycle Approach (or) Cash Working Capital Method.

(1) Percentage of Sales Method: This is simple and traditional method. According to percentage of sales method, the requirement of working capital can be determined on the basis of sales, amount of working capital required and prior year's experiences. In this method, the working capital is calculated and expressed it as a percentage to sales. This method is much useful in planning short term working capital requirements. However, the basic criticism of this method is that it assumes a linear relationship between sales and working capital. Therefore, this method is not universally accepted.

(2) Estimation of Components of Working Capital Method: The second method is useful in estimating working capital requirements on the basis of the components current assets and current liabilities. These components includes inventories, Accounts receivables, Accounts payables, Marketable investments, Short Term Obligations etc. This method is widely discussed in the chapter of cash management of this book. It is practically suitable for long term forecasting. Symbolically, it can be expressed as:

Working Capital = Current Assets – Current Liabilities

(3) Operating Cycle (or) Cash Working Capital Method: Operating cycle method is otherwise known as 'cash working capital method'. In estimating the working capital cycle require for a business, the volume of cash needed to finance the entire process of the cycle is to be taken in to consideration. Accordingly, this method suggests that actual level of working capital requirement of a firm in a period can be appropriately determined with reference to the length of net operating cycle and the volume of cash needed to meet the operation expenses for the period. In other words, the operating cycle refers to the period that a firm takes from the acquisition of raw materials and ends with the collection of receivables or collection of cash for sales. The periods may be the holding period of various type of inventories, the credit collection period and the credit payment period. The operating cycle generally involved in the different stages of operation such as :

Stage I – Holding inventories *i.e.*, stock of raw materials and consumable stores for production

Stage II – Stock of semi-finished goods or work-in-progress

Stage III – Stock of finished goods for sale

Stage IV – Collection of Accounts Receivable or Book Debts

The duration of the operating cycle for the purpose of determining working capital requirement is equal to the number of days involved in the different stage of operation commencing from purchase of raw material and ending up with the collection of sale proceeds from debtors against which the number of days credit allowed by suppliers are to be adjusted.

The following formula may be used to express the duration of the working capital cycle or operating cycle :

$$O = R + W + F + D - C$$

Where

O = Total period of the operating cycle or working capital cycle in Number of days

R = Period or number of days for holding stock of raw materials and stores

W = Period or number of days for holding stock of work-in-progress with regard to cost of production

F = Period or number of days for holding stock of finished goods ready for sale

D = Debtors collection period *i.e.*, period of unpaid credits extended to Debtors

C = Creditors Payment period *i.e.*, period of unpaid credits received from Suppliers

The estimate of inventory period, the accounts receivable period, and the accounts payable period can be calculated as follows:

R – (Period of holding Stock of Raw material) $= \dfrac{\text{Average stock of raw materials and stores}}{\text{Average consumption of raw materials and stores per day}}$

W – Period of holding Stock of Work in progress $= \dfrac{\text{Averagestock of work in progress}}{\text{Averagecost of productionper day}}$

F – Finished Stock Inventory Period $= \dfrac{\text{Averageinventory of finshed goods}}{\text{Averagecost of sales per day}}$

D – Accounts Receivable Period (or) Debtor's collection period $= \dfrac{\text{Average accounts receivable}}{\text{Average credit sales per day}}$

C – Accounts payable period (or) Credit payment period $= \dfrac{\text{Averagetrade creditors}}{\text{Averagecredit purchases}}$

The given below specimen format used to computing the period of one operating cycle:

R – Period of holding stock of raw material and Stores	* * *
W – Period of holding stock of work in progress	* * *
F – Finished stock inventory period	* * *
D – Accounts receivable period	* * *
Total period of holding inventory and accounts receivable	* * *
Less : C – Accounts payable period	* * *
Period of one operating cycle	* * *

After computing the period of one operating cycle, the total number of operating cycles, period during particular year can be calculated as follows:

$$\text{Total number of operating cycle} = \frac{365}{\text{Total operating cycle period}}$$

Once the number of operating cycle has been determined, the actual working capital requirement can be calculated as follows:

$$\text{Actual working capital requirements} = \frac{\text{Total operating cost}}{\text{Number of operating cycles in a year}}$$

Actual working capital requirements = Amount required per day × Period of operating cycles

Factors to be Considered

The following factors to be consider by a manufacturing company while making an estimation of working capital requirements:

(1) Total units of output manufactured by a firm throughout the year.

(2) The length of time for which raw materials and consumable stores are to maintain in stores before they are issued for production.

(3) The length of the production cycle or work-in-progress *i.e.*, the time taken for conversion of raw materials into finished goods.

(4) The length of sales cycle *i.e.*, the time taken for finished goods remain in stores for ready to sale.

(5) The average period of credit allowed to debtors.

(6) The average period of credit allowed by supplies.

(7) The amount of cash required to meet day to day expenses of the business.

(8) The amount of cash required to make advance payments, if any.

(9) Time-lag in the payment of wages and overheads *i.e.*, general and administrative expenses, selling and distribution expenses.

Illustration: 1

Sam Industries Ltd. plans to sell 30000 units next year. The expected cost of goods sold is as follows :

	Per unit
	Rs.
Raw materials	200
Manufacturing expenses	60
Operating expenses including selling and distribution expenses	40
Selling price	400

The duration at various stages of the operating cycle is expected to be as follows :

Raw materials stage	2 months
Work-in-progress stage	1 month
Finished goods stage	½ month
Debtors stage	1 month

Assuming the monthly sales level of 2500 units :

(1) Calculate the investment in various current assets.

(2) Estimated the working capital requirement if the desired cash balance is 5% of the working capital requirements.

Solution :

Calculation of profitability:

			Rs.
Proposed sales	=	30000 units	
Selling price per unit	=	Rs. 400	
Sales for the year 30000 × Rs. 400	=	1,20,00,000	
Less : Raw material 30,000 × 200	=	60,00,000	
Manufacturing expenses 30000 × 60	=	18,00,000	
Operating expenses 30000 × 40	=	12,00,000	90,00,000
Net profit			30,00,000

Calculation of investment in various current assets:

			Rs.
(a) Raw material (1/6 of Rs.60,00,000)		=	10,00,000
(b) Work-in-progress (Taken to be complete 25% as to manufacturing expenses) :			
Raw Material	Rs. 60,00,000		
Manufacturing expenses 25% of Rs.18,00,000	Rs. 4,50,000		
	Rs. 64,50,000		
Stage of work-in-progress for one month (64,50,000 x 1/12)		=	5,37,500
(c) Finished goods :			
Raw Materials	Rs. 60,00,000		
Manufacturing expenses	Rs. 18,00,000		
	Rs. 78,00,000		

Stage of finished goods for half month of (1/2/12 × 78,00,000)	=	3,25,000
(d) Debtors one month of Rs.1,20,00,000 (1,20,00,000 × 1/12)	=	10,00,000
Total Current Assets (a + b + c + d)	=	28,62,500

Estimation of Working Capital Requirement

	Rs.
Stock of raw materials	10,00,000
Stock of work-in-progress	5,37,500
Finished goods	3,25,000
Debtors	10,00,000
	28,62,500
Cash balance $\left(\frac{5}{95} \times 28{,}62{,}500\right)$	1,50,658
Working capital required	30,13,158

Illustration: 2

X Y Ltd, a trading company, provides the following information. Annual sales during the year Rs.24,00,000:

Analysis	60%
Operating Expenses	15%
Profit	25%

Average credit allowed to debtors – 2 ½ months

Average credit period allowed by creditors – 1 ½ months

Raw materials are remain in store on average – 1 month

Processing period on average – 2 months

Finished goods remain in ware house on average 3 months

Bank overdraft Rs.10,00,000

10% of the total working capital (including contingencies) is to be kept in hand for contingencies.

You are required to determine the working capital requirement of X Y Ltd on the basis of above information.

Solution:

Sales per month $= \frac{\text{Rs. } 24{,}00{,}000}{12} =$ Rs. 2,00,000

Amount to be blocked in material and operating expenses per month are:

Material	=	Rs. 2,00,000 × 60%	=	Rs. 1,20,000
Operating Expenses	=	Rs. 2,00,000 × 15%	=	Rs. 30,000

Working Capital Requirement

Particulars	Amount Rs.	Amount Rs.
Current Assets:		
(1) Stock of Raw materials (1 month):		
Raw materials Rs.1,20,000 × 1	1;20,000	
(2) Work-in-progress (2 months):		
Raw materials Rs.1,20,000 × 2	2,40,000	
Operating expenses Rs.30,000 × 2	60,000	
(3) Stock of Finished goods (3 months):		
Raw materials Rs.1,20,000 × 3	3,60,000	
Operating Expenses Rs.30,000 × 3	90,000	
(4) Debtors (2 ½ months) :		
Raw materials Rs.1,20,000 × 2½	3,00,000	
Operating expenses Rs.30,000 × 2½	75,000	
Profit credit to debtors (1/3rd of cost) (3,00,000 + 75,000 × 1/3)	1,25,000	13,70,000
Total current assets (A)		13,70,000
Less : Current Liabilities:		
Less : Current Liabilities		
(1) Creditors (1 ½ months)		
Raw materials 1,20,000 × 1½	1,80,000	1,80,000
		11,90,000
Add : Cash required for contingencies (1/9 of the above)		1,32,220
Total estimated working capital		13,22,220
Less : Bank Overdraft		10,00,000
Working Capital required		3,22,220

Illustration: 3

Ram Co Cements (P) Ltd sells its products on a gross profit of 20% on sales. The following information is extracted from its annual accounts for the year ended 31st December 2004 :

	Amount Rs.
Sales at 3 months credit	80,00,000
Raw materials	24,00,000
Wages paid – 15 days in arrears	19,20,000
Manufacturing expenses paid one month in arrears	24,00,000
Administrative expenses paid one month in arrears	9,60,000
Sales promotion expenses payable half yearly in advance	4,00,000

The company enjoys one months credit from the suppliers of raw materials and maintains 2 months stock of raw materials and one and half months finished goods. Cash balance is maintained at Rs.20,00,000 as a precautionary balance. Assuming a 10% margin, find out the working capital requirements of Ram Co Cements (P) Ltd.

Solution:

Calculation of Working Capital Requirements :

		Amount Rs.
Current Assets:		
Inventories:		
Stock of Raw materials (1/6 × 24,00,000)		4,00,000
Stock of Finished goods – 1 ½ months of cost of production : Cost of production being 80% of sales of Rs.80,00,000		8,00,000
Sundry Debtors (Rs.80,00,000 × 3/12)		20,00,000
Advance payment of Sales promotion		2,00,000
Cash		2,00,000
Total Current Assets (A)		36,00,000
Less : Current Liabilities:		
Sundry Creditors (goods) one month of Rs.24,00,000 x 1/12	2,00,000	
Wages – arrear for 15 days (1/24 × 19,20,000)	80,000	
Manufacturing expenses arrear for one month 1/12 × 24,00,000	2,00,000	
Administrative expenses arrear for one month 1/12 × 9,60,000	80,000	
Total Current Liabilities	5,60,000	5,60,000
Net Working Capital (A – B)		30,40,000
Working capital including 10% margin (30,40,000 × 10/100)		3,04,000
Working capital required		33,44,000

Illustration: 4

From the following information you are required to estimate the net working capital requirement :

	Cost per unit Rs.
Raw materials	400
Direct Labour	150
Overheads (excluding depreciation)	300
Total Cost	850

Additional Information:

Selling price	Rs.1000 per unit
Out put	52000 units per annum
Raw materials in stock	average 4 weeks

Working progress (assume 50% completion stage with full material consumption)	average 2 weeks
Finished goods in stock	average 4 weeks
Credit allowed by suppliers	average 4 weeks
Credit allowed by debtors	average 8 weeks
Cash at bank is expect to be	Rs. 50,000

Assume that production is sustained at an even pace during the 52 weeks of the year. All sales are on credit basis. State any other assumption that you might have made while computing.

Solution :

Statement Showing Net Working Capital Requirements

Particulars	*Amount Rs.*	*Amount Rs.*
Current Assets:		
Stock of Raw materials (4 weeks)		
$52{,}000 \times 400 \times \frac{4}{52}$		16,00,000
Stock of work-in-progress (2 weeks)		
Raw Material $52{,}000 \times 400 \times \frac{2}{52}$	8,00,000	
Direct Labour (50% completion)		
$52{,}000 \times 150 \times \frac{2}{52} \times \frac{50}{100}$	1,50,000	
Overheads (50% completion)		
$52{,}000 \times 300 \times \frac{2}{52} \times \frac{50}{100}$	3,00,000	12,50,000
Stock of finished goods (4 weeks)		
$52{,}000 \times 850 \times \frac{4}{52}$		34,00,000
Amount blocked in debtors at cost (8 weeks)		
$52{,}000 \times 850 \times \frac{8}{52}$		68,00,000
Cash at bank		50,000
Total Current Assets		1,31,00,000
Less : Current Liabilities:		
Creditors for Raw material (4 weeks)		
$52{,}000 \times 400 \times \frac{4}{52}$		16,00,000
Net working capital required		1,15,00,000

Illustration: 5

A B C Ltd, sells goods on a gross profit of 25% Depreciation is taken into account as part of cost of production. The following are the annual figures given to you :

	Rs.
Sales (two months credit)	36,00,000
Materials consumed (one months credit)	9,00,000
Wages paid (one month lag in payment)	7,20,000
Cash manufacturing expenses (one month lag in payment)	9,60,000
Administration expenses (one month lag in payment)	2,40,000
Selling expenses (paid quarterly in advance)	1,20,000
Income tax payable in 4 installment of which one lies the next year	3,20,000

The company keeps one months stock each of raw materials and finished goods. It also keeps Rs.2,00,000 in cash. You are required to estimate the working capital requirements of the company on cash basis assuming 15% safety margin.

Solution:

		Rs.
(1) Total Manufacturing Expenses :		
Sales		36,00,000
Less : Gross Profit 25% of sales		9,00,000
Total Cost		27,00,000
Less : Cost of material	Rs. 9,00,000	
Wages	Rs. 7,20,000	16,20,000
Manufacturing Expenses		10,80,000
(2) Depreciation :		
Total Manufacturing Expenses		10,80,000
Less : Cash Manufacturing Expenses		9,60,000
Depreciation		1,20,000
(3) Total Cash Cost :		
Total Manufacturing Cost		27,00,000
Less : Depreciation		1,20,000
		25,80,000
Add : Administration Expenses		2,40,000
Selling Expenses		1,20,000
Total Cash Cost		29,40,000

Statement of Working Capital Requirements

Particulars	*Amount Rs.*	*Amount Rs.*
Current Assets :		
Debtors (cash cost of goods sold) 29,40,000 × 20/12	4,90,000	
Prepaid sales expenses	30,000	
Inventories :		
Raw Materials 9,00,000/12	75,000	
Finished goods 25,80,000/12	2,15,000	
Cash in hand	2,00,000	10,10,000
Total Current Assets (A)		10,10,000
Current Liabilities :		
Sundry Creditors 9,00,000/12	75,000	
Outstanding Manufacturing Expenses 9,60,000/12	80,000	
Outstanding Administration Expenses 2,40,000/12	20,000	
Provision for taxation 3,00,00/4	75,000	
Outstanding Wages 7,20,000/12	60,000	
Total Current Liabilities (B)	3,10,000	3,10,000
Working Capital (A – B)		7,00,000
(Current Assets – Current Liabilities)		
Add : 15% for contingencies		1,05,000
Total Working Capital Required		8,05,000

Illustration: 6

From the following information you are required to estimate working capital requirement. A B C Ltd, company plan to attain a sales of Rs.5 crores. It has the following information for production and selling activity. It is assumed that the activities are evenly spread throughout the year.

(1) Average period raw materials are kept in stores prior to issue for production—2 months.

(2) Production cycle period—work-in-progress cycle period—2 months.

(3) Average time finished stocks are kept in stores in unsold condition—½ month.

(4) Average credit allowed from suppliers 1 ½ month.

(5) Average credit allowed to customers 1 ½ month.

(6) Analysis of cost plus profit for above sales.

Particulars	*Percentage*	*Rs. in Crores*
Raw Materials	50	2.50
Direct Labour	20	1.00
Overheads	10	0.50
Profit	20	1.00
Total	100	5.00

Solution:

Calculation of Working Capital Requirement:

(1) Total months to be financed to Raw Materials:

Periods of holding raw material in stores	2
Periods of work-in-progress cycle	2
Periods of holding finished good in stores	½
Credit allowed to customers	1½
	6
Less : Credit allowed by suppliers	1½
Total months to be financed to raw materials	4½ month

(2) Total months to be financed to Labour:

Periods of production cycle	2 months
Periods of holding finished goods in stores	½ month
Periods of credit allowed to customers	1½ months
Total months to be financed	4 months

(3) Total months to be financed to overhead:

Periods of production cycle	2 months
Periods of holding finished goods in stores	½ month
Periods of credit allowed to customers	1½ months
	4 months
Less : Periods of credit allowed by suppliers	1½ months
Total month to be financed	2½ months

(4) Maximum Working Capital Required: *Rs. in Crore*

Raw materials $\frac{4\frac{1}{2}}{12} \times 2.50$ Crore = = 0.94 Crore

Direct Labour $\frac{4}{12} \times 1.00$ Crore = = 0.33 Crore

Overheads $\frac{2\frac{1}{2}}{12} \times 0.50$ Crore = = 0.10 Crore

Total Working Capital Requirement = 1.37 Crore

Illustration: 7

From the following information prepare a statement showing the estimated working capital needs, in total and for each constituent.

Budgeted Sales	Rs. 52,00,000 per Annum
Analysis per Unit of sales	(Rs)
Raw Materials (Rs)	25
Direct Labour (Rs)	45

Overheads	(Rs)	20
Cost of Sales	(Rs)	90
Profit	(Rs)	10
Sales Price per unit		100

It is estimated that (a) Raw materials will be carried in stock for two weeks and finished goods for three weeks (b) Factory processing will take four weeks (c) Suppliers will give four weeks credit and customers will require seven weeks credit.

It may be assumed that production and overheads arise evenly throughout the year.

Solution:

Statement showing Estimated Working Capital Required

Particulars	*Amount Rs.*	*Amount Rs.*
Current Assets :		
Inventories :		
Stock of raw materials $\frac{2}{5} \times \frac{2}{20} \times 52{,}00{,}000$		50,000
Stock of work-in-progress :		
Materials $\frac{4}{52} \times \frac{5}{20} \times 52{,}00{,}000$	1,00,000	
Labour $\frac{1}{2} \times \frac{4}{52} \times \frac{9}{20} \times 52{,}00{,}000$	90,000	
Overheads $\frac{1}{2} \times \frac{4}{52} \times \frac{4}{20} \times 52{,}00{,}000$	40,000	2,30,000
Stock of finished goods $\frac{3}{52} \times \frac{18}{20} \times 52{,}00{,}000$	2,70,000	
Accounts Receivable (Debtors) $\frac{7}{52} \times 52{,}00{,}000$	7,00,000	9,70,000
Total Current Assets (A)		12,50,000
Less : Current Liabilities :		
Creditors $\frac{4}{52} \times \frac{5}{52} \times 52{,}00{,}000$	1,00,000	1,00,000
Estimate Working Capital (CA – CL)		11,50,000

Illustration: 8

X and Y who want to buy a business seek your advice about the average working capital requirements in the first years trading. The following estimates are available and you are asked to add 10% to allow for contingencies.

	Rs. Per Annum
(1) Average amount locked up in Stock :	
Stock of finished goods and WIP	50,000
Stock of stores, materials	80,000
(2) Average Credit given :	
Local Sales – 2 week credit	7,80,000
Outside the state – 6 weeks credit	31,20,000
(3) Time available for payment :	
For purchases – 4 weeks	9.60,000
For wages – 4 weeks	26,00,000

Calculate the average amount of working capital requirements.

Solution:

Statement showing the Amount of Working Capital Requirements (WC = CA – CL)

Particulars	*Amount Rs.*	*Amount Rs.*
Current Assets:		
Inventories:		
Stock of finished product and WIP	50,000	
Stock of stores, materials	80,000	1,30,000
Accounts Receivable:		
Local Sales (780000 × 2/52)	30,000	
Outside the state (31,20,000 × 2/52)	3,60,000	3,90,000
Total Current Assets		5,20,000
Less : Current Liabilities:		
Accounts payable (9,60,000 × 4/52)	73,850	
Outstanding wages (26,00,000 × 2/52)	1,00,000	1,73,850
Total Current Liabilities		3,46,150
Add : 10% for contingencies (10% of 346150)		34,615
Working Capital Required		3,11,535

Illustration: 9

A firm is engaged in large scale manufacturing company. From the following information you are required to forecast their working capital requirements projected monthly sales of 32000 units at Rs.10 per unit The excepted ratio of cost to selling price are :

Raw materials	40%
Labour	30%

Budgeted overheads Rs.16000 per week

Stock will include raw materials for Rs.96,000 and 16000 units of finished goods

Materials will stay in process for 2 weeks

Credit allowed to debtors is 5 weeks

Credit allowed by creditors is 1 month

Lag in payment of overhead is 2 weeks

Wages will be paid at the beginning of the week following the week of work

Cash in hand is expected to be 10% of Net working capital

Assume that production is carried on evenly throughout the year and overhead accrue similarly and a time period of 4 weeks is equivalent to a month.

Solution:

Elements of Cost		Per units
		Rs.
Materials (Rs.10 × 40%)	=	4
Labour (Rs. 10 × 30%)	=	3
Overheads (Rs. 16000 ÷ 8000)	=	2
Total Cost of production	=	9
Profit	=	1
Selling price	=	10

Weekly Production $\frac{32,000}{4}$ = 8000 units

Cost of Materials per week = 8000 × Rs. 4 per units = Rs. 32,000

∴ Time lag in store $= \frac{\text{Rs. } 96,000}{\text{Rs. } 32,000} = 3$ weeks

Average staying period of finished goods in store $= \frac{16,000 \text{ units}}{8000 \text{ units}} = 2$ weeks

Average cost of labour per week = 8000 units × Rs.3 per unit = Rs. 24000

Average cost of overhead per week = 8000 units × Rs.2 per unit = Rs.16000

Average profit per week = 8000 units × Rs.1 per unit = Rs.8000

Working Capital Requirement Forecast

Particulars	*Period in week*	*Total* Rs.	*Raw Materials* Rs.	*Work in Progress* Rs.	*Finished Goods* Rs.	*Debtors* Rs.	*Creditors* Rs.
(1) Materials:							
in Stores	3		96,000				
in Work-in-Progress	2			64,000			
in Finished foods	2				64,000		
with Debtors	5					1,60,000	
	12						

Less : Credit from Creditors	4						1,28,000
	8	2,56,000					
(2) Wages :							
in Work-in-Progress	1			24,000			
in Finished foods	2				48,000		
with Debtors	5					1,20,000	
	8	1,92,000					
(3) Overheads :							
in Work-in-Progress	1			16,000			
in Finished foods	2				32,000		
with Debtors	5					80,000	
	8						
Less : Credit from Creditors	2						32,000
	6	96,000					
(4) Profit :							
Credit to Debtors	5	40,000				40,000	
Total		5,84,000	96,000	1,04,000	1,44,000	4,00,000	1,60,000

		Rs.
Estimated requirement of working capital as per above statement	=	5,84,000
Add : Expected cash in hand @10% of total requirement (*i.e.*, Rs.5,84,000 × 1/9)	=	64,829
∴ Total requirement of working capital	=	6,48,829

Illustration: 10

The following annual figures relate to MNP Limited :

	Rs.
Sales (at three months credit)	90,00,000
Materials consumed (suppliers extend one and half month's credit)	22,50,000
Wages paid (one month in arrear)	18,00,000
Manufacturing expenses outstanding at the end of the year (cash expenses are paid one month in arrear)	2,00,000
Total administrative expenses for the year (cash expenses are paid one month in arrear)	6,00,000
Sales Promotion expenses for the year (paid quarterly in advance)	12,00,000

The company sells its products on gross-profit of 25% assuming depreciation as a part of cost of production. It keeps two month's stock of finished goods and one month's stock of raw materials as inventory. It keeps cash balance of Rs. 2,50,000.

Assume a 5% safety margin, work out the working capital requirements of the company on cash cost basis. Ignore work-in-progress.

Solution:

Statement of Working Requirements (CA – CL)

Particulars	*Amount Rs.*	*Amount Rs.*
Estimation of Current Assets :		
Debtors (Total cash cost × 3/12) = (8250000 × 3/12)	4,90,000	
Stock of Raw materials (Material cost × 1/12) = (2250000 × 1/12)	1,87,500	
Stock of Finished goods (cash manufacturing × 2 /12) = (8250000 × 2/12)	13,75,000	
Prepaid Sales promotion expenses (1200000 × ¼)	3,00,000	
Cash balance	2,50,000	26,02,500
Total Current Assets (A)		26,02,500
Less : Estimation of current Liabilities :		
Sundry creditors (Material cost × 1.5/12) = 2250000 × 1.5/12	2,81,250	
Manufacturing expenses outstanding	2,00,000	
Wages outstanding (18,00,000 × 1/12)	1,50,000	
Administrative Expenses Outstanding (6,00,000 × 1/12)	50,000	
Total Current Liabilities (B)	6,81,250	6,81,250
Working Capital (CA – CL)		19,21,250
Add : 5% safety margin		96,062
Working Capital Required		20,17,312

Working Notes:

Manufacturing Expenses :		Rs.
Sales		90,00,000
Less : Gross Profit (25%of Rs.90,00,000)		22,50,000
Total Manufacturing cost		67,50,000
Less : Materials	22,50,000	
Wages	18,00,000	40,50,000
Total Manufacturing expenses (i)		27,00,000
Cash Manufacturing Expenses (ii) :		
(Rs.2,00,000 x 12)		24,00,000
Depreciation (iii)		3,00,000

Total Cash Cost IV :

Total Manufacturing Cost	67,50,000
Less : Depreciation	3,00,000
	64,50,000
Add : Administrative Expenses	6,00,000
Add : Sales Promotion Expenses	12,00,000
Total Cash Cost	82,50,000

Illustration: 11

Financial Director of RR Ltd, desires to know the amount of working capital which the company require during 2004. He has assigned this task to the company's finance manager.

The fiancé manager in course of his discussions with other executives gathered the following information.

(1) The total production during the previous year amounted to 1,60,000 units. The company planned to maintain this level of output during the current year.

The estimated costs in terms of percentage to the selling price were as below :

Raw materials	60%
Direct wages	10%
Overheads	20%

(2) Raw materials would remain in stores for about two months

(3) The production process were expected to take one month

(4) The company purchased raw materials from suppliers on credit, the average credit period being 3 months

(5) The company would sell the entire production on credit

(6) The average time lag between the storage and time of despatch of finished products to customers was about 3 months

(7) The company expects to have sales revenue of the order of Rs.72,00,000 during the year 2004.

(8) Sales and production would be carried on regularly and on even scale throughout the year.

(9) Direct Labour charges for a month would be paid on the 1st day of the following month

(10) The company's policy is to carry a minimum cash balance of Rs.6,00,000 throughout the year.

On the basis of the above information the fiancé executive of the company has to compute its working capital requirements for the year 2004.

Solution:

Statement of Working Requirements for 2004

Particulars	Amount Rs.	Amount Rs.
Current Assets :		
Cash		6,00,000
Sundry Debtors		18,00,000
Inventories :		
Stock of Raw material	7,20,000	
Stock of Work in progress	4,50,000	
Stock of Finished goods	16,20,000	27,90,000
Total Current Assets		51,90,000
Less : Current Liabilities :		
Sundry Creditors	10,80,000	
Expenses Payable (wages)	60,000	11,40,000
Working Capital required		40,50,000

Working Notes:

(1) Calculation of Sundry Debtors (3 months) :

Sundry Debtors = Average Sales per month × Credit period

$$\text{Average Sales Per moth} = \frac{72,00,000}{12} = \text{Rs. } 6,00,000$$

∴ Sundry Debtors = 6,00,000 x 3 = Rs18,00,000

(2) Stock of Raw Materials (2 months) :

= Cost of raw materials for a month × Storage Time

$$\text{Cost of raw materials for a month} = 72,00,000 \times \frac{60}{100} \times \frac{1}{2}$$

$$= \text{Rs.}3,60,000$$

Stock of raw materials for 2 months = Rs. 3,60,000 × 2 = Rs. 7,20,000

(3) Stock of work-in-progress :

= (Cost of raw materials in process + Labour Cost + Overheads) × Process Time

(a) Raw materials are in process for one month

$$\text{Rs. } 72,00,000 \times \frac{60}{100} \times \frac{1}{12} = \text{Rs. } 3,60,000$$

(c) Overhead costs for work-in-progress (half of the overhead costs for a month)

$$\text{Rs. } 72,00,000 \times \frac{20}{100} \times \frac{½}{12} = \text{Rs.}3,60,000$$

Total amount required for working-in-progress (Rs. 3,60,000 + Rs. 30,000 + Rs. 60,000) } = Rs. 4,50,000

(4) Stock of Finished goods :

= Cost of raw materials + Labour cost + Overhead cost

(a) Cost of Raw Materials :

= Cost of raw materials for one month × Period of storage of finished goods.

= Rs. 3,60,000 × 3 months

= Rs. 10,80,000

(b) Cost of labour blocked in finished goods inventory :

= Labour cost for one month × Period of storage of finished goods

= Rs. 60,000 × 3 months

= Rs. 1,80,000

(c) Cost of overheads blocked in finished inventory :

Overhead cost for one month × Period of storage of finished goods

Overhead cost for one month = Rs. 72,00,000 × $\frac{20}{100}$ × $\frac{1}{12}$ = Rs. 1,20,000

= Rs. 1,20,000 × 3 months = Rs. 3,60,000

∴ Capital required for finished goods inventory

= Rs. 10,80,000 + Rs. 1,80,000 + Rs. 1,20,000

= Rs. 16,20,000

(5) Estimation of Sundry Creditors :

= Credit purchase for a month x period of credit allowed by suppliers of raw materials

= Rs. 3,60,000 × 3 months = Rs. 10,80,000

(6). Calculation of Wages Payable :

= Amount of wage for a month × Time lag between incurrence of ways and payment of wage (1 month)

= Rs. 60,000 × 1 month = Rs. 60,000

Illustration: 12

Sharma Ltd, a newly formed company started business in 2004 and has the under mentioned projected Profit and Loss A/c:

		Amount *Rs.*
Sales		21,00,000
Less : Cost of goods sold		15,30,000
Gross Profit		5,70,000
Less : Administrative expense	Rs. 1,40,000	
Selling expenses	Rs. 1,30,000	2,70,000
Profit before tax		3,00,000
Less : Provision for taxation		1,00,000
Profit after tax		2,00,000

The cost of goods sold has been arrived at as under :

	Amount Rs.
Materials used	8,40,000
Wages and manufacturing expenses	6,25,000
Depreciation	2,35,000
	17,00,000
Less : Stock of finished goods (10% of goods produced not yet sold)	1,70,000
	15,30,000

The figures given above relate only to finished goods and not to work-in-progress equal to 15% of the years production (in terms of physical units) will be in process on the average requiring full materials but only 40% of the other expenses. The company believes in keeping equal to 2 months consumption in stock.

All expenses will be paid one month in advance. Suppliers of materials will extend 1½ months credit. Sales will be 20% for cash and the rest at 2 months credit. 70% of the income tax will be paid in advance in quarterly installments. The company wishes to keep Rs.80,000 in cash prepare an estimate of *(i)* Working capital, *(ii)* Cash cost of working capital.

Solution:

	Amount Rs.
(1) Estimation of work-in-progress :	
15% of material consumed for finished goods $\text{Rs. } 8{,}40{,}000 \times \frac{15}{100}$	1,26,000
15% of 40% of wages and expenses $\text{Rs. } 6{,}25{,}000 \times \frac{6}{100}$	37,500
15% of 40% of Depreciation $\text{Rs. } 2{,}35{,}000 \times \frac{6}{100}$	14,100
Total Work in progress	1,77,600

(2) Estimation of Raw Materials :

Materials used in finished goods	=	Rs. 8,40,000
Materials used in work-in-progress	=	Rs. 1,26,000
Total consumed	=	Rs. 9,66,000
2 month's consumption in stock $\text{Rs. } 9{,}66{,}000 \times \frac{2}{12}$	=	Rs. 1,61,000

(3) Estimation of Debtors :

80% of credit sales on Total sales

$$\text{Rs. } 21{,}00{,}000 \times \frac{80}{100} = \text{Rs. } 16{,}80{,}000$$

$$\text{Debtors for 2 months} \left(\text{Rs. } 16{,}80{,}000 \times \frac{2}{12}\right) = \text{Rs. } 2{,}80{,}000$$

(4) Materials consumed = Rs. 9,66,000

Add : Closing Stock = Rs. 1,61,000

Purchases = Rs. 11,27,000

$$\therefore \text{Creditors for } 1\tfrac{1}{2} \text{ months} \left(\text{Rs. } 11{,}27{,}000 \times \frac{1\tfrac{1}{2}}{12}\right) = \text{Rs. } 1{,}40{,}880$$

(5) Prepaid wages :

$$(\text{Rs. } 6{,}25{,}000 + \text{Rs. } 37{,}500) \times \frac{1}{12} = \text{Rs. } 55{,}210$$

(6) Prepaid Administrative and selling expenses

$$\text{Rs.}2{,}70{,}000 \times \frac{1}{12} = \text{Rs.}22{,}500$$

(7) Depreciation and profit included in the cost of current assets :

Depreciation :		*Rs.*
Finished goods $2{,}35{,}000 \times \frac{10}{100}$	=	23,500
Work-in-progress	=	14,100
Debtors	=	28,200
	=	65,800
Profit included in debtors Rs. $2{,}80{,}000 \times \frac{1}{7}$	=	40,000
	=	1,05,800

(8) Profit before tax

$$\frac{1}{7} \times 21{,}00{,}000 \text{ (sales)} = \text{Rs. } 3{,}00{,}000$$

Statement of Working Required

Particulars	*Amount Rs.*	*Amount Rs.*
Current Assets :		
Stock of Raw materials	1,61,000	
Stock of Work-in-progress	1,77,600	
Stock of Finished goods	1,70,000	5,08,600
Debtors		2,80,000
Prepaid expenses (Rs. 55210 + Rs. 22500)		77,710
Cash in hand		80,000
Total current assets		9,46,310
Less : Current Liabilities :		
Creditors	1,40,880	
Provision for tax 100 – 70 = 30% of 1,00,000	30,000	1,70,880
Working capital requirement		7,75,430

Estimate of cash cost of working capital:	*Rs.*
Working capital	7,75,430
Less : Depreciation and profit included in current assets	1,05,800
Cash cost of working capital	6,69,630

Illustration: 13

A proforma cost sheet of a company provides the following particulars.

	Per units
Elements of Cost :	Rs.
Raw materials	80
Direct labour	30
Overheads	60
Total cost	170
Profit	30
Selling price	200

The following additional information are :

Raw materials are in stock on average one month. Materials are in process, on average, half a month. Finished goods are in stock on average on month.

Credit allowed by suppliers is one month

Credit allowed to Debtors is two months

Lag in payment of wages is 1½ weeks

Lag in payment of overhead expenses one month

One fourth of the output is sold against cash and cash in hand and at bank is expected to be Rs. 25,000

You are required to prepare a statement showing the net working capital needed to finance a level of activity of 104000 units of production.

You may be assume that production is carried on evenly throughout the year, wages and overheads accure similarly and a time period of 4 weeks is equivalent to a month.

Solution :

Statement of working Capital Requirement

Particulars	*Amount Rs.*	*Amcunt Rs.*
Current Assets :		
(1) Stock of materials (4 weeks)		
Raw materials Rs. 1,60,000 × 4		6,40,000
(2) Work in progress (2 weeks) :		
Raw Materials Rs. 1,60,000 × 2	3,20,000	
Direct Labour Rs. 60,000 × 2	1,20,000	
Overheads Rs. 1,20,000 × 2	2,40,000	6,80,000
(3) Stock of Finished goods (4 weeks) :		
Raw materials Rs. 1,60,000 × 4	6,40,000	
Direct Labour Rs. 60,000 × 4	2,40,000	
Overheads Rs. 1,20,000 × 4	4,80,000	13,60,000
(4) Sundry Debtors (8 weeks) :		
Raw materials Rs. 1,60,000 × ¾ × 8	9,60,000	
Direct labour Rs. 60,000 × ¾ × 8	3,60,000	
Overheads Rs. 1,20,000 × ¾ × 8	7,20,000	20,40,000
(5) Cash on hand at bank :		25,000
Total Current Assets		47,45,000
Less : Current Liabilities :		
Sundry Creditors Rs. 1,60,000 × 4	6,40,000	
O/S Wages Rs. 60,000 × 1½ weeks	90,000	
O/S Overhead Rs. 1,20,000 × 4	4,80,000	12,10,000
Estimated working capital requirement		35,35,000

Note : (i) It has been assumed that direct labour and overheads are in process, on average half a month

(ii) Profit has been ignored and debtors have been taken at cost

Working Notes:

Sales for the year = 1040000 units × Rs. 200 = Rs. 2,08,00,000

Sales per week = Rs. 2,08,00,000 ÷ 52 = Rs. 4,00,000

Amount to be blocked per week :

In material = Rs. 4,00,000 × 80/200 = Rs. 1,60,000

In Labour = Rs. 4,00,000 × 30/200 = Rs. 60,000

In Overheads = Rs. 4,00,000 × 60/200 = Rs. 1,20,000

Illustration: 14

Prepare an estimate of working capital as at the end of 31st December 2004 from the following details supplied by Thomas Ltd.

Budgeted sales for the year Rs. 12,00,000

Ratio between cash and credit sales 1 : 5

Debtors Turnover ratio 73 days

Creditors Turnover ratio 30 days

Estimated gross profit 30% of sales

Proprietary ratio to fixed assets 0.80

Operating ratio 90%

Direct expenses ratio 75%

Stock turnover ratio 5 times

Lag in payment of expenses (except wages) 36.5 days

Liquid ratio 2.5 : 1

Net profit to proprietors fund ratio 10%

Closing stock will be Rs. 20,000 more than the opening stock

Solution:

(1) Estimation of Debtors:

$$\text{Debtors Turnover Ratio} = \frac{\text{Debtors}}{\text{Credit sales}} \times 365 \text{ days}$$

$$73 = \frac{\text{Debtors}}{10000} \times 365$$

$$\therefore \text{Debtors} = \frac{7,30,000}{365} = \text{Rs. } 2,00,000$$

$$\text{Total Sales} = \text{Rs. } 12,00,000$$

$$\therefore \text{Cash sales} = \frac{1}{6} \times 12,00,000 = \text{Rs. } 2,00,000$$

$$\therefore \text{Credit sales} = \frac{5}{6} \times 12,00,000 = \text{Rs. } 10,00,000$$

(2) Calculation of Stock:

$$\text{Stock Turnover Ratio} = \frac{\text{Cost of Goods Sold}}{\text{Average Stock}}$$

Where

$$\text{Cost of goods sold} = \text{Sales} - \text{Gross profit}$$

$$= \text{Rs. } 12,00,000 - 30\% \text{ of Rs. } 12,00,000$$

$$= \text{Rs. } 12,00,000 - \frac{30}{100} \times \text{Rs. } 12,00,000$$

$$= \text{Rs. } 12,00,000 - \text{Rs. } 3,60,000 = \text{Rs. } 8,40,000$$

$$\text{(or)} \quad 5 = \frac{\text{Rs. } 8,40,000}{\text{Average Stock}}$$

$$\therefore \text{Average Stock} = \frac{\text{Rs. } 8,40,000}{5} = \text{Rs. } 1,68,000$$

Total Stock (opening + Closing) will be Rs. 1,68,000 × 2 = Rs. 3,36,000

Closing stock is more than the opening stock by Rs. 20,000

$$\therefore \text{Opening Stock} = \text{Rs. } 3,36,000 - \text{Rs. } 20,000 \times \frac{1}{2}$$

$$= \text{Rs.} 1,58,000$$

$$\therefore \text{Closing Stock} = \text{Rs. } 1,58,000 + \text{Rs. } 20,000 = \text{Rs. } 1,78,000$$

(3) Calculation of Creditors :

$$\text{Creditor's Turnover Ratio} = \frac{\text{Creditors}}{\text{Credit purchases}} \times 365 \text{ days}$$

Where,

Credit Purchase = Cost of goods sold + Closing stock – Opening stock

= Rs. 8,40,000 + Rs. 1,78,000 – Rs. 1,58,000 = Rs. 8,60,000

$$\therefore 30 = \frac{\text{Creditors}}{\text{Rs. } 8,60,000} \times 365 \text{ days}$$

∴ Creditors = Rs. 70,685

(4) Creditors for expenses :

Other expenses ratio = Operating ratio – Direct expenses ratio

= 90% – 75% = 15%

$$= \frac{15}{100} \times \text{Rs. } 12,00,000 = \text{Rs. } 1,80,000$$

Since the expenses are outstanding for 36.5 days, the O/S amount for expenses will be:

$$= \frac{\text{Rs. } 1,80,000}{365} \times 36.5 \text{ days} = \text{Rs. } 18,000$$

(5) Calculation of Cash Balance :

$$\text{Liquid Ratio} = \frac{\text{Liquid Assets}}{\text{Current Liabilities}}$$

$$2.5 = \frac{\text{Liquid Assets}}{\text{Current Liabilities}}$$

Current Liabilities = Creditors + O/S expenses

= Rs. 70865 + Rs. 18000 = Rs. 88865

$$2.5 = \frac{\text{Liquid Assets}}{\text{Rs. } 88685}$$

∴ Liquid Assets = Rs. 88865 × 2.5 = Rs. 2,22,162

Now Liquid Assets = Cash + Debtors (Assumed)

Rs. 221713 = Cash + Rs. 2,00,000

Cash = Rs. 222162 – Rs. 2,00,000 = Rs. 22162

(6) Calculation of Proprietors Fund :

$$\text{Net Profit to proprietors fund} = \frac{\text{Net Profit}}{\text{Proprietors Fund}}$$

$$\text{Net Profit} = \frac{10}{100} \times \text{Sales} = \frac{10}{100} \times \text{Rs. } 12,00,000$$

$$= \text{Rs. } 1,20,000$$

$$\therefore 10\% = \frac{\text{Rs. } 1,20,000}{\text{Proprietors fund}}$$

∴ Proprietors fund = Rs. 2,00,000

(7) Working Capital Cost of proprietor's fund :

$$20\% \text{ of Rs. } 12,00,000 = \frac{20}{100} \times \text{Rs. } 12,00,000 = \text{Rs. } 2,40,000$$

Statement of Working Requirements

Particulars	*Amount Rs.*	*Amount Rs.*
Current Assets :		
Cash	22,162	
Debtors	2,00,000	
Stock	1,68,000	
Total Current Assets	3,90,162	3,90,162
Less : Current Liabilities :		
Creditors	70865	
Creditors for expenses	18,000	
Total Current Liabilities	88,685	88,685
Net working Capital (CA – CL)		3,01,477
Less : Financed by proprietors or long term funds		2,40,000
Working capital to be required		61,477

Illustration: 15

A Client of yours, Care Ltd, are about to commence a new business, and finance has been provided in respect of fixed assets. They have, however, asked you to advise the additional amount which they should make available for working capital.

They provided you with the following estimate for their first year and inform you that they have arranged an overdraft limit with their banker of Rs. 1,50,000.

	Average Period of credit	*Estimated for the first year (Rs.)*
Purchase of materials	6 weeks	26,00,000
Wages	172 weeks	19,50,000

Overheads :		
Rent	6 months	1,00,000
Director's & Manager's salaries	1 month	3,60,000
Traveler's commission	2 weeks	4,55,000
Other overheads	3 months	6,00,000
Sales :		
Cash	–	1,40,000
Credit	7 weeks	6,50,000
Average amount of stock & work in progress	-	3,00,000
Average amount of undrawn profits	-	3,10,000

Sales were made at an even rate for the year. You are required to prepare from the above figures and information, a table for submission to your client, giving an estimate of the average amount of working capital which are provide.

Solution:

Statement of Working Requirements

Particulars	*Amount Rs.*	*Amount Rs.*
Current Assets :		
Average amount of stock and WIP	3,00,000	
Average debtors	8,75,000	
Total Current Assets (A)	11,75,000	
Less : Current Liabilities : (Lag in Payments)		
Purchases (Rs. 26,00,000 × 6/52)	3,00,000	
Wages	56,250	
Rent (Rs. 1,00,000 × 6/12)	50,000	
Director's salaries	30,000	
Traveler's commission (Rs. 4,55,000 × 2/52)	17,500	
Other overheads (Rs. 6,00,000 × 3/12)	1,50,000	
Total current liabilities (B)	6,03,750	6,03,750
Total Working Capital Requirements (WC = CA – CL)		5,71,250
Less : Average amount of undrawn profit overdraft limit (Rs.3,10,000 – Rs.1,50,000)		4,60,000
Additional amount of working capital requirements		1,11,250

Note : Since profit on cash sales is also included in the average figure of undrawn profit, no allowance for cash sales been made.

TEST QUESTIONS

Objective Type : Choose the correct answer :

(1) Net Working Capital is the excess of current assets over - - - - - - - - - - -

(a) Current Liabilities (b) Liquid Assets

(c) Long Term Liabilities (d) Capital Employed

(2) The Gross working capital is a - - - - - - - - - - concept.

(a) Business Entity (b) Dual Aspect

(c) Going Concern (d) Money Measurement

(3) Working Capital is also known as - - - - - - - - - -

(a) Circulating Capital (b) Revolving Capital

(c) Operating Capital (d) Both a and b

(4) Gross Working Capital refers to capital invested total of - - - - - - - - - -

(a) Current Assets (b) Fixed Assets

(c) Circulating Assets (d) Both a and c

(5) Temporary working capital is otherwise called as - - - - - - - - - -

(a) Fluctuating working capital (b) Revolving working capital

(c) Variable working capital (d) Both a and c

(6) Permanent working capital is also termed as - - - - - - - - - -

(a) Regular working capital (b) Core working capital

(c) Fixed working capital (d) All the above

(7) The fixed proportion of working capital generally financed from the - - - - - - - - - -

(a) Fixed capital resources (b) Government assistance

(c) Private loans (d) Reserve and provisions

(8) The rate of return on investments - - - - - - - - - - with the shortage of working capital

(a) Larger (b) Falls (c) Adequate (d) None of these

(9) Operating cycle method is also known as - - - - - - - - - -

(a) Cash working capital method (b) Percentage of sales method

(c) Estimation of components of working capital method

(d) None of the above

(**Ans** : 1 – (a) Current Liabilities; 2 – (c) Going Concern; 3 – (d) Both a and b;
4 – (d) Both a and c; 5 – (d) Both a and c; 6 – (d) All the above
7 – (a) Fixed capital resources; 8 – (b) Falls
9 – (a) Cash working capital method)

(10) Define working capital.

(11) What do you understand by circulating of current assets?

(12) Explain the components of working capital.

(13) Explain the charactertics of current assets.

(14) What are the importance of working capital?

(15) Write detailed note on operating cycle of manufacturing firm.

(16) Describe the types of working capital.

(17) What do you understand by Net Working Capital?

(18) Write Short note on:

(a) Gross working capital.

(b) Permanent working capital.

(c) Net working capital.

(19) What are the difference between net working capital and gross working capital?

(20) Explain and illustration of temporary working capital and permanent working capital

(21) Explain the reasons for changes in working capital

(22) Explain the dangers of excess working capital

(23) Describe the dangers of inadequate working capital

(24) Discuss the determination of working capital

(25) What are the factors influence the working capital requirement? Discuss their importance

(26) Explain the assessment of working capital requirements

(27) Explain the techniques used for determination of working capital requirements

(28) Write detailed note on :

(a) Percentage of sales method

(b) Estimation of components working capital method

(c) Operating cycle approach or cash working capital method

(d) Balance sheet working capital

Practical Problems:

(1) From the following information prepare a statement showing the estimated working capital requirements:

(1) Projected annual sales – 26000 units

(2) Selling price per unit Rs.60

(3) Analysis of selling price

Materials	40%
Labour	30%

(4) Time lag (on average)

Raw materials in stock	—3 weeks
Production process	—4 weeks
Credit to debtors	—5 weeks
Credit from supplies	—3 weeks
Lag in payment of wages and overheads	—2 weeks
Finished goods in warehouse	—2 weeks

(5) Cash in hand is expected to be 10% of net working capital

(**Ans** : The working capital requirements Rs. 2,52,000)

(2) On 1st January of the year, 2004 the Managing Director of the company wanted to know the amount of working capital that will be required during the years

From the following information prepare the forecast of working capital requirements, production in the last year was 60000 units. The same will be the production this year.

Estimated ratios of different costs to selling price are :

Raw materials	60%
Direct Labour	10%
Overheads	20%

Raw materials will remain in store, on an average, for 12 months, before issue for production. Each unit will be in production process for the month the raw materials being fed into pipeline immediately. The labour and overhead costs will occur evenly throughout the period. Finished goods stay in the warehouse, awaiting dispatch to customers for approximately 3 months.

Credit allowed by Creditors is 2 months from the date of delivery of raw materials

Credit allowed to Debtors is 3 months from the date of despatch

There are regular production and sales cycles company keeps normally Rs.20,000 as cash in hand and selling price is Rs.5 per unit.

(**Ans** : Working capital requirements Rs.28,000 including profit)

(3) X Y Z Ltd, have approached their bankers for their working capital requirements who have agreed to sanction the same by retaining the margins as under :

Raw Material	20%
Stock in progress	30%
Finished goods	25%
Debtors	10%

From the following projections for 2003-04, you are required to work out

(1) The working capital required by the company and

(2) The working capital limits likely to be approved by bankers

Estimates for 2003-04.	Rs.
Annual sales	14,40,000
Cost of production	12,00,000
Raw material purchases	7,05,000
Monthly expenditure	25,000
Anticipated opening stock of raw materials	1,40,000
Anticipated closing stock of raw materials	1,25,000

Inventory Norms :

Raw Materials	2 months
Work in progress	15 days
Finished goods	1 month

The firm enjoys a credit of 15 days on its purchases and allows one month credit on its

suppliers. On sales orders the company has received an advance of Rs.15,000. State your assumption, if any

(**Ans** : (A) Working Capital required Rs.3,70,625

(B) Limits to be approved by bankers Rs.3,32,750)

(4) Prepare an estimate of working capital requirements from the following information of a trading concern

(1) Projected annual sales 100000 units

(2) Selling price Rs.8 per unit

(3) Percentage of net profit on sales 25%

(4) Average credit period allowed to customers 8 weeks

(5) Average credit period allowed by suppliers 4 weeks

(6) Average stock holding interms of sales requirement 12 weeks

(7) Allow 10% for contingencies

(**Ans** : Working Capital required Rs.2,03,078)

(5) The annual capacity of a manufacturing company is to produce 10000 units. But owing to scarcity of resources the normal level of activity has been 60%. From the information given below, calculate the working capital requirement on an estimated basis to sustain the normal activity level.

	Per unit
(1) Element of Cost	Rs.
Direct Material	40
Direct Labour	30

Overhead 100% of Direct Labour

(2) Profit per unit : 1/6 of selling price

(3) Other particulars :

(a) Raw materials storages period	– 2 months
(b) processing time	– 3 months
(c) Finished goods in stores	– 1 month
(d) Credit to Debtors	– 2 months
(e) Credit from creditors	– 1 month
(f) Lag in wage payment	– 1 month

It may be assumed that production and overheads accrue evenly throughout the year.

(**Ans** : Estimated requirement of working capital Rs.2,80,000)

(6) A newly formed company has applied to the commercial bank for the first time for financing its working capital requirements. The following information is available about the projections for the current year

Estimated level of activity : 1,04,000 completed units of production plus 4000 units of work in progress based on the above activity, estimated cost per unit is :

	Fer unit Rs.
Raw Material	80
Direct wages	30
Overheads (exclusive of depreciation)	60
Total cost	170
Selling price	200

Raw materials in stock : average 4 weeks consumption, work-in-progress (assume 50% completion stage in respect of conversion cost ; materials issued at the start of processing)

Finished goods in stock	8000 units
Credit allowed by suppliers	Average 4 weeks
Credit allowed to debtors/receivables	Average 8 weeks
Lag in payment of wages	Average 1 ½ weeks

Cash at bank (for smooth operation) is expected to be Rs.25,000

Assume that production is carried on evenly throughout the year (52 weeks) and wages and overheads accure similarly. All sales are on credit basis only. Find out working capital required.

(**Ans** : Working capital required Rs.4695990)

(7) Manufacturing company sells goods in the home market and earn a gross profit of 25% on sales. 1st annual figures are as follows :

	Rs.
Sales	3,00,000
Materials used	1,08,000
Wages	96,000
Manufacturing expenses	1,20,000
Administrative and other expenses	30,000
Selling and distribution expenses	18,000
Depreciation	12,000
Income tax payable in four installments of which one falls in the next financial year	60,000

Additional information is as follows :

(1) Credit give by suppliers of materials is 2 months

(2) Credit allowed to customers is one month

(3) Wages are paid half month in arrear

(4) Manufacturing and administrative expenses are paid one month in arrear

(5) Selling and distribution expenses are paid quarterly in advance

(6) The company wishes to keep one month stock of raw material and also of finished goods

(7) The company believes in keeping cash of Rs.50,000 including the overdraft limit of Rs.20,000 not yet utilized by the company.

You are required to prepare a statement showing the working capital requirement of the company adding 10% margin for contingencies.

(**Ans** : Working capital required Rs.53,900)

(8) A company has been operating on single shift basis manufacture its product with the following cost price structure :

	Per unit Rs.
Raw Materials	12
Wages (60% variable)	10
Overheads (20% variable)	10
	32
Profit	4
Selling price	36

Sales for the year ended 30th June 2003 amounted to Rs.8640000. As at 30.06.2003, the company held :

	Rs.
Stock of raw materials	7,20,000
Work in progress (valued at prime cost)	4,40,000
Finished goods (Value at total cost)	14,40,000
Sundry Debtors	2,16,000

At present, the company receives 2 months credit from suppliers of materials and there is a lag of payment of wages and expenses at half a month.

In view of increased market demand, it is proposed to double production by working an extra shift from suppliers of raw materials, in view of increased volume of production. Extra production can be sold at the existing price. There will not be any change in the credit policy. Credit from suppliers of material and time lag in payment of wages and expenses will continue to remain at present level.

You may asked by management to ascertain the effects of working capital or introduction shift working.

(**Ans** : Working capital required Rs. 40,80,000 ; shift working capital required (double production) Rs. 79,56,000)

(9) Prepare a working capital forecast from the following information :

Issue of share capital	40,00,000
6% Debenture	15,00,000

The fixed assets are value at 30 lakhs. Production during the previous year is one lakh units. The same level of activity is intended during the current year.

The expected ratios of cost to selling price are :

Raw materials	50%
Direct wages	10%
Overheads	25%

The raw materials ordinarily remain in store for 2 months before production. Every unit of production remain in process for 2 months, finished goods remain in warehouse for 4 months. Credit allowed by creditors is 3 months from the date of delivery of raw materials and credit given to debtors is 3 months from the date of despatch. Selling price per unit is Rs.6. Both production and sales are in regular cycle.

(**Ans** : Working capital required Rs.35,75,000)

(10) Prepare a working capital estimate from the following information :

Issue of share capital	Rs. 80,00,000
6% Debentures	Rs. 15,00,000

The fixed assets are valued at 30 lakhs, production during the previous year is one lakh units. The same level of activity is indented during the current year. The expected ratios of cost to selling price are :

Raw materials	50%
Direct wages	10%
Overheads	25%

The raw materials ordinarily remain in stores for 2 months before production. Every unit of production remains on process for 2 months. Finished goods remain in the warehouse for 4 months. Credit allowed by creditors in 3 months from the date of delivery of raw materials and credit given to debtors is 3 months from the date of despatch. Selling price is Rs.6 per unit Both production and sales are in a regular cycle.

(**Ans** : Working capital required Rs.3,57,500)

(11) Prepare an estimate of working capital requirements from the following information of a ABC Ltd, projected level of activity of 1,56,000 units of production.

	Per unit Rs.
Raw materials	90
Direct labour	40
Overheads	75
	205
Profits	60
Selling price per unit	265

(b) Raw materials are in stock on average one month

(c) Materials are in process, on average two weeks

(d) Finished goods are in stock on average one month

(e) Credit allowed by suppliers one month

(f) Time lag in payment from debtors 2 months

(g) Lag in payment of wages 1 ½ weeks

(h) Lag in payment of overheads is one month

20% of the output is sold against cash. Cash in hand and at bank is expected to be Rs.60,000. It is to be assumed that production is carried on evenly throughout the year, wages and overheads accure similarly and a time period of 4 weeks is equivalent to a month.

(**Ans** : Working capital required Rs.74,13,000)

(12) From the following details concerning manufacturing enterprise estimate the amount of working capital needed to finance an activity level of 50%. The capacity of the concern to produce 480000 units p.a. Expected selling price per unit Rs.100; cost of raw materials per unit Rs.30 ; direct labour cost per unit Rs.25 ; other overhead (including depreciation Rs.50,000) Rs.50,00,000 p.a.

Raw materials are in stock on an average for one month. Materials are in process on average for 2 months. Finished goods are in stock on an average for 2 months. Finished goods are in stock on an average for 2 months. Credit allowed to debtors 3 months and that received from the suppliers of raw materials is one month cash in hand and at bank is 10% of the net working capital you may assume that production is carried on evenly throughout the year and other overhead accure similarly. ¼ th of the output is sold against cash.

PLANNING AND FINANCING OF WORKING CAPITAL

Objectives of Working Capital

Procurement of required amount of working capital and its effect utilization is the important functions of working capital management. To ensure that the working capital financial plan serves as a guide to the future course of action of the financial department, the financial manager will keep in mind the following objectives which preparing the working capital financial plan.

(1) Availability of adequate funds

(2) Minimum cost

(3) Matching (balance) between profitability and liquidity

(4) Flexibility

(5) Optimum use of funds

(1) Availability of Adequate Funds : A sound working capital financial plan must ensure the supply of adequate amount of working capital needed by the business enterprises, both for current and future needs.

(2) Minimum Cost : The fund required by the firm should be made available at the lowest cost. It is made possible through planning—considering in advance various cost factors and trends of capital market and suggesting the best course of action.

(3) Matching (Balance) Between Profitability and Liquidity : A judicious balance between profitability and liquidity is one of the fundamental principles of successful finance planning. Profitability and liquidity are inversely related. The working capital financial plan must ensure sufficient amount of investment in those assets which are liquid cash and near—cash assets.

(4) Flexibility : The working capital financial plan should be dynamic in nature. In other words, it should provide sufficient scope for change and re-adjustment in the financial structure. Such changes become necessary due to changes in business conditions in future.

(5) Optimum Use of Funds : An important focal point of a financial working capital plan is the best use of the funds raised through various sources. All the possible efforts should be made that funds do not remain idle.

Working Capital Requirement of Different Concern

The below table shows the relative proportion of investment in current assets and fixed assets for certain industries.

Proportion of Current Assets and Fixed Assets

Industries	*Fixed Assets (%)*	*Current Assets (%)*
Hotel and Restaurants	80—90	10—20
Electricity Generation and Distribution	70—80	20—30
Aluminium, Shipping	60—70	30—40
Iron and Steel, Basic Industrial Chemicals	50—60	40—50
Tea Plantation	40—50	50—60
Cotton Textiles, Sugar Manufacturing	30—40	60—70
Ediable oils, Tobacco	20—30	70—80
Trading, Construction	10—20	80—90

The above table shows that investment in current assets represent a very significant portion of the total investment in assets. In the case of Cotton Textile, Sugar, Ediable oils, Tobacco, Trading and Construction companies in India, required investment in current assets constituted from 60 to 80 percent of total assets or total capital employed. On the other hand, Hotel and Restaurants, Electricity Genration and Distribution, Aluminium, Shipping, Iron and Steel Basic Industrial Chemical and Tea Plantation are not have much investment in current assets but it has to investment in fixed assets. These companies invest in current assets constituted from 10 to 50 percent respectively. This is very clearly indicates that the financial manager should pay special attention to the management of current assets on a continuing basis.

Elements of Working Capital

Working Capital Management refers to the administration of all aspects of current assets and current liabilities. The financial manager must determine the levels and composition of current assets. The following are the important elements of working capital.

(1) Inventories

(2) Accounts Receivables

(3) Marketable (Temporary) Investments

(4) Cash

(5) Creditors

(1) Inventories : Inventories include all requirements in raw materials, work-in-progress, consumable items, spare parts and finished goods. They constitute an important part of the current assets. The purchase of raw materials and stock of inventories involves investment which must be properly controlled. There are many aspects of inventory management which must be taken into consideration as:

(a) Fixing of level of inventories

(b) Determining economic ordering quantity

(c) Deciding the issue price of policy

(d) Setting up the procedure for receipts and issues

(e) Ensure proper storage facilities

(f) Setting up effective information system

(g) Determining the size of inventory to be carried

(h) Ensure Cost Control

(2) Accounts Receivables : One of the most commonly used methods of sales by the business organizations is the credit sales where in the companies sell their goods and services to the customers on credit basis in accordance with the credit policies formulated by them. The credit sales are recorded in the books of the selling company as debtors. The debtors are called book debts in accounting language. Further goods are sold on credit also said to the customers who agree to give their acceptance for the bills in consideration of sales payments. The bills so received from the customers are called Bills Receivable or Notes Receivable. Regarding accounts receivable in working capital management, the financial manager must be taken into consideration as:

(a) Ensure liberal credit policies

(b) Cost of recovering debts

(c) Interest Charges

(d) Risk associated with advancing credit

(e) Impact on promotion of sales

(f) Legal formalities

(g) Setting up the procedure for creation of bills

(3) Marketable (Temporary) Investments : Firm hold temporary investments for surplus cash flows arising either during seasonal operations or out of sale of long term securities. In other words, the amount of revenue realized from the sale of short term or temporary investment would be the cash inflow to the extent of actual sale proceeds. That means, the inflow of cash include even the profit on the sale of short-term investments. If the firm need to maintain sound working capital position, it should be consideration as:

(a) Determining the size of temporary investments

(b) Cash forecast

(c) Ensure the cash liquidity position

(d) Shortage of bank credit facilities

(e) Speculative needs

(f) Period of short-term investments

(g) Interest earned on investment

(h) Risk associated with short-term investments

(4) Cash : Cash is the significant portion of the working capital. There must be adequate cash to meet the requirements of all segments of the organization. The major source of cash is the amount of profit earned during the year from its business operations. Similarly, whenever there is an increase in any existing liability or when a new liability is created, cash inflows into the organization. On the other hand, when an organization purchases an asset or when a liability is discharged it would result in an outflow of cash. Therefore, it is necessary that every segment of the organization must consider the

(a) Sources of cash inflows

(b) Application or uses of cash out flows

(c) Cash expenses

(d) Position of excess cash or less cash

(e) Cash forecast

(f) Cash requirements to meets its current obligations

(5) Creditors : Creditors is one of the important elements of working capital. If the payment of creditors is delayed there is a possibility of saving of some interest but it can be very costly because it will spoil the goodwill of the concern in the market. If try to get liberal credit loans the payment may be made at the stipulated time.

Sources of Working Capital

The financial executives is always interest in obtaining the working capital at the right time, at a reasonable cost and at the best possible favourable terms. In any concern, a part of the working capital investment are permanent investment in fixed assets. Because, there is always a minimum level of current assets which are continuously required by the enterprise to carry out its day to day business operations. The long term working capital can be conveniently financed by (a) Owner's Equity (b) Genders Equity and (c) Reduction of fixed assets. Medium term working capital funds are ordinarily raised for a period varying from 3 to 7 years through loans which are repayable in installments. The short-term working capital fund can be obtained for financing day to day business requirements through trade credit, bank credit, discounting bills and factoring of account receivable. The following are the important sources of working capital available to a concern.

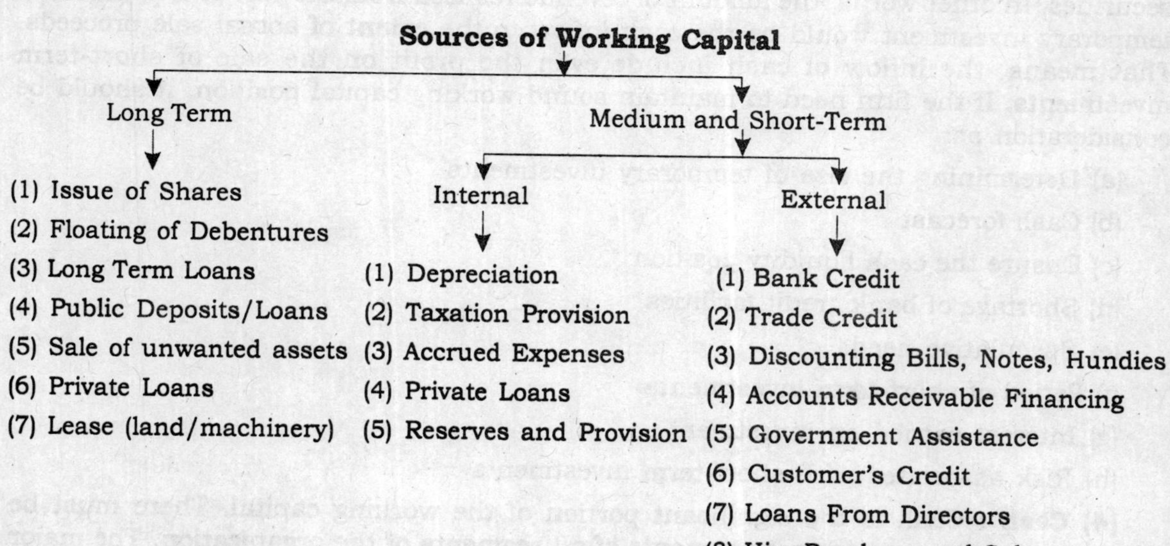

I. Long Term Source of Working Capital

(1) Issue of Shares : This is the most common method of raising the permanent working capital. Every company generally uses this method. According to companies Act, the term "Shares" may be defined as "the share in the capital of a company and includes stock expect where a distinction between stock and share is expressed or implied". The maximum amount of permanent working capital can be raised by the issue of shares. Share are of two types. Equity shares and preference shares.

(2) Floating of Debentures : It is also an important source of long term working capital. A debenture is a document issued by a company as an evidence of a debt due from the company with or without a charge on the asset of the company. According to Companies Act, the term debenture includes debenture stock, bonds and any other securities of a company whether constituting a charge on the assets of the company or not. Debenture are of many types such as Naked Debentures, Mortgage Debentures, Redeemable Debentures and Convertible Debentures etc.

(3) Long Term Loans : Long term loans is one of the important source of permanent working capital. Financial institutions and commercial banks provide loans for augmenting long term working capital needs and for meeting additional margin money requirements for working capital arising out of increase in volume of operations, expansion, diversifications etc.

(4) Public Deposits/Loans : The next alternative is public deposits. The issue of tapping public deposits is directly related to the image of the company seeking to invite public deposits. Many companies accept deposits as permanent working capital from their members, directors and the general public. This mode of raising funds is becoming popular these days on account of bank credit becoming quiet costlier.

(5) Sale of Unwanted Assets : It is also one of the alternative sources of permanent working capital. Considerable amount of working capital can be raised by the sale of unwanted or unutilized assets of land, building, machinery, furniture, scrap and loose tools etc.

(6) Private Loans : Lending private institutions and private banks are granting permanent working capital at a fixed rate of interest against securities to meet the operational expenses.

(7) Equipment Leasing : Companies can get the permanent working capital assistance by offering equipment leasing facilities. Financial institutions and commercial banks provides facilities for leases indigenously procured imported machinery and equipment for a period of 5 to 8 years with a 90% principal amortization through lease rentals over the period.

II Medium and Short Term Sources of Working Capital

Internal Sources

(1) Depreciation : Depreciation means decrease in the value of asset due to wear and tear, lapse of time, obsolescence, exhaustion and accident. Depreciation reserve provides a good source of funds for working capital. It is as a non-cash expense, and it does not represent any cash outlay with the result that part of the profits adjusted for depreciation can be used by management to increase any of the current assets or pay taxes, dividend etc.

(2) Taxation Provision : Provision for taxation is one of the internal sources of medium and short-term working capital. According to Income Tax Act, firms are liable to pay income tax on the assessable net profit as per rate prescribed for the same by Finance Act from time to time. As such, once the net profit of a firm has been ascertained, it makes provisions out of the said profit for payment of income tax. Normally, there is a time—lag between the creation of the provision for taxes and their actual payment. And in the period the resources as against this provision which remain within the enterprise may be used as a source of working capital.

(3) Accrued Expenses : Accrued expenses otherwise known as outstanding expenses. The firm can postpone the payment of expenses for shorter periods. This constitute as a internal source of medium and short-term working capital.

(4) Private loans : Lending private institutions and private banks are granting medium and short-term working capital at a fixed rate of interest against securities to meet the operational expenses.

(5) Reserves and Provisions : It is provided for meeting prospective losses or liabilities, creation of reserve and provision to increase the working capital in the business and strengthen its financial position. Sometimes, the amount is not kept in the business as additional working capital but is invested in purchase of outside securities, then it is called reserve fund.

External Sources

(1) Bank Credit : Bank credit is one of the important external sources of medium and short-term sources of working capital. It is arranged by which a banker allow his customer to borrow money up to a certain limit. Cash credit arrangements are usually made against the security of commodities hypothecated or pledged with the bank.

(2) Trade Credit : Trade credit is a form of medium and short-term financing common to all type of business firm. As a matter of fact, it is the largest source of temporary working capital. In an advanced economy, most buyers are not required to pay for goods on delivery. Trade credit is also granted by the seller of raw materials and goods to manufactures and/or wholeseller. It generally takes the form of discount for cash payment on delivery and net for future payment. This credit may take the form of (a) Open account credit arrangement (b) Acceptance credit arrangement. In the case of an open account credit arrangement, the buyer does not sign a formal debt instrument as an evidence of the amount due by him to the seller while in the case of acceptance.

(3) Discounting Bills : Companies can get the medium and short-term working capital assistance by discounting their bill of exchange, promissory notes and hundies from banks. These documents are discounted by the banks at a price lower than their face value.

(4) Accounts Receivable Financing : Under this arrangement, the account receivable of a business concern are bought by a financing company or money may be advanced on securing of accounts receivable. Normally, 60% of the value of accounts receivable pledged is advanced by the finance companies. If there is any bad debts, it is to be borne by the business concern itself.

(5) Government Assistance : Government undertakes a variety of promotional activities including provides subsidies and short-term working capital assistance for the acquisition and installation of energy conversion equipment. It extends the facility of granting loans, tax concessions for projects involving the development and use of indigenous technology and for adopting and development of imported technology, as well as high risk, high return ventures.

(6) Customer Credit : This is also known as installment credit as it is usually allowed y retailers for selling consumer durable goods. Some portion of the cost price of the sset is paid at the time of delivery and the balance is paid in number of installments long with interest. Sometimes, installment credit is granted by financial companies or ommercial banks which have special arrangements with the suppliers.

(7) Loans from Directors : A business firm may resort to miscellaneous source of nance in periods of pressing working capital needs. Such sources may include loan om Directors or Sister business units. Specialized financial institutions also provide hort-term finance to their client units in times of need. The cost of these funds is sually nominal.

(8) Hire Purchase and Sale : Financial institutions and commercial banks grant bans as medium and short-term working capital to companies engaged in leasing and ire purchase financing or industrial plant and machinery or durable customer goods.

Vorking Capital Control and Banking Policy

rade credit and bank credit are the important sources of working capital finance. uidelines for effective control and equitable productive distribution of resources to arious sectors of the Indian Economy. To achieve the objectives, the guidelines for vorking capital financing have been formulated on the basis of the reports submitted by ne Tandon committee (1975) and Chore committee (1980) respectively.

'andon Committee and its recommendations

n July 1974, the Reserve Bank of India appointed a committee under the chairmanship f Sri P. L. Tandon to suggest guidelines for the follow-up and supervision of bank credit. he Tandon committee interviewed with commercial banks, customers, large number f professionals industrialists and others before formulating their recommendations. To rame necessary guidelines on bank credit particularly the following :

(1) To suggest guidelines for commercial banks for safety of the fund vis-à-vis supervise credit for optimum end use of funds and to develop an information base required by banks periodically from borrowers and also by RBI such lending banks.

(2) To give recommendation on prescribed inventory norms for different industries.

(3) To make suggestions on sources for financing the minimum working capital requirements.

(4) To suggest criteria regarding satisfactory future credit norms.

(5) To suggest/recommend any other related matters.

'inding of the Study Group

'he study Group analyzed the existing system of working capital financing and identified he major short coming as follows :

(1) Under existing cash credit system, the borrower can draw freely with in limits.

(2) Lack of sound credit planning on the part of banker will lead to financial indiscipline in the borrower.

(3) Improper utilization of short-term credit. In practice, sanctioned cash credit was diverted for purchase of non-current assets.

(4) The bank credit is considered as the first source of finance and not as supplementary to other source of finance.

(5) Relatively easy access to working capital finance led to large inventory level with industry.

(6) Granting credit without proper securities and projected financial statements.

(7) The amount of credit limits sanctioned on the basis of security available, not o the operational efficiency of the borrower.

Recommendations by the Committee

The Tandon Committee submitted its report in August 1975. Most of its recommendation were accepted and implemented by Reserve Bank of India. On the basis of th recommendations banking sectors were advised to follow them.

Norms For Inventory

The Tandon committee has suggested prescribed broad inventory norms for the give below industries. According to the norms raw material has been expressed interms o monthly consumption, semi-finished products or WIP interms of monthly production valu and finished goods of monthly sales. In some industries, finished goods have bee separated from the accounts receivables. These inventory norms are presented in th below table :

Inventory Norms

Industry	*Raw Materials*	*Work in Progress*	*Finished Goods*	*Accounts Receivable*
Cotton, Synthetic Textiles	2.50	0.75	—	—
Man-made fiber	1.50	0.50	—	—
Jute Textile	2.50	0.25	1	1.50
Rubber	2	0.25	—	—
Fertilizers	2	0.25	—	1.25
Vegetable Oils	1	—	—	—
Dyes and Dyes Stuff	2.25	0.50	2	1.25
Chemicals	2.75	0.25	1	1.25
Cement	1.50	0.50	—	—
Pharmaceuticals	2.75	0.50	2	1.25
Paper	2 to 6	—	1	1
Engineering Auto	2.25	0.75	—	—
Engineering Durable	2	0.75	—	—
Engineering Ancillaries	2	0.75	—	—
Machineries	2.75	1.25	—	—

Lending Norms

Tandon committee has also suggested three important methods of lending norms to be followed by commercial bank for determining maximum permissible bank borrowings for working capital finance. This implies:

Method—I : In the first method, the borrower will have to contribute minimum of 5% of the working capital gap-defined as current assets minus current liabilities other ıan bank borrowings. Thus, 75% can be financed from bank borrowings. According to ıis method, the maximum permissible bank finance is determined as 0.75 (current ssets—current liabilities). This method will reflect the current ratio of 1 : 1.

Method—II : According to this method, the borrower will have to provide a minimum f 25% of the total current assets from long term funds and the balance of the working apital will be financed by bank credit (*i.e.*, the working capital gap less the borrowing ontribution) In short, under this method, the maximum permissible bank finance is alculated as 0.75 (Current Assets—Current Liabilities). This method will give a minimum atio of 1 : 3 : 1.

Method—III : Under this method, the borrower will have to contribute a major portion om the core current assets (permanent current assets) and a minimum portion of the alance of current assets. The remaining balance of the working capital gap will have to e financed by bank credit. In short, the maximum permissible bank finance is etermined as 0.75 (Current Assets—Core Current Assets)—Current Liabilities. This ıethod will reflect the high current ratio. In all three methods, accepted for nplementation by RBI, are further interpretation with help of given in the form of lustrations.

llustration:

urrent Liabilities	*Rs.*	*Current Assets*	*Rs. in lakhs*
ank borrowings	1,000	Raw Materials	800
undry creditors	800	Work in progress	500
ther Current Liabilities	200	Finished goods	360
		Sundry Debtors	500
		Other Current Assets	100
	2,000		2,260

'hus,

Current Assets	=	Rs. 2260
Current liabilities other than bank borrowings	=	Rs. 2000 – 1000 = 1000

lethod—I

	Rs. in lakhs
(1) Total Current Assets	2,260
(2) Less : Other Current Liabilities	1,000
(3) Working Capital Gap (1 – 2)	1,260
(4) Less : 25% Margin on working capital gap (to be funded from long-term sources)	314
(5) Maximum permissible bank finance (3 – 4)	946
(6) Excess borrowings (Bank borrowings *i.e.*, 1000 – 946)	54

Method—II

	Rs.
(1) Total Current Assets	2,260
(2) Less : 25% margin on (1) to be funded from long term sources	566
	1,694
(3) Less : Other Current Liabilities	1,000
(4) Maximum Permissible Bank Finance	694
(5) Excess borrowings (Bank borrowings *i.e.*, 1000 – 694)	306

Method—III

	Rs.
(1) Total Current Assets	2,260
(2) Less : Permissible Current Asset or Core Current Asset to be funded from long term sources	500
(3) Effective Current Asset for this purpose	1,760
(4) Less : 25% of (3)	440
(5) Less : Other Current Liabilities	1,320
(6) Maximum Permissible Bank Finance	1,000
(7) Excess Borrowings (Bank borrowing *i.e.*, 1000 – 320)	680

It may be noted that demand from borrower for long term fund from long term i increasing as we go from Method—I to Method—II and to Method—III. It is 314, 566, an 940 (500 + 440) respectively in Method—I, Method—II and Method—III.

Chore Committee Report

In 1979, Reserve Bank of India appointed a committee under the chairmanship of Shri K. B. Chore to find out and review the system of cash credit.

Terms of Reference

To frame necessary guidelines on working capital credit system, the Study Group review the following aspects:

(1) To analyze the gap between the credit limits sanctioned and credit limits utilized

(2) To study on the limits fixed on the basis of the maximum requirements o individual borrowers and draws are made according to actual needs at any poin of time.

(3) To give suggestions for modification of existing cash credit system to ensure th effective utilization of credit facilities to increase in out put or other product way

Recommendations

The major recommendations submitted by chore committee which were accepted by Reserve Bank of India, which has directed the banks to implement them:

(1) The existing system working capital facility extending credit by a combinatior of three types of lending such as cash credit, loans and bills facilities.

(2) All commercial banks are required to continuous assessment of accounts of the borrowers regarding sanctioned loan of working capital limit of Rs.10 lakhs and above.

(3) The committee further advised the commercial banks to streamline the withdrawal of funds. It has been regulated through submission of simplified quarterly statements on projection of actual performance and half-early statements for operating and fund flow statements.

(4) If borrowers limits exceed by Rs.50 lakhs and over will have to submit their quarterly projected working capital statement.

(5) The Study Group recommends that in case of extra-ordinary situations if further sanctions limit may be allowed by the additional rate of interest may be charged at 2% per annum over the rate applicable on the relative cash credit limit.

(6) While evaluating the peak-level and non-peak level credit requirements, the commercial banks are advised to appraise and fix separate credit limits to meet the needs of the industries.

(7) The Chore Group has also advised that the over dependence on bank credit by medium and large borrowers must be reduced by requiring them to increase their contribution towards working capital.

(8) The Study committee has also suggested to the commercial banks not to encourage frequent sanctions of temporary limits even for short period.

(9) The committee has recommend to encourage the bills system of finance and to facilitate call money operations an autonomous financial institution on the lines of the discount houses in the UK may be set up .

(10) In case of borrowers fails to submission of the return in time due to bring additional features in the form themselves a working capital term loan will have to be sanctioned to such borrowers for meeting above guidelines, he should be penalized by charging the whole outstanding in the account at an enhanced rate by 1 percent over the rate of interest cash credit.

QUESTIONS

(1) Explain the important objectives of working capital.

(2) Explain with illustrations of working capital requirements of different concern.

(3) What are the elements of working capital? Explain it in details.

(4) What are the important sources of working capital? Explain it in details.

(5) Explain the long term sources of working capital.

(6) What are the medium and short term sources of working capital? Explain it in details.

(7) Explain in details of Tandon Committee and its recommendation.

(8) Discuss in details about chore Committee Reports.

LIQUIDITY AND ITS TEST

Meaning and Definition

The term 'Liquidity' refers to the ability of a firm to meet its obligations in the short run usually one year. The liquidity resources of a firm may be kept in various forms : cash in hand and cash at bank in current assets, reserve drawing power under a cash credit or overdraft arrangement and short term deposits. Cash balances in current account provides the highest degree of liquidity.

According Hrishikes Bhattacharya, the term liquidity may be defined as "a firm can maintain liquidity if it hold assets that could be shifted or sold quickly with minimum transaction cost and loss in value. The test of liquidity is the ability of the firm to meet its cash obligations when they are due and to exploit sudden opportunities in the market.

According to Solomon, E and Springle J. Whenever one speaks of a firm's liquidity, he tries to measure firm's ability to meet expected and unexpected cash requirements, expand its assets, reduce its liabilities or cover any operating losses.

Factors Determining Liquidity

In efficient cash management the finance manager has to be consider the following factors for determining liquidity :

(1) Certainty of firm's cash flow pattern.

(2) Maturity schedule of its current obligations.

(3) Availability of inventories at right time and right place.

(4) Ability to procure extra funds in case of needs.

(5) Ability of the firm to meet its cash obligations.

(6) Ensure the cash ability of non-cash assets.

(7) Utilization of unavailed credit limits.

(8) Enhancement of short-term credit facilities with bank and other financial institutions.

(9) Minimization of cost of financing.

(10) Risk involved in short-term borrowings.

(11) Ability of the firm to raise non-bank funds.

(12) Efficiency of cash management regarding financial planning and cash control.

(13) Ability to speed the collection of accounts receivable.

(14) Ability to defer payment of bills until the latest possible moment.

Measurement of Liquidity

The measure of liquidity helps to indicate the level of solvency and financial flexibility of the firm. In order to ensure a desire level of solvency and provide to enough financial flexibility to attain the strategic goals of the enterprise, the following important liquidity ratio's are used to measure the liquidity of a concern.

Ratios

(1) Current Ratio

(2) Liquidity Ratio

(3) Cash Position Ratio

(4) Stock Ratio

(5) Debtor Velocity Ratio

(6) Creditors Velocity Ratio

Liquidity Ratio

The term 'ratio' refers to the mathematical relationship between any two inter- related variables. In otherwords, it establishes relationship between two items expressed in quantitative form. Ratio can be used in the form of (i) Percentage (10%) (ii) Quotient (say 20) and (iii) Rates. In other worlds, it can be expressed a to b; a : b (a is to b) or as a simple fraction, integer and decimal. It can be calculated by dividing one item or figure by another item or figure.

Liquidity Ratios are also termed as "Short Term Solvency Ratios". Here, the word 'Liquidity' means the extent of quick convertibility of short term nature. Accordingly, liquidity ratios are useful in obtaining and indication of a firms ability to meet its current liabilities, but it does not reveal how effectively the resources can be managed.

Liquidity Ratio can be grouped into

(1) Current Ratio

(2) Liquidity Ratio or Acid Test Ratio

(3) Cash Position Ratio or Absolute Liquidity Ratio

(4) Net Working Capital Turnover Ratio

(5) Current Assets to Fixed Assets Ratio

(1) Current Ratio : This ratio also termed as "working capital ratio". Current ratio is the most common ratio for determining liquidity. It establishes the relationship between current assets and current liabilities. It attempts to measures the ability of a firm to meet its current obligations or short-term solvency. Current ratio is calculated by dividing current assets and total current liabilities. Thus, the below presented formula is :

$$\text{Current Ratio} = \frac{\text{Current Assets}}{\text{Current Liabilities}}$$

The two basic components of this ratio are current assets and current liabilities. The term current assets normally mean that assets which can be easily converted into cash with in a year time. On the other hand, current liabilities represent those liabilities which are payable with in a year. The following table represents the components of current assets and current liabilities in order to measure the current ratios.

Components of current Assets and Current Liabilities

Current Assets	*Current Liabilities*
(1) Cash in hand	(1) Sundry Creditors
(2) Cash at bank	(2) Bills Payable
(3) Sundry Debtors	(3) Outstanding and Accrued Expenses
(4) Bills Receivable	(4) Income Tax Payable
(5) Marketable Securities	(5) Short-term Advances
(6) Other short-term investments	(6) Unpaid or Unclaimed dividend
(7) Inventories :	(7) Bank overdraft (short term period)
(a) Stock of raw materials	
(b) Stock of work-in-progress	
(c) Stock of finished goods	

Interpretation of Current Ratio

The ideal current ratio is 2 : 1. It indicates that current assets double the current liabilities is considered to be satisfactory. The higher the current ratio represents that the more liquid and greater the safety of funds the firm is ability to meet its current liabilities. On the other hand, low current ratio indicates that the liquidity position of the firm is not good and the firm may find it difficult to pay its current liabilities. If current liquidity position is not good even though it appears that after realizing all the amount of current assets and current liabilities can be paid off. A very high current ratio is also not desirable since it means less efficient use of funds. As the working capital is equivalent to the difference between current assets and current liabilities, or as the working capital is the excess of current assets over current liabilities, this ratio is also called working capital ratio.

Advantages of Current Ratio

The following are the advantages of current ratio:

(1) Current ratio helps to measure the liquidity and solvency of a firm.

(2) It represents general picture of the adequacy of the working capital position of a company.

(3) It represents a margin of safety *i.e.*, cushion of protection against current creditors.

(4) It helps to measure the short term financial position of a firm.

(5) It evaluates the operational efficiency of a concern.

(6) It discloses the over trading or under capitalization.

(7) Poor current ratio indicates a danger signal to the management to take corrective measures.

Change in Current Ratio

The significance of the current ratio varies with the following factors are:

(1) The seasonal influence.

(2) The extent to which the balance sheet reflects the current realizable values at the date of the balance sheet.

(3) The proportions of the different current assets. Cash being more stable than receivables, and receivable more stable than inventories.

(4) The degree of risk of possible value fluctuation in the particular kind of business.

(5) The probable expansion or contraction of operations likely to occur subsequent to the balance sheet date.

(6) The forms of current assets.

Calculation of Current Ratio

Illustration: 1

The following information relates to Mishra & Co for the year 2004 calculate

Current Ratio :

Current Assets Rs. 5,00,000

Current Liabilities Rs. 2,00,000

Solution:

$$\text{Current Ratio} = \frac{\text{Current Assets}}{\text{Current Liabilities}}$$

$$= \frac{\text{Rs. 5,00,000}}{\text{Rs. 2,00,000}}$$

$$= 2.5 \text{ or } 2.5 : 1$$

Comments

The current ratios 2.5 or 2.5 : 1. It means that the current assets are 2.5 times of current liabilities. The ideal current ratio is 2 : 1, it implies that for every one rupee of current liabilities, 2 rupees of current assets are available to meet them. In the above calculation we can observed that the liquidity position is more satisfactory with higher current ratio.

Illustration: 2

Calculate Current Ratio from the following particulars

Liabilities	*Amount* Rs.	*Assets*	*Amount* Rs.
Sundry Creditors	40,000	Inventories	1,20,000
Bills Payable	30,000	Sundry Debtors	1,40,000
Dividend Payable	36,000	Cash at bank	40,000
Accrued Expenses	14,000	Bills Receivable	60,000
Short term Advances	50,000	Prepaid Expenses	20,000
Share Capital	1,50,000	Machinery	2,00,000
Debenture	2,00,000	Patents	50,000
		Land & Building	1,50,000

Solution:

$$\text{Current Ratio} = \frac{\text{Current Assets}}{\text{Current Liabilities}}$$

Current Assets = Rs. 1,20,000 + Rs. 1,40,000 + Rs. 40,000 + Rs. 60,000 + Rs. 20,000 = Rs. 3,80,000

Current Liabilities = Rs. 40,000 + Rs. 30,000 + Rs. 36,000 + Rs. 14,000 + Rs. 50,000 = Rs. 1,70,000

$$\text{Current Ratio} = \frac{\text{Rs. } 3{,}80{,}000}{\text{Rs. } 1{,}70{,}000} = 2.24 \text{ or } 2.24 : 1$$

Comments

The Current Ratio is 2.24 : 1 which is considered satisfactory because the ratio is much higher than the accepted standard of 2 : 1. It indicates that a firm with higher current ratio has better liquidity short-term solvency.

(2) Quick Ratio (or) Acid Test Ratio

The Quick Ratio which is also known as Liquid Ratio or Acid Test Ratio or Near Cash Ratio. It is complementary to the current ratio. This ratio is concerned with the establishment of relationship between the liquid assets and quick liabilities. The Liquid Assets refers to those assets which can be immediately or at a short notice, be converted into cash without loss or diminution in value. The quick assets usually include all current assets excepts inventories (stock of raw materials, work in progress and finished goods) and prepaid expenses. The reasons as to why inventories are to be excluded for computing quick ratio is, inventories requires more time to become the most liquid assets. Prepaid expenses can not be termed to be liquid assets because they can not be normally converted in to cash. Liquid liabilities usually refers to current liabilities less bank overdraft. Bank overdraft is not included in current liabilities because it is not required to be paid off in the immediate future. Test of a firm's ability to pay its short term obligations as and when they become due. In order to compute this ratio, the below presented formula is used :

$$\text{Liquid Ratio} = \frac{\text{Liquid Assets (Current Assets Less Stock and Prepaid Expenses)}}{\text{Quick or Liquid Liabilities (Current Liabilities Less Overdraft)}}$$

Some times, the Liquid Ratio is also calculated by using current liabilities instead of Liquid Liabilities. Thus, the formula is :

$$\text{Quick Ratio} = \frac{\text{Quick Assets}}{\text{Current Liabilities}}$$

Where,

Quick Assets = Current Assets – Inventories and Prepaid Expenses

Current Liabilities represent those liabilities which are payable with in a year. However, in qu~stions liquid assets and current liabilities have been used for calculating quick ratio.

Components of Quick or Liquid Ratio

Quick Assets	*Liquid Liabilities*
Cash in hand	Outstanding / Accrued Expenses
Cash at bank	Sundry Creditors
Bills Receivable	Short term Loans
Sundry Debtors	Bills Payable
Marketable Securities	Income Tax Payable
Temporary Investments	Dividend Payable
	Bank Overdraft

Interpretation of Quick Ratio

The ideal Quick Ratio of 1 : 1 is considered to be satisfactory. Because the quick assets are equal to current liabilities then the firm can easily meet all current obligations. If the ratio is more than 1 : 1 indicates that the firm has sound liquidity position. At the same time, a quick ratio of less than 1 : 1 does not necessarily imply poor liquidity position. Because the conclusion is to be drawn after a careful analysis of the contents of quick assets. For example, Sundry Debtors can not be realized and cash is needed immediately to the current liabilities. In the same way, inventory which has been excluded is not necessarily fully non-liquid. A part of inventory may immediately be realized and used for discharging current liabilities.

Significance of Quick Ratio

(1) It used as a complementary to the current ratio.

(2) Quick ratio helps to measure the liquidity position of the firm.

(3) It is used to remove inherent defects of current ratio.

(4) It is used as a tool to evaluate the solvency of a concern.

(5) It gives the correct picture about the firm's ability to meet its immediate obligations.

(6) Higher Quick Ratio (more than 1 : 1) indicates sound liquidity position or adequate liquidity position.

(7) A Quick Ratio less than 1 : 1 indicates that the firm's liquidity position is not good.

(8) It is a more rigorous test of liquidity than the current ratio.

(9) This is an important ratio of financial institutions.

Illustration: 3

Calculate Quick Ratio from the information given below

	Rs.
Current Assets	40,00,000
Liquid Liabilities	20,00,000
Inventories	2,50,000
Prepaid Expenses	2,50,000
Land and Building	40,00,000
Share Capital	30,00,000
Good will	20,00,000

Solution:

$$\text{Quick Ratio} = \frac{\text{Quick Assets}}{\text{Liquid Liabilities}}$$

Quick Assets = Current Assets – (Inventories + Prepaid Expenses)

= Rs. 40,00,000 – (Rs. 2,50,000 + Rs. 2,50,000)

= Rs. 35,00,000

Liquid Liabilities = Rs. 20,00,000

$$\text{Quick Ratio} = \frac{\text{Rs. } 35{,}00{,}000}{\text{Rs. } 20{,}00{,}000}$$

= 1.75 or 1.75 : 1

Comments

The quick ratio is 1.75 : 1 which is considered satisfactory. It indicates that the firm has sound financial position because of the quick ratio is more than the standard (1 : 1). The firm can able to meet its immediate obligations in time. It can also be observed that liquid assets are more than one and half times the liquid liabilities.

(3) Absolute-Liquid Ratio

Absolute Liquid Ratio is also called as Cash Position Ratio or Over Due Liability Ratio. This ratio establishes the relationship between the absolute liquid assets and current liabilities. Absolute Liquid Assets include cash in hand, cash at bank and Marketable Securities or Temporary investments. Both the sundry debtors and bills receivables are excluded as there is always an uncertainty with respect to their realization. The absolute liquid ratio can be calculated by dividing the total of the absolute liquid assets by total current liabilities. Thus,

$$\text{Absolute Liquid Ratio} = \frac{\text{Absolute Liquid Assets}}{\text{Current Liabilities}}$$

Interpretation

The optimum value for this ratio should be one *i.e.*, 1 : 2. It indicates that 50% worth of absolute liquid assets are considered adequate to pay the 100% claims of current liabilities in time. It the ratio is relatively lower than one, it indicates that the company's day to day cash management is poor. If the ratio is considerably more than one, the absolute liquid ratio represents enough funds in the form of cash to meet its short term obligations in time.

Illustration: 4

Calculate absolute liquid ratio from the following information

Liabilities	*Amount* Rs.	*Assets*	*Amount* Rs.
Bills Payable	3,00,000	Goodwill	20,00,000
Sundry Creditors	2,00,000	Land & Building	20,00,000
Share Capital	10,00,000	Inventories	5,00,000
Debenture	20,00,000	Cash in hand	3,00,000
Bank Overdraft	2,50,000	Cash at bank	2,00,000
		Sundry Debtors	5,00,000
		Bills Payable	7,50,000
		Marketable Securities	1,00,000

Solution:

$$\text{Absolute Liquid Ratio} = \frac{\text{Absolute Liquid Assets}}{\text{Current Liabilities}}$$

Absolute Liquid Assets = Cash in hand + Cash at bank + Marketable Securities

= Rs. 3,00,000 + Rs. 2,00,000 + Rs. 1,00,000

= Rs. 6,00,000

Current Liabilities = Rs. 3,00,000 + Rs. 2,00,000 + Rs. 2,50,000

= Rs. 7,50,000

$$\text{Absolute Liquid Ratio} = \frac{\text{Rs. } 6{,}00{,}000}{\text{Rs. } 7{,}50{,}000}$$

= 0.8 or 0.8 : 1

Comment

The ratio of 0.8 is quite satisfactory because it is much higher than the optimum value of 50% or 0.5 : 1. It indicates firm's sound liquidity position to immediately meet its current obligations.

Illustration: 5

You are given the following information :

	Rs.
Cash in hand	1,00,000
Cash at bank	1,50,000
Sundry Debtors	7,50,000
Stock	6,00,000
Bills Payable	2,50,000
Bills Receivable	3,00,000
Sundry Creditors	4,00,000
Outstanding Expenses	2,00,000
Prepaid Expenses	1,00,000
Dividend Payable	1,50,000
Land and Building	20,00,000
Goodwill	10,00,000

Calculate (a) Current Ratio (b) Liquid Ratio and (c) Absolute Liquidity Ratio

Solution:

$$\text{(a) Current Ratio} = \frac{\text{Current Assets}}{\text{Current Liabilities}}$$

Current Assets :	Rs.	*Current Liabilities :*	Rs.
Cash in hand	1,00,000	Bills Payable	2,50,000
Cash at bank	1,50,000	Sundry Creditors	4,00,000
Sundry Debtors	7,50,000	Outstanding Expenses	2,00,000
Stock	6,00,000	Dividend Payable	1,50,000
Bills Receivable	3,00,000	Total Current Liabilities	10,00000
Prepaid Expenses	1,00,000		
Total Current Assets	20,00,000		

$$\text{Current Ratio} = \frac{\text{Rs. } 20,00,000}{\text{Rs. } 10,00,000}$$

$$= 2 \text{ times or } 2 : 1$$

$$\text{(b) Quick Ratio} = \frac{\text{Liquid Assets}}{\text{Current Liabilities}}$$

Liquid Assets = Current Assets – (Stock and Prepaid Expenses)

= Rs. 20,00,000 – (Rs. 6,00,000 + Rs. 1,00,000)

= Rs. 20,00,000 – Rs. 7,00,000 = Rs. 13,00,000

Liquid Ratio = $\frac{\text{Rs. } 13,00,000}{\text{Rs. } 10,00,000}$ = 1.3 times (or) 1.3 : 1

(c) Absolute Liquid Ratio = $\frac{\text{Absolute Liquid Assets}}{\text{Current Liabilities}}$

Absolute Liquid Assets = Cash in hand + Cash at bank + Marketable Securities

= Rs. 1,00,000 + Rs. 1,50,000 + Nil

= Rs. 2,50,000

Absolute Liquid Ratio = $\frac{\text{Rs. } 2,50,000}{\text{Rs. } 10,00,000}$ = 0.25 or 0.25 : 1

Comments

The current ratio of 2: 1 means that current assets are 2 times of current liabilities. It is considered to be satisfactory as a rule of thumb (2:1). An high liquid ratio 1.3 :1 is an indictation that the firm has sound liquid position can easily meet its all current obligation in time. But Absolute Liquid Ratio is below the optimum of 0.50 : 1 indicating that the liquidity position of the firm is not satisfactory. The firm can meet its current obligations only to the extent of 0.25%.

Illustration: 6

Following is the Balance sheet of William & Co Ltd as on December 31st 2004.

Liabilities	*Amount* Rs.	*Assets*	*Amount* Rs.
Equity Share Capital	20,00,000	Goodwill	12,00,000
Capital Reserve	4,00,000	Fixed Assets	28,00,000
8% Loan on Mortgage	16,00,000	Inventories	6,00,000
Sundry Creditors	8,00,000	Sundry Debtors	6,00,000
Bank Overdraft	2,00,000	Investments (short-term)	2,00,000
Taxation : Current	2,00,000	Cash Balances	6,00,000
Future	2,00,000		
Profit & A/c			
Profit for 2004 after taxation			
and interest on Mortgage :			
Loan Rs. 12,00,000			
Less : Transfer to			
reserve 4,00,000			
Less : Dividend 2,00,000	6,00,000		
	60,00,000		60,00,000

Sales amounted to Rs.1,20,00,000. Calculate (1) Current Ratio (2) Liquid Ratio and (3) Absolute Liquid Ratio

Solution:

(1) Current Ratio = $\frac{\text{Current Assets}}{\text{Current Liabilities}}$

Current Assets :

Stock / Inventories	=	Rs. 6,00,000
Sundry Debtors	=	Rs. 6,00,000
Short Term Investment	=	Rs. 2,00,000
Cash Balances	=	Rs. 6,00,000
Total Current Assets	=	Rs. 20,00,000

Current Liabilities :

Sundry Creditors	=	Rs. 8,00,000
Bank Overdraft	=	Rs. 2,00,000
Tax Payable	=	Rs. 2,00,000
Total Current Liabilities	=	Rs. 12,00,000

Current Ratio = $\frac{\text{Rs. } 20,00,000}{\text{Rs. } 12,00,000}$ = 1.67 or 1.67 : 1

(2) Liquid Ratio = $\frac{\text{Liquid Assets}}{\text{Current Liabilities}}$

Liquid Assets = Current Assets – Inventories and Prepaid Expenses

= Rs. 20,00,000 – Rs. 6,00,000

= Rs. 14,00,000

Liquid Ratio = $\frac{\text{Rs. } 14,00,000}{\text{Rs. } 12,00,000}$ = 1.17 Or 1.17 :1

(3) Absolute Liquid Ratio = $\frac{\text{Absolute Liquid Assets}}{\text{Current Liabilities}}$

Absolute Liquid Assets = Cash Balances + Short Term Investments

= Rs. 6,00,000 + Rs. 2,00,000

= Rs. 8,00,000

Absolute Liquid Ratio = $\frac{\text{Rs. } 8,00,000}{\text{Rs. } 12,00,000}$ 0.66 (or) 0.66 :1

Comments

The current ratio is 2 :1. The ratio is only 1.67 hence, the liquidity position is not much satisfactory. At the same time, Liquid Ratio and Absolute Liquid Ratio is 1.17 and 0.66

espectively. It is also observed that both Acid Test ratio are considered as more than deal and the ratios indicate very much favourable to company. The Liquid position of he company can be termed as satisfactory and thus the firm can able to meet to its urrent obligations in time.

llustration: 7

s credit manager of the State Bank of India, you have been approached by two companies or a loan of Rs.4,00,000 for six months, with no collateral offered. Since the bank has lmost exhausted its quota for loans of this type, only one of these requests can be granted. he relevant information supplied to you by the two companies is presented below.

articulars	Company A	Company B
	Rs.	Rs.
sets :		
ash Balance	3,40,000	6,00,000
undry Debtors	5,48,000	8,48,000
nventories	18,00,000	27,00,000
ixed Assets	20,00,000	20,40,000
otal Assets	46,88,000	61,88,000
urrent Liabilities & Capital :		
urrent Liabilities	10,00,000	12,80,000
ong Term Loans	16,00,000	20,00,000
quity Share Capital	16,00,000	24,00,000
etained Earnings	4,88,000	5,08,000
	46,88,000	61,88,000

Additional Information :

Sales	Rs. 48,00,000	Rs. 34,00,000
Rate of Gross Profit on Sales	30%	40%

Considering the above data, specify the company which should be granted the credit. Explain your answer with reasons :

Solution:

Liquidity Ratios are relevant for the bank :

(1) Current Ratio

(2) Acid Test Ratio

Calculations :

$$(1) \text{ Current Ratio} = \frac{\text{Current Assets}}{\text{Current Liabilities}}$$

	Company – A	Company – B
	Rs.	Rs.
Current Assets :		
Cash Balances	3,40,000	6,00,000
Sundry Debtors	5,48,000	8,48,000
Inventories	18,00,000	27,00,000
Total Current Assets	26,88,000	41,48,000
Total Current Liabilities	10,00,000	12,80,000

Current Ratio :

$$\text{Company – A} = \frac{26,88,000}{10,00,000} = 2.69 \text{ or } 2.69:1$$

$$\text{Company – B} = \frac{41,48,000}{12,80,000} = 3.24 \text{ or } 3.24:1$$

(2) $\text{Acid Test Ratio} = \dfrac{\text{Liquid Assets}}{\text{Current Liabilities}}$

	Company – A	Company – B
	Rs.	Rs.
Liquid Assets		
Cash Balances	3,40,000	6,00,000
Sundry Debtors	5,48,000	8,48,000
Total Liquid Assets	8,88,000	14,48,000

Liquid or Acid Test Ratio :

$$\text{Company – A} = \frac{\text{Rs. } 8,88,000}{\text{Rs. } 10,00,000} = 2.89 \text{ or } 0.89:1$$

$$\text{Company – B} = \frac{\text{Rs. } 14,48,000}{\text{Rs. } 12,80,000} = 1.13 \text{ or } 1.13:1$$

Commend

Company – B is, therefore, recommended for being granted the loan as its liquidity ratios are better than those of Company – A.

Illustration: 8

Find out (a) Current Assets (b) Current Liabilities (c) Liquid Assets and

(d) Stock from the following information :

Current ratio	=	2.8 : 1
Acid-Test ratio	=	1.5 : 1
Working Capital	=	Rs. 1,62,000

Solution:

a) Calculation of Current Assets and Current Liabilities :

$$\text{Current Ratio} = \frac{\text{Current Assets}}{\text{Current Liabilities}}$$

Current Ratio is given = 2.8 : 1 or $\frac{2.8}{1}$

Vhere,

Current assets are 2.8 and current liabilities are,

$\therefore$ Working Capital = Current Assets – Current Liabilities

= 2.8 – 1

= 1.8

Working Capital is given = Rs. 1,62,000

$\therefore$ 1.8 = Rs. 1,62,000

ote : Excess of current assets over current liabilities is referred to as working capital

(a) Current Assets = $\frac{2.8}{1.8} \times$ Rs. 1,62,000

= Rs. 2,52,000

(b) Current Liabilities = $\frac{1}{1.8} \times$ Rs. 1,62,000

= Rs. 90,000

) Calculation of Liquid Assets :

$$\text{Liquid Ratio} = \frac{\text{Liquid Assets}}{\text{Current Liabilities}}$$

Liquid Ratio (given) = 1.5 : 1

$$1.5 = \frac{\text{Liquid Assets}}{\text{Rs. } 90{,}000}$$

Liquid Assets = Rs. 90,000 × 1.5 = Rs. 35,000

Calculation of Stock :

Liquid Assets = Current Assets – Stock

Rs. 1,35,000 = Rs. 2,52,000 – Stock

Stock = Current Assets – Liquid Assets

= Rs. 2,52,000 – Rs. 1,35,000

= Rs. 1,17,000

Illustration: 9

Extracts from the financial accounts of M/s Rahave Ltd are given below :

Particulars	*Balance sheet as on 31st Dec.2003*		*Balance sheet as on 31st Dec.2004*	
	Assets Rs.	Liabilities Rs.	Assets Rs.	Liabilities Rs.
Stock	2,00,000	—	4,00,000	—
Debtors	6,00,000	—	6,00,000	—
Prepaid Expenses	40,000	—	—	—
Sundry Creditors	—	5,00,000	—	6,00,000
Bank Overdraft	—	—	—	1,00,000
Bills Payable	—	3,00,000	—	2,40,000
Cash in hand	4,00,000	—	3,00,000	—
Total	12,40,000	8,00,000	13,00,000	9,40,000

Sales amounted to Rs.75,00,000 in the year 2003 and Rs.60,00,000 in the year 200 You are required to comment on the solvency position of the concern with the help accounting ratios.

Solution:

(1) Analysis of the short-term solvency :

Ratios : (1) Current Ratio

(2) Acid Test Ratio or Quick Ratio

(3) Inventory Turnover Ratio

(4) Average Collection Period

$$\text{(1) Current Ratio} = \frac{\text{Current Assets}}{\text{Current Liabilities}}$$

Current Assets (2003) = Rs. 2,00,000 + Rs. 6,00,000 + Rs. 40,000 + Rs. 4,00,(

= Rs. 12,40,000

Current Assets (2004) = Rs. 4,00,000 + Rs. 6,00,000 + Rs. 3,00,000

= Rs. 13,00,000

Current Liabilities (2003) = Rs. 5,00,000 + Rs. 3,00,000

= Rs. 8,00,000

Current Liabilities (2204) = Rs. 6,00,000 + Rs. 1,00,000 + Rs. 2,40,000

= Rs. 9,40,000

$$\text{So, Current Ratio (2003)} = \frac{\text{Rs. }12{,}40{,}000}{\text{Rs. }8{,}00{,}000} = 1.55 \text{ (or) } 1.55$$

$$\text{Current Ratio (2004)} = \frac{\text{Rs. }13{,}00{,}000}{\text{Rs. }9{,}40{,}000} = 1.38 \text{ (or) } 1.38 : 1$$

(2) Acid – Test Ratio or Liquid Ratio :

$$\text{Liquid Ratio} = \frac{\text{Liquid Assets}}{\text{Current Liabilities}}$$

Liquid Assets = Current Assets – Inventories & Prepaid Expenses

Liquid Assets (2003) = Rs. 12,40,000 – (Rs. 2,00,000 + Rs. 40,000)

= Rs. 10,00,000

Liquid Assets (2004) = Rs. 13,00,000 – Rs. 4,00,000

= Rs. 9,00,000

$$\text{So Liquid Ratio(2003)} = \frac{\text{Rs. } 10,00,000}{\text{Rs. } 8,00,000} = 1.25 \text{ (or) } 1.25 : 1$$

$$\text{Liquid Ratio(2004)} = \frac{\text{Rs. } 9,00,000}{\text{Rs. } 9,40,000} = 0.96 \text{ (or) } 0.96 : 1$$

(3) Inventory Turnover Ratio :

$$\text{Inventory Turnover Ratio} = \frac{\text{Net Sales}}{\text{Average Inventory}}$$

$$\text{For 2003} = \frac{\text{Rs. } 75,00,000}{\text{Rs. } 2,00,000} = 37.5 \text{ times}$$

$$\text{Average Inventory (2004)} = \frac{\text{Opening Inventory} = \text{Closing Inventory}}{2}$$

$$= \frac{\text{Rs. } 2,00,000 + \text{Rs. } 4,00,000}{2}$$

$$= \frac{\text{Rs. } 6,00,000}{2} = \text{Rs. } 3,00,000$$

$$\text{Inventory Turnover Ratio (2004)} = \frac{\text{Rs. } 60,00,000}{\text{Rs. } 3,00,000} = 20 \text{ times}$$

Note : During the year 2003, opening inventory has not been given in the problem. Hence Rs.2,00,000 has been taken as average inventory.

Average Collection Period :

$$= \frac{\text{Trade Debtors (including Bills Receivable)}}{\text{Net Sales per day}}$$

(or)

$$= \frac{\text{Trade Debtors}}{\text{Net Sales}} \times \text{No. of working days}$$

$$\text{For 2003} = \frac{\text{Rs. } 6,00,000}{\text{Rs. } 75,00,000} \times 365 \text{ days} = 29.2 \text{ days}$$

For 2004 $= \dfrac{\text{Rs. } 6{,}00{,}000}{\text{Rs. } 60{,}00{,}000} \times 365 \text{ days} = 36.5 \text{ days}$

Comments on Short—term Solvency Position

From the above analysis, it is observed that the short-term solvency position of the company is not sound. An ideal current ratio is 2 : 1. In the year 2003, the current ratio is 1.55 : 1. which indicates much below the standard norms. During the year 2004, the results in current ratio has lowering down to 1.38. The current ratio of both years indicate that the liquidity position of the company has not satisfied. On the other hand, the liquid ratio which is 1.25 indicates a satisfactory position in the year 2003 as it is well above the ideal ratio of 1 : 1. At the same time, during the year 2004, the quick ratio has fallen to 0.96 : 1. It indicates that firm's short-term liquidity position is not satisfied. It is difficult to meet its current obligations in time.

While analyzing the inventory turnover ratio, it is highlighted that the inventory turnover ratio has fallen from 37.5 times in the year 2003 to 20 times in the year 2004. This indicates that the company's efficiency in managing its liquid assets has been not satisfied. Similarly, average collection period has increased from 29.2 days in the 2003 to 36.5 days in 2004. This also proves firm's inefficiency in the collection debts.

(4) Net Working Capital Turnover Ratio : This ratio highlight the effective utilization of working capital with regard to sales. This ratio indicates the firm's liquid position and number of times the working capital is turned over in the course of a year. It establishes relationship between cost of sales and net working capital. It is computed by dividing the amount of sales revenue by the amount of net working capital. Thus,

$$\text{Working Capital Turnover Ratio} = \frac{\text{Net Sales}}{\text{Net Working Capital}}$$

Net working capital = Current Assets – Current Liabilities

Net Sales = Gross Sales – Sales Return

Significance

(1) It is an index to know whether the working capital has been efficiently utilized or not in making sales.

(2) It highlight the liquidity position of a concern.

(3) High working capital turnover ratio indicates the favourable turnover of inventories into sales and then to cash.

(4) Low working capital turnover ratio shows that inadequacy of liquid position accompanied by slow turnover inventories and lower sales.

Illustration: 10

Calculate Working Capital Turnover Ratio

Current Assets	Rs. 3,20,000
Current Liabilities	Rs. 1,10,000
Gross Sales	Rs. 4,00,000
Sales Return	Rs. 20,000

Solution:

$$\text{Working Capital Turnover Ratio} = \frac{\text{Net Sales}}{\text{Net Working Capital}}$$

Net Sales = Gross Sales – Sales Return

= Rs. 4,00,000 – Rs. 20,000 = Rs. 3,80,000

Net Working Capital = Current Assets – Current Liabilities

= Rs. 3,20,000 – Rs. 1,10,000

= Rs. 2,10,000

$$\text{Working Capital Turnover Ratio} = \frac{\text{Rs. } 3{,}80{,}000}{\text{Rs. } 2{,}10{,}000} = 1.80 \text{ times}$$

Comments

The working capital turnover ratio of 1.80 signifies that working capital has been utilized in making sales of 1.80 times in year. This also indicates the favourable turnover of inventories and receivables.

(5) Current Assets to Fixed Assets Ratio : Current assets are invested in various fixed assets to make production and earn considerable profit. The efficiency with which assets are managed directly affect the production and volume of sales. Current assets to fixed assets ratio helps to measure the efficiency of a firm's to utilize its level of current assets to fixed assets. It establishes the relationship between current assets and fixed assets on the basis of liquidity, risk, level of output and returns. It also helps to determining working capital investment policies. It is most wisely use to make the analysis of a short-term financial investment and liquidity of a firm.

The level of current assets to fixed assets can be calculated by dividing the total of current assets by total of the fixed assets. Thus,

$$\text{Current Assets to Fixed Asset Ratio} = \frac{\text{Current Assets}}{\text{Fixed Assets}}$$

This ratio helps to examining the following the alternative working capital policies are :

(a) Conservative policies

(b) Moderate policies

(c) Aggressive policies

(a) Conservative policies : Assuming a constant level of fixed assets a higher current assets to fixed assets ratio refers to conservative policies. It indicates that firm's sound liquidity position and lower risk in order to meet its current obligations and investments. This policy is also termed flexible policy. It also indicates current assets are efficiently utilized at every levels of output.

Moderate policies otherwise termed as Average Current Assets policy. This ratio occurs between higher and lower ratio of current assets to fixed assets ratio. In other words, the current assets policy of most firms may fall between the conservative policies and aggressive policies. This indicates moderate risk and average liquidity position of a firm.

(3) Aggressive policy : Lower level of current Assets to Fixed Assets Ratio represents aggressive policy. This aggressive policy indicates higher risk and poor liquidity position of a firm. It also indicates that the current assets are inefficiently utilized at all levels of output. This policy is also termed as restrictive policy.

The alternative working capital policies may shown in the given below figure :

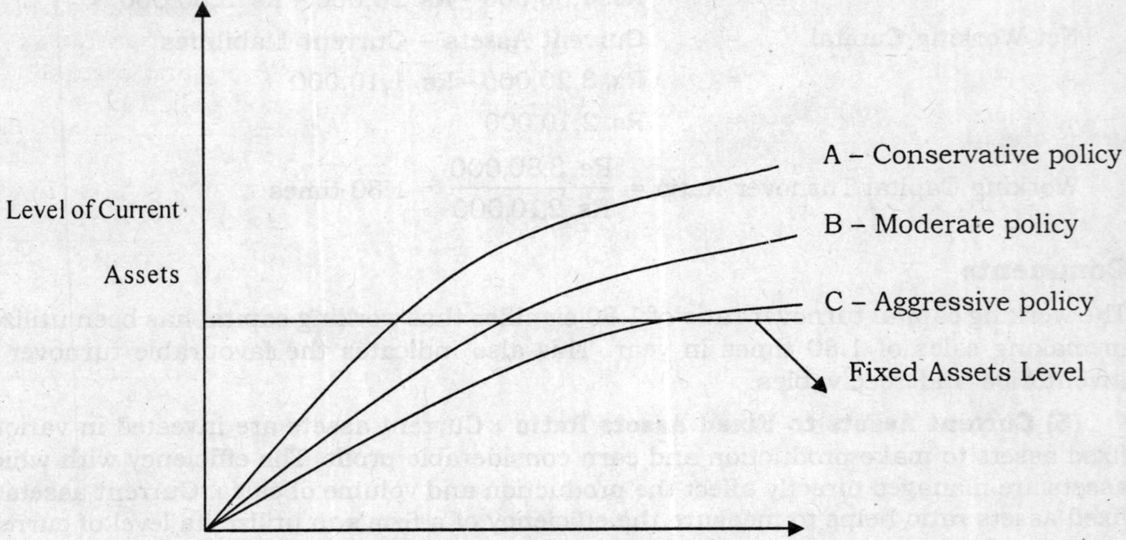

Fig 3.1 : Alternative Working Capital Policies.

A—Conservative policy indicates :

(1) Sound Liquidity.

(2) Lower Risk.

(3) Current assets are efficiently utilized in production.

(4) No bottlenecks in production due to maintenance of huge stock.

(5) Prompt payment of accounts payable because of huge liquid cash in hand.

(6) Prompt payment of accounts payable because of huge liquid cash in hand.

B—Moderate policy indicates :

(1) Moderate Risk.

(2) Average Liquidity Position.

(3) Current assets moderately used in production.

(4) Maintenance of stock of raw materials and work-in-progress and finished goods at an average level.

C—Aggressive Policy indicates :

(1) Poor Liquidity Position.

(2) Higher risk.

(3) Current assets are utilized at lowest in all levels of output.

(4) Maintenance of small stock levels.

(5) Declining size of sales due to rare credit sales facilities.

(6) Stoppage and bottlenecks in production due to lack of stock.

(7) Slower accounts payable payments due to low cash balance in hand.

Illustration: 11

An engineering company is considering its working capital investment for the year 2003-04. The estimated fixed assets and current liabilities for the next year are Rs.6.63 crore and Rs.5.967 crore respectively. The sales and earnings before interest and taxes (EBIT) depend on investment in its current assets—particularly inventory and receivables. The company is examining the following alternative working capital policies:

Working capital policy	*Investment in Current Assets (Rs. Crore)*	*Estimated Sales (Rs. Crore)*	*EBIT (Rs. Crore)*
Conservative	11.475	31.365	3.1365
Moderate	9.945	29.325	2.9325
Aggressive	6.63	25.50	2.55

Your are required to calculate the following for each policy :

(i) Rate of return on total assets.

(ii) Net working capital position.

(iii) Current assets to fixed assets ratio.

(iv) Discuss the risk-return trade off of each working capital policy.

(CA – May 2004)

Solution:

Working Capital Investment Policy (Rs. in Crore)

Particulars	*Conservative*	*Moderate*	*Aggressive*
(i) Current Assets (CA)	11.475	9.945	6.63
(ii) Fixed Assets (FA)	6.63	6.63	6.63
(iii) Total Assets	18.105	16.575	13.26
(iv) Current Liabilities (CL)	5.967	5.967	5.967
(v) Forecast Sales	31.365	29.325	25.50
(vi) Forecast Earning before Interest and Taxes (EBIT)	3.1365	2.9325	2.55
(vii) Rate of return (vi ÷ iii)	17.32%	17.69%	19.23%
(viii) Net working capital (i – iv)	5.508	3.978	0.663
(ix) Current Ratio (i ÷ iv)	1.92	1.67	1.11
(x) CA/FA	1.73	1.50	100

Working Notes :

(1) Calculation of Rate of Return :

$$\text{Rate of Return} = \frac{\text{Forecast or Estimate EBIT (vi)}}{\text{Total Assets (iii)}} \times 100$$

(a) Conservative = $\frac{3.1365}{18.105} \times 100 = 17.32\%$

(b) Moderate = $\frac{2.9325}{16.575} \times 100 = 17.69\%$

(c) Aggressive = $\frac{2.55}{13.26} \times 100 = 19.23\%$

(2) Net Working Capital = Current Assets (i) – Current Liabilities (iv)

(a) Conservative = 11.475 – 5.967 = 5.508 Crores

(b) Moderate = 9.945 – 5.967 = 3.978 Crores

(c) Aggressive = 6.63 – 5.967 = 0.663 Crores

(3) Calculation of Current Ratio :

Current Ratio = $\frac{\text{Current Assets (i)}}{\text{Current Liabilities (iv)}}$

(a) Conservative = $\frac{11.475}{5.967} = 1.92$

(b) Moderate = $\frac{9.945}{5.967} = 1.67$

(c) Aggressive = $\frac{6.63}{5.967} = 1.11$

(4) Calculation of Current Assets to Fixed Assets Ratio :

Current Assets to Fixed Assets Ratio = $\frac{\text{Current Assets (i)}}{\text{Fixed Assets (ii)}}$

(a) Conservative = $\frac{11.475}{6.63} = 1.73$

(b) Moderate = $\frac{9.945}{6.63} = 1.50$

(c) Aggressive = $\frac{6.63}{6.63} = 1.00$

Risk—return trade off

The Networking Capital Position or current ratio is a measure of risk and rate of return on total assets is a measure of return. The expected risk and return are minimum in case of conservative investment policy and maximum in case of aggressive investment policy. The firm can improve profitability by reducing investment in working capital.

Choose the correct answer :

(1) Current assets and current liabilities are the elements:

(a) Current Ratio (b) Liquid Ratio

(c) Absolute Liquid Ratio (d) Gross Profit Ratio

(2) Liquid Ratio is also termed as:

(a) Turnover Ratio (b) Acid Test Ratio

(c) Gross Profit Ratio (d) Proprietary Ratio

(3) Current Liabilities are payable in:

(a) More than 5 years (b) Between 2 to 5 years

(c) Less than a year (d) More than two years

(4) The ideal thump of Current Ratio is:

(a) 1 : 1 (b) 3 : 1 (c) 2 : 1 (d) 2 : 3

(5) Inventory is a part of ————

(a) Current Assets (b) Fixed Assets

(c) Non-Current Assets (d) Liquid Assets

(6) The ideal standard for Liquid Ratio is ————

(a) 2 : 1 (b) 1 : 1 (c) 2 : 3 (d) 0.5 : 1

(7) ———— is to measure the short term solvency of a firm:

(a) Gross profit ratio (b) Net profit ratio

(c) Liquid ratio (d) Price earning ratio

(8) Which of the following item is not included in current ratio?

(a) Goodwill (b) Sundry Debtor

(c) Sundry Creditor (d) Bills Receivable

(9) Which of the following ratios will be useful in indicating liquidity crisis:

(a) Gross profit ratio (b) Net profit ratio

(c) Debt equity ratio (d) Current ratio

(10) ———— indicates borrowing of short term funds:

(a) Stock – Turnover Ratio (b) Debt – Coverage Ratio

(c) Current Ratio (d) Fixed Assets Turnover Ratio

(11) Conservative Current Assets Policy indicates ————

(a) Greater Liquidity (b) Higher Risk

(c) Poor Liquidity (d) Moderate Risk

(12) Poor Liquidity and higher risk represent:

(a) Conservative Current Asset Policy

(b) Aggressive Current Asset Policy

(c) Moderate Current Asset Policy

(d) None of the above

(13) Moderate Current Asset Policy indicates:

(a) Moderate Risk (b) Poor Liquidity

(c) Average Liquidity Position (d) Both a and c

[**Ans** : 1. (a) Current Assets 2. (b) Acid – Test Ratio 3. (c) Less than a year

4. (c) 2 : 1 5. (d) Liquid Assets 6. (b) 1 : 1 7. (c) Liquid Ratio

8. (a) Goodwill 9. (d) Current Ratio 10. (c) Current Ratio

11. (a) Greater Liquidity 12. (b) Aggressive Current Asset Policy

13. (d) Both a and c.

Questions:

(1) What is mean by Liquidity?

(2) What are the factors determining liquidity of a concern?

(3) Explain briefly the measurement of liquidity.

(4) Explain the significant of current ratio. How it is used to measure of liquidity?

(5) What are the liquidity ratio? Explain it in details.

(6) Explain the advantages of current ratio.

(7) What are the important components of liquid ratio. How it is used to measure liquidity?

(8) Explain the significance of quick ratio.

(9) Examine critically the different liquidity ratios to measure liquidity of a concern.

(10) What is Net Working Capital Turnover Ratio? Explain it significance.

(11) Write short notes on :

(a) Conservative Policies

(b) Moderate Policies

(c) Aggressive Policies

(d) Current Assets to Fixed Assets Ratio

Practical Problems :

(1) Your are given the following information

Cash	1,80,000
Debtors	1,42,000
Closing Stock	18,00,000
Bill Payable	2,70,000
Sundry Creditors	5,00,000
Outstanding expenses	1,50,000
Tax payable	7,50,000

Calculate (a) Current Ratio (b) Liquidity Ratio and (c) Absolute Liquidity Ratio

(**Ans** : (a) Current Ratio 2.036 : 1

(b) Liquidity Ratio 0.96 : 1

(c) Absolute Liquid Ratio 0.11 : 1

(2) From the following details, find out :

(1) Current Assets

(2) Current Liabilities

(3) Liquid Assets

(4) Stock

Given : Current Ratio 2.5

Liquid Ratio 1.5

Working Capital Rs. 6,00,000

(**Ans** : Current Assets Rs. 10,00,000

Current Liabilities Rs. 4,00,000

Liquid Assets Rs. 6,00,000

Stock Rs. 4,00,000)

(3) The following are the extracts from the financial statements of Rahave Ltd. as on 31st Dec. 2003 and 2004 respectively.

	31st Dec.2003	*31st Dec. 2004*
	Rs.	*Rs.*
Inventories	1,00,000	2,50,000
Sundry Debtors	2,00,000	2,00,000
Bills Receivable	1,00,000	50,000
Advances (recoverable in cash)	20,000	—
Cash balances	1,80,000	1,50,000
Sundry Creditors	2,50,000	3,00,000
Bills Payable	1,50,000	2,00,000
Bank Overdraft	—	20,000
9% Debentures	50,00,000	50,00,000
Sales for the year	35,00,000	30,00,000

You are required to compute for both the years

(1) Current Ratio (2) Liquid Ratio (3) Absolute Liquid Ratio

(5) Stock Turnover Ratio

	2003	2004
(**Ans** : (1) Current Ratio	1.5 : 1	1.25 : 1
(2) Liquid Ratio	0.77 : 1	0.80 : 1
(3) Absolute Liquid Ratio	0.77 : 1	0.80 : 1
(4) Stock Turnover Ratio	0.5 : 1	1.92 : 1

(4) Following is the Balance sheet of ABC Ltd. as in 31st December 2004

Liabilities	*Rs.*	*Assets*	*Rs.*
Equity Share Capital	10,00,000	Goodwill	5,00,000
General Reserve	2,50,000	Fixed Assets	15,00,000

Profit and Loss A/c	4,00,000	Stock	4,00,000
Secured Loans	7,00,000	Sundry Debtors	4,90,000
Sundry Creditors	5,00,000	Advances	1,00,000
Bank Overdraft	3,00,000	Bank Balances	2,00,000
Provision for Taxation	2,00,000	Cash in hand	1,60,000
	33,50,000		33,50,000

You are required to calculate

(a) Current Ratio (b) Liquid Ratio (c) Absolute Liquid Ratio

(**Ans** : (a) Current Ratio 1.35 : 1 (b) Liquid Ratio 0.95 : 1 (c) Absolute Liquid Ratio 0.36 : 1.

CASH MANAGEMENT

Introduction

Cash plays a vital role in the entire economic life of a business. Cash is the basic components of input required to make payment to its suppliers, to met day to day operating expenses of any firm, Therefore, it is essential for a business to maintain adequate balance of cash. Thus, cash management is one of the key area of working capital management. The basic objective of financial management is to match the inflows and outflows of cash and ensure the liquidity and adequate cash position of a concern during a particular period. This may be because, the present chapter focuses on the following aspect of cash management :

(1) Meaning and nature of cash

(2) Issues of cash management

(3) Motives for holding cash

(4) Cash planning

(5) Factors determining cash needs

(6) Cash Management Model :

(a) Baumol Model

(b) Miller-Orr Model

(7) Various Tools of Cash Planning :

(a) Cash Budget (Receipts and Payments Method)

(b) Cash Flow From Operation

(c) Cash Inflow And Cash Outflow Statements (Financial)

(d) Statement of Working Capital Forecast

Meaning of Cash

The term cash has a variety of meanings. In a narrow sense, that it includes coins, currency notes, bank draft, with draws by cheques on demand and bank balances in bank accounts. In a broader sense, the term cash refers to as near cash assets. Such cash equivalent assets are marketable securities, time deposit in banks and treasury bills etc. : The basic charactertics of these is that they can be easily converted into cash. In fact, what blood is to a human body, cash is the company's liquid asset and can be used immediately to make payments. Both cash and near-cash assets are used in cash management. Cash is therefore apply described as the oil to lubricate the ever-turning wheels of business; without it the process grinds to a stop.

(1) Cash serves as a liquid asset

(2) Cash as the medium of exchange on the common purchasing power

(3) Cash and near-cash assets can be immediately sold and converted into cash

(4) Cash as a working asset to meet in day to day payment of operational obligations.

(5) Cash as a most significant and least productive asset

(6) Cash is an asset, it earns only when it is in use.

(7) Cash is the basic input needed to keep the business running on a continuous basis

Motives For Holding Cash

John Maynard Keynes has identified the following motives for cash is held by the firm

(1) Transaction Motive

(2) Precautionary Motive

(3) Speculative Motive

(4) Compensation Motive

(1) Transaction Motive : Transaction motive refers to the holding of cash required by a firm to carry its day to day business transactions in the ordinary course of business. The firm required to maintain purchase of raw materials, wages, operating expenses, interest, taxes, dividends and so on. In other words, any transaction result in decreasing the cash position is refers to cash outflow or cash payments or application of cash or uses of cash. Similarly, any transaction results in increase the cash position is represent cash inflow or cash receipts. Thus, the cash receipts and cash payments constitute a continuous two-way flow of cash. Since, the receipt of cash is not perfectly synchronized with the outflow of cash, the firm should maintain some adequate cash balance to be able to make the required payments. The requirement of cash balance to meet the routine business obligations is known as the transaction motive and such cash balances are termed as transaction balances.

(2) Precautionary Motive : According to this motive, the firm keep sufficient cash balances to meet unexpected cash needs arising at short notice may be the result of :

(a) Floods, strikes, droughts and failure of important customers

(b) Bills may be presented for payment earlier than expected

(c) Unexpected slow down in collection of accounts receivable

(d) Cancellation of some orders for goods as the customer is not satisfied

(e) Share increase in the cost of raw materials and labour

This is why, it is necessary to reserve sufficient cash balances to protect against such uncertainties are called as precautionary balances. The size of the cash balances to be maintained may depends upon

(1) Possibility of unforeseen fluctuations
(2) Ability of the firm to borrow cash at short notice
(3) Investment in short-term or marketable securities
(4) Risk associated with marketable securities or short term investments
(5) Availability of short-term credit
(6) Loss or return on precautionary balances
(7) Costs to meet the unforeseen obligations
(8) Degree of liquidity about marketable securities
(9) Maximum credit limit, company policies, investment plan etc.

(3) Speculative Motive : An important reason for holding cash balances is the speculative motive. This refers to maintaining cash balance, the firm to take advantage of investing in profit making opportunities and which typically outside the normal course of business. Such motive, is therefore, of purely a defensive in nature, the firm must carry additional liquidity. Thus, the speculative motive represent a positive and aggressive approach. The speculative motive helps to take advantage of :

(a) The opportunity to make profit arising from fluctuations in commodity prices.
(b) Purchase of raw materials at a reduced rate on payment of immediate cash *i.e.* benefit of cash discount and trade discount
(c) A chance to speculate on interest rates, security prices and foreign exchange rate by buying securities when rates are expected to decline.
(d) Delay purchases of raw materials on the anticipation of decline in prices.
(e) To make purchases at favourable prices.

(4) Compensation Motive : This motive for holding cash balances is to compensate banks for providing certain services to their clients free of charge. Banks provide variety of services to business firms, such as clearance of cheque, supply of credit information transfer of funds etc. While for some of the services banks charges a commission or fee, for others they seek indirect compensation. In other words, usually clients are required to maintain a minimum cash balances at the bank, which help them to earn interest and thus compensate them for the free services so provided.

Objectives of Cash Management

The chief objectives of cash management are of two fold:

(a) Meeting Cash Disbursements (Payment Schedule)
(b) Minimizing funds committed to cash balances

(a) Meeting Cash Disbursements : The basic objective of management is to make payment of cash in connection with normal course of business. In other words, the primary objective of cash management is to meet the payment schedule *i.e.*, to have sufficient cash to make payments for purchase of raw materials, wages, operating expenses, taxes, dividend etc. Thus, the financial manager to ensure sufficient cash balances to meet the payment schedule at minimum costs.

(b) Minimizing Funds Committed to Cash Balances : In addition to primary objective, the cash management ensure to minimize the amount locked up as cash balances. In minimizing the cash balances two conflicting aspect have to be reconciled. A high leve or sufficient cash balances ensures proper payment together with all the advantages But it also implies that large balance of cash remaining idle. A low level of cash balances may result in failure to meet the payment schedule. The aim of cash managemen should be to have an optimum amount of cash balances.

Factors Determining Cash Needs

The following factors are to be considered before determining the amount of cash requirements for the operations of the business :

(1) Synchronization of cash flows
(2) Consideration of short costs
(3) Position of accounts receivable
(4) Nature of product / business
(5) Availability of other sources of funds
(6) Management's attitude regarding procurement
(7) Operating and cash cycle
(8) Market conditions in relation to assets
(9) Control of cash disbursements

(1) Synchronization of Cash Flows : Cash inflows and outflows should be so planne as it would help in determining cash surplus or deficit for the period for which the plan i related. With this object in view, the first consideration to ascertain the discrepancie between cash receipts and cash payments on the basis of normal business activities For this purpose, cash budget to be prepared. Under this method, shows the timing an magnitude of expected cash collection and uses over the budgeted period.

(2) Consideration of Short Costs : Cost of Short falls in the firm's cash needs nc only influence the need for working capital but also increase the cost of productior Such costs incurred as result of borrowing cash at high rate of interest, cost associate with legal formalities, transaction cost incurred with raising cash and loss of trad discount etc.

(3) Position of Accounts Receivable : Another general factor to be considered i determining cash needs is the time required for converting the accounts receivabl into cash. The higher rate of receivable turnover is necessary for a firm to conduct larg volume of business.

(4) Nature of Product / Business : The cash requirements of a firm mainly depen on the nature of its business. Trading concerns have operates large volume of tradin activities, need for cash requirements are very large. On the other hand, manufacturin or public utility concerns need for cash is much less. Further, cash requirement influenced by the firm's demand.

(5) Availability of Other Sources of Fund : Before determining the cash needs, company must ascertain the availability of other sources of fund. In order to meet th emergency obligations, the financial manager to negotiate short-term financir arrangement with banks or private financial institutions.

(6) Management's Attitude Regarding Procurement : Cash requirement of a fir is influency by the attitude of management, staff and activities. To enhance the efficiency of cash management procurement or collection of cash, process the cheques received, and alternative cash sources should be properly monitored.

(7) Operating and cash cycle : Another factor affecting the cash requirement is the operating and cash cycle. The operating and cash cycle refers to the length of the period of manufacture which starts with the procurement of raw materials converts into finished goods and then sells the same. The time that elapses between the purchase of raw materials and the collection of cash for sales is referred to as the operating cycle, where as the time length between the payment for raw material purchases and the collection of cash for sales referred to as cash cycle.

(8) Market conditions in relation to assets : Market conditions and volume of sales are the important factors to a great extent, the volume of cash requirements. In case of increase in the volume of sales and change in the demand for the products and services correspondingly there will be maintaining huge cash balances to investment in inventories and accounts receivable.

(9) Control of cash disbursements : Cash needs of a firm is closely related to the control of cash disbursements. The firm need cash to invest inventories, receivables and fixed assets and to make payments for operating expenses in order to maintain growth in sales and earnings. At the same time, the cash management must ensure the controlling the use of cash. It involves a projection of future cash inflows and cash disbursements of the firm over various intervals of time.

Advantages of Maintaining Optimum or Adequate Cash

A firm holding sufficient cash balances can drive the following benefits from it:

(1) Sufficient cash balances help to increases efficiency of operations and higher productivity.

(2) It ensures higher liquidity and enhance the rate of earnings.

(3) Ample cash helps to availed cash discount and trade discounts from the suppliers.

(4) It helps to maintaining goods will of the concern.

(5) It ensures the credit worthiness and financial soundness of a concern.

(6) It facilitates new investments and expanding its future market.

(7) It creates good confidence among the investors, creditors customers, employees and general public.

(8) Ample cash balances ensure regular flow of cash for meeting routine course of business operations.

(9) It ensures regular flow of raw materials to the process of production.

(10) It facilitates to enjoy the new business opportunities.

(11) It ensures inventories for steady supplying the needs of customers.

(12) It helps to overcome the short term crises caused by depression.

Issues in Cash Management

The chief aim of cash management is to match the inflows and outflows of cash in such a way that the numerous demands for cash like payment for expenses, payment to suppliers etc. are promptly managed without maintaining excessive cash balance. It is very essential for a business to maintain an adequate balance of cash. But many times, a concern operates profitability and yet it becomes very difficult to predict cash flows accurately and that there is no perfect coincidence between the inflows and outflows of cash. This may be because, huge cash collection from sale of goods and services, sale of assets and additional financing will exceed the cash payments. During some periods, cash outflows will be more than cash inflows because payment for purchase of goods and services, acquisition of capital assets and meeting other obligations. At other times holding of cash balance has an implicit cost in the form of opportunity cost. The higher the amount of idle cash lead to a loss of earning power if a company is unable to finance attractive investments. Reducing cash balance by reinvesting in an liquid assets that gives a higher return may increase the risk that there will be insufficient cash to meet future obligations.

Cash management is important since it is very difficult to correct prediction of cash flows. Practically, it is not so easy to resolve about lack of synchronization between cash receipts and cash payments. To control a company's cash flows, the firm should develop some strategies for cash management for the following:

(1) Cash Planning

(2) Managing the Cash Flows

(3) Optimum Cash Level

(4) Investing Idle Cash

(1) Cash Planning : Cash budget or cash forecast is an important device prepared to ascertain the expected cash receipts and cash payments over the budget period. It helps to determine the cash surplus or deficit of a firm through the inflows and outflows of cash.

(2) Managing the Cash Flows : Managing the cash flows is vital importance in financial management. For short-term planning, controlling of cash inflows and cash outflows should be properly managed. So that the synchronization between inflows and outflows is possible.

(3) Optimum Cash Level : The firm should determine to hold optimum level of cash balances. Financing cash shortage and cost of running out of cash also to determine the optimum level of cash. Thus, it is necessary to avoid excessive or insufficient cash balances.

(4) Investing Idle Cash : The basic strategies for efficient management of cash is to surplus or idle cash should be properly invested to earn profits.

Avoiding Cash Deficit or Cash Insolvency

While maintaining cash inflows and outflows the management should be very particular in striking a desired level of cash balance to meet the payment schedule and to minimize funds committed to cash balances. If the cash flow is inadequate or holding deficit cash balances leads to create many problems. A cash deficit may be dealt with in the following ways:

(1) Utilize unavailed credit limits.

(2) Sell marketable securities.

(3) The collections from customers and sundry debtors should be accelerated.

(4) The deficit may be met temporarily by interdepartmental transfer to excess cash

(5) Negotiate spacing of repayment schedules of term liabilities.

(6) Negotiate for enhancement of short-term loan with banks.

(7) Account receivable may be discounted with a bank.

(8) Defer payment of suppliers bills may be extent to the possible.

(9) Sell redundant assets.

(10) Overhead expenditure should be brought under control.

(11) Cash management should take necessary steps to reduce cash outflows.

(12) Investing in marketable securities should be delayed.

(13) The cash management should ensure the easy availability working capital finance from banks.

Utilization of Cash Surplus or Excess Cash

A excess or surplus cash balance represent the excess volume of money a company keeps with banks on current or deposit account or invested in short term (marketable securities) investments and the money it holds in the company's cash departments. In other words, excess or surplus cash is the cash in excess of the firm's normal cash requirements. Excessive cash balance or Idle cash can lead to a loss of earning power if a company is unable to finance attractive investments. Cash surplus or Idle cash should utilized in the following ways :

(1) Surplus cash to be invested in temporary investments which are readily marketable to fetch desired quantum of profit.

(2) Idle cash to be invested in fixed assets for development, modernization and expansion of business units for the purpose of earning revenue.

(3) To avoid solvency or unable to meet its future obligations, the management often resort to interdepartmental transfer of excess cash.

(4) Excess cash to be used for reduce the firm's term loan or borrowed capital availed at higher rate of interest.

(5) Idle cash to be invested in high liquid and low risk marketable securities.

(6) Surplus cash to be utilized when it is expected that interest rates will rise and security prices will fall.

The cash management should consider the following aspects before surplus cash investing in marketable securities:

(1) High Return / Yield

(2) Low Risk

(3) High Liquidity

(4) Period of Maturity

(5) Terms of Investments

Marketable Securities

If the firm has excess cash balances, it may decide to convert it to short-term investments. The financial manager will purchase low risk, high liquidity money market investments that can be converted back to cash without delays if the need arises. This is known as marketable securities.

Types of Marketable Securities

There are variety of options are available a firm can invest its excess cash used as short term investment. In practice, short-term investments may be in the form of marketable securities. Each security offers different characteristics that it suitable for different firm. These securities are:

(1) Treasury Securities

(2) Banker's Acceptance

(3) Commercial Paper

(4) Global Depository Receipts

(5) Factoring

(6) Repurchase Agreement

(7) Negotiable Certificates of Deposits

(1) Treasury Securities : This type of marketable securities popular in US. These are obligations of the Government Treasury and are issued weekly on an auction basis. The treasury weekly auctions bills with maturities of 91 days and 182 days. In addition, nine month and one year bills are sold every month. In practice, Treasury bills are sold every month bidding, going to the highest bidding. These securities are extremely popular with companies as short transaction cost are small in the sales of Treasury bills in the secondary market.

(2) Banker's Acceptance : Banker's Acceptance is an instrument that are accepted by banks, and they are used in financing international trade. A draft is drawn by a Importer, in order to finance a foreign purchase ordering a commercial bank to pay some amount of money to the holder or exporter at some specified future date. When the order is accepted by the bank it becomes an obligation of the bank. Acceptances generally have maturities of less than six months and are of high quality. The rate on banker's acceptances trend to be slightly higher than rates on treasury bill of like maturity.

(3) Commercial Paper : The companies, which are financially sound and has a good track record can access to an instrument, known as the Commercial Paper (CP). To give a boost to he money market and reducing the dependence of high rated corporate borrowers on bank finance for meeting their working capital requirement corporate borrowers were permitted to arrange short-term borrowing by issue of commercial paper w.e.f. 1st January 1990. Commercial paper is a new instrument used for financing working capital requirements of corporate enterprises.

A commercial paper is a short-term usance promissory note issued by a company, negotiable by endorsement & delivery, issued at such a discount on face value as any be determined by the issuing company. Commercial Papers can be sold either directly or through dealers. These notes are issued by firm's needing cash for periods 3 days to 270 days. Many large fiancé companies have found it profitable, because of the volume, to sell their paper directly to investors, thus by passing dealers. Commercial paper is normally purchased through a bank or securities dealers. Each commercial paper will bear a certificate from the bank verifying the signature of the executants.

(4) Global Depository Receipts : Depository Receipts issued by a company anywhere in the global other than USA are known as Global Depository Receipts (GDR). A depository receipt is basically a negotiable certificate, denominated in US company's publically traded local currency (Indian Rupee) equity shares. In theory, though a depository receipt can also signify debt instrument, in practice it rarely does. Depository Receipts are created when the local currency shares of an Indian company are delivered to the depository's local custodian bank against which the depository bank issues Depository Receipts in US Dollars. These overseas markets like any other dollar denominated security via either a foreign stock exchange or through a over counter market or among restricted group such as Qualified Institutional Buyers. Rule 144 A of Security and Exchange Commission of USA permits companies from outside USA to offer their GDR's to Qualified Institutional Buyers. The Global Depository Receipts are traded on US exchange but not listed.

(5) Factoring : Factoring is a new financial service that is presently being developed in India. Factoring involves provision of specialized services relating to credit investigation, sales ledger management, purchase & collection of debts, credit protection as well as provision of finance against receivables and risk bearing. In factoring, account receivables are generally sold to financial institutions (a subsidiary of commercial bank called factor) who charges commission and bears the credit risk associated with the accounts receivable purchased by it. Factoring offers the following advantages.

(1) Immediate conversion of accounts receivable in to cash.

(2) Ensures a definite pattern of cash inflows.

(3) Continuous factoring eliminates the need for credit department.

(4) Saving of substantial credit and collections costs.

(6) Repurchase Agreements : A repurchase agreements is not a specific security, it an effort to tap important sources of financing. These involve the sale of securities by a government security dealers offers repurchase agreements to company. The repurchase agreement or "repo" is the sale of specific marketable securities to a firm and agrees to repurchase the securities at a specified price at a specified point of time. The repurchase agreements give the investor a great deal of flexibility with respect to maturity.

(7) Negotiable Certificate of Deposits : Certificate of Deposits are negotiable instruments evidencing of the deposits of funds at a commercial bank for a specified period of time at a specified rate of interest. In other worlds, the bank agrees to pay the bearer the amount of the deposit plus a stipulated amount of interest at maturity. The yield on Certificate of Deposit is typically above that on treasury bills and slightly above the yield on commercial paper.

Short Costs Or Cost of Being Short of Cash

The term short cost refers to the expenses incurred as a result of short fall of cash. In other words, cost associated with a shortage of cash in the firm's cash requirements. Such costs may be incurred in any of the following forms :

(1) Loss of Discount

(2) Transaction Cost

(3) Borrowing Cost

(1) Loss of Discounts : Substantial loss incurred in the form of cash discount and trade discount due to shortage of cash.

(2) Transaction Cost :

(a) Cost associated when a firm must incur to remedy the liquid situation to arrest a crisis.

(b) Brokerage incurred in relation to the sale of marketable securities

(3) Borrowing Costs :

(a) Cost involved when a firm must incur to procure urgently the amount needed to restore the liquidity.

(b) High rate of interest, commitment charges and other expenses relating to the loan or credit facilities availed from banks or private financial institutions.

(c) Cost associated in the form of penalty rates charged by the banks for not meeting the obligations in time.

(d) Borrowing costs or opportunity costs incurred a firm to maintaining liquidity.

Cash Cycles and Cash Turnover

Cash Cycle refers to the process by which cash is used to purchase of raw materials from which are produced finished goods, which are then sold to customers who later pay bills. The firm receives cash from customers and the cycle repeat itself.

The term Cash Turnover means the number of times each year the firm's cash is actually turned over.

The concept of cash cycle and cash turnover involves several questions to be answered are :

(1) How long does the raw materials remain in stock before working-in-progress beings?

(2) What is the duration of the work in-progress?

(3) How long do the finished goods remain in stock?

(4) How long do the debtors take to pay?

(5) What is the period of credit taken from suppliers?

Based on the above questions, the cash cycle identified the several stages along the way as fund flow from the firm's account.

Different Stages in Cash Cycle Model

(1) Purchase of raw materials on account

(2) Average time (days) involved in holding stock of inventory (stock of raw materials, work-in-progress and finished goods)

(3) Sell finished goods on account

(4) Average time (days) involved in accounts receivable or book debts

(5) Collect account receivable (Inflow of cash)

(6) Average time (days) involved in accounts payable

(7) Pay accounts payable (Outflow of cash)

The stock of raw materials related to the purchases, and so must the credit taken from the suppliers—since the total paid or payable to the suppliers in a period will be the total of the purchases. The work-in-progress will be related to the costs of goods sold and so will the finished goods stock. The credit taken by the customer (the debtors) must be related to the credit sales. It also may be noted that the cash cycle of the firm can be measured by finding the average number of days that elapses between the cash outflows associated with paying accounts payable and the cash inflows associated with collecting accounts receivable. In order to credit control procedure, production process and inventory policy are working efficiently the cash management executive the given below each possible course of action would need to be considered carefully.

(1) Implication of holding smaller stock of raw materials for shorter period before beginning to work on them.

(2) Possibility of production period to be reduced.

(3) Impact on stock of finished goods are held to be reduced.

(4) Implication about the amount and duration of credit allowed to customers be reduced.

(5) Impact on sales decline.

(6) Effect on the goodwill of customers and or suppliers be damaged.

(7) Possibility on loss of production or output of the factory.

(8) Percentage of cash to the current assets.

(9) Percentage of cash to the total resources/assets.

(10) Rate of rotation of cash : This is calculated by dividing the annual sales with average cash balances.

(11) Percentage of cash to the net annual sales.

(12) Number of days sales the cash balances represent.

Function of Cash Management

The following basic functions are involved in cash management:

I. Controlling inflow of cash or sources of cash

(a) Accelerating Collection

(b) Concentration Banking

(c) Lock-box System

(d) Efficient Inventory Production Management

II. Control Over Cash Outflows or Application of Cash

(a) Efficient System of Cash Disbursement

(b) Billing Float

(c) Mail Float

(d) Check Processing Float

(e) Bank Processing Float

III. Optimum investment of surplus cash

IV. Controlling Level of Cash

(a) Preparing cash of cash

(b) Providing unpredictable discrepancies

(c) Consideration of short cost

(d) Exploring other source of finance

I. Controlling Inflow of Cash or Sources of Cash : It is the important function of cash management. In order to ensure effective cash management, it is attempt to accelerate collection, slow up disbursement and maximize available cash, the following methods can be adopted.

(1) Accelerating Collection

(2) Concentration Banking

(3) Lock-box System

(4) Efficient Inventory Production Management

(1) Accelerating Collections : Collections can be accelerated by way of

(a) Speed the mailing time of payments from customers to the firm.

(b) Reduce the time during which payments received by the firm remain collected funds.

(c) speed the movement of funds to the disbursement banks.

(d) Reducing the firm's operating cash requirements is to speed up the collection of accounts receivable.

(2) Concentration Banking : Concentration of banking is a system of decentralized collection of accounts receivable. In other words, under this system number of centres are opened for collection of payments against sales. The purpose is to reduce the time gap between despatch of cheques by customers and actual receipts of same by the concerned firms. Accordingly, all the collections from customers are deposited in the local banks of the collection centers and there after funds are transferred to main office or in other words all the funds are concentrated in the main bank of the head accounts receivable is known as Concentration Banking. It ensures controlling the firm's funds and minimizing idle cash balances.

(3) Lock-box System : Another means of accelerating the flow of funds is a lock-box arrangement. The lock-box system differs from concentration banking in that the customer, instead of mailing payment to a collection center, send it to a post office box. The purpose of a lock-box arrangement is to reduce the amount of time between the receipts of remittances by the company and their deposit in the bank. A lock-box arrangement usually is on a regional basis the company choosing regional banks according to its billing patterns. It eliminates the check processing float completely because the firm does not record the checks until after they have been deposited.

(4) Efficient Inventory Production Management : Another way of minimizing required cash is to increase the inventory turnover rate. It can be achieved by:

(a) Increasing the raw materials turnover.

(b) Decreasing the production cycle—by initiating better production planning and control technique, the firm can reduce the length of production cycle.

(c) Increasing the finished goods turnover.

II. Control Over Cash Outflows or Application Of Cash : Efficient system of cash disbursement, it is essentials to consider the following terms :

Float : The term float refers to the periods that affect cash as it moves through the different stages of the collection process. In other words, the word float indicates that the amount of money tied up in checks that have been written but have yet to be collected or paid on. The following are the four kinds of float are identified :

(1) Billing Float

(2) Mail Float

(3) Check Processing Float

(4) Bank Processing Float

(1) Billing Float : An invoice is the formal document a seller prepares and sends to a purchaser as the payment request for goods sold or services provided. The time between the sale and the mailing of the invoice is the billing float.

(2) Mail Float : This is the time period that a check is being processed by the post office, messenger service or other means of delivery.

(3) Check Processing Float : This is the time required by a company to process checks internally. This internal extends from the moment a check is received to the moment it is deposited with a bank for credit to the company account.

(4) Bank Processing Float : This aspect of float involves the time consumed in clearing the check through the banking system. A check becomes collected funds when it is presented to the advance bank and actually paid by that bank.

III. Optimum Investment of Surplus Cash :

Cash Management Models : Liquidity is maintained in the form of cash, bank balances and marketable securities (nearer cash assets). It may be necessary for a cash management to know what should be the optimum cash and bank balances must be maintain, and for that purpose how often and in what quantity marketable securities should be purchased or sold. There are number cash management models developed so far to determine the optimum level of cash balances. The following two important cash models are :

(1) William J. Baumol Model

(2) Merton Miller and Daniel Orr Model

(1) William J. Baumal Model (Inventory Model) : William J. Baumal's mathematical model is based on the combination of inventory theory with monetary theory. In determination of optimum level of cash of a company, Economic Order Quantity Model is used in the standard inventory situation. According to this model, the optimum cash level is that level of cash where the carrying costs and transaction cost are the minimum. In other words, the optimumal level of cash is one at which cost of carrying the inventory of cash and cost of going to the market satisfying cash requirements is minimum. The carrying cost of holding cash refers to the interest foregone on marketable securities where as transaction cost represents the cost of liquidating marketable securities in cash. The formula for determining optimum cash balances is :

$$C = \sqrt{\frac{2UP}{S}}$$

Where :

C = Optimum cash balances *i.e.*, (optimum amount of cash to be with drawn each time).

U = Annual (monthly) cash disbursement (total amount of transaction demand).

P = Fixed cost per transaction.

S = Opportunity cost of one Re. P.a (Cost of carrying cash Inventory interest rate on marketable securities for the period involved)

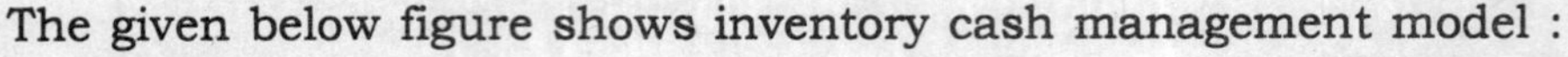

The given below figure shows inventory cash management model :

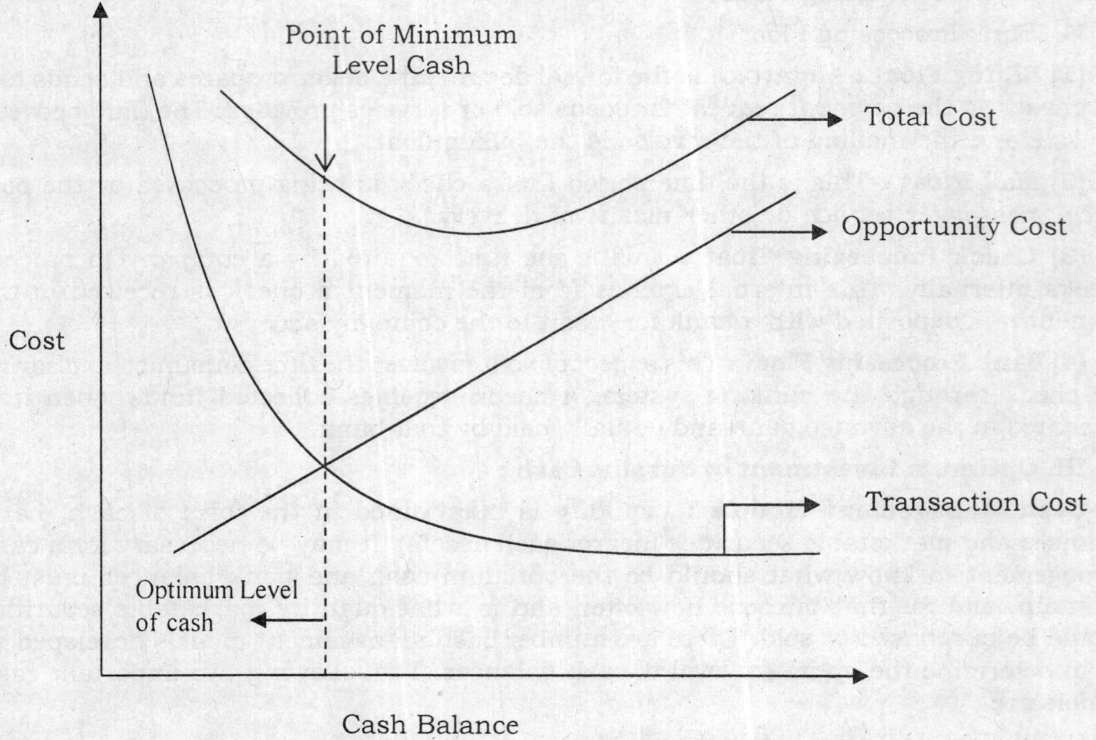

Fig 4.1 : Optimal Cash Level.

Assumption

The model can be applied with the following assumptions :

(1) Cash payments are predictable.

(2) Constant demand for cash during the period under consideration.

(3) Transaction cost of obtaining cash and holding cost for a particular period are given and do not change during the period.

Illustration:

A B C Ltd, estimated cash payments of 40 lakhs for a one month period. The average fixed cost for securing capital from market is Rs.100 and the interest rate on marketable securities is 12% per annum or 1.0 per cent for the one month period. What is the economic order size of cash?

Solution:

The optimum size of cash balance in this instance will be :

$$C = \sqrt{\frac{2UP}{S}}$$

Where :

C = Optimum cash balance

U = Rs. 40,00,000 (monthly cash payment)
P = Rs.100 (fixed cost per-transaction)
S = 12% p.a or 1% for the month (opportunity cost)

$$C = \sqrt{\frac{2 \times 100 \times 40,00,000}{.01}}$$

The optimal transaction of the company is Rs. 2,82,487.

(2) Miller—Orr Cash Management Model : Their view was that cash balance of business world is not as simple as that prescribed by William J. Baumal. This model set control of 'h' as upper limit, "Z" as the return point; and zero as the lower limit. When cash balance reaches the upper limit, the transfer of cash equal to "h – z" is invested in marketable securities account. When it touches the lower limit, a transfer from marketable securities account to cash account is made. The objective of the model is to maximize earning by investing in securities. It should noted that the determination of optimum value of "h" and "z" depends upon the result of fluctuation in the trend of operating receipts and payments and the fixed and opportunity cost. The optimal value of "Z", the return to point for security transaction is determined by the given below formula:

$$Z = \sqrt{\frac{3b\sigma^2}{4i}}$$

Where :

b = Fixed cost associated with a security transaction.
σ^2 = Variance of daily net cash flows.
i = Interest rate per day on marketable securities.

The optimal value of 'h' is simply 3Z

The following diagram illustrates the Miller—Orr Model

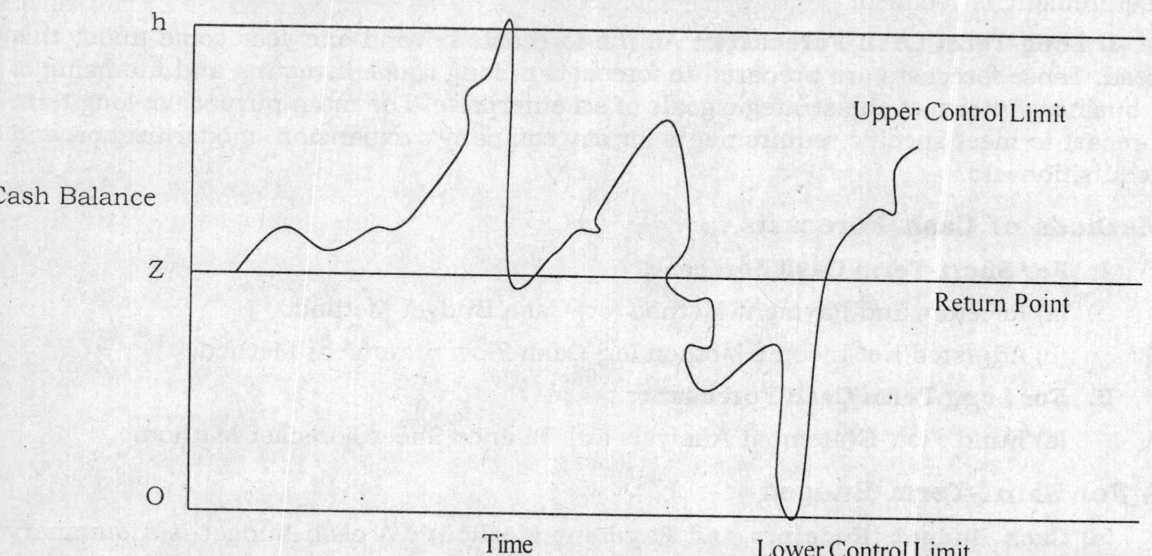

Fig 4.2 : Uncertain cash flow pattern and cash control limit.

It is observed from the diagram that when cash balances reaches the highest level, an amount equal to "h – z" is invested in marketable securities. Cash balance touches at zero level the amount of securities held earlier will be sold and transferred back to cash so that cash balance again goes up to 'Z' level.

Assumption

(1) The main assumption about the model is that only two forms of assets exist : cash and marketable securities.

(2) It also assumes that transfer of cash is done with out any delay but there is some transfer of cost.

(3) It also assumes that net cash flows are completely stochastic.

IV. Controlling Level of Cash : Controlling level of cash is one of the importance functions of cash management. Cash forecast is also an essential part of effective controlling the optimum level of cash. For successful working capital management, a firm should consider to preparing cash budgets, providing unpredictable discrepancies, consideration of short costs and exploring other sources of finance etc.

Cash Forecasts

Cash forecasts are essential to establish a cash budget. It is mainly concerned with an assessment of probable future events. The term cash forecast refers to a summary of expected cash inflows and outflows over a period of time.

Types of Cash Forecasts

Cash forecasting may be used with different objectives, it grouped into :

I. Short-Term Cash Forecasts

II. Long-Term Cash Forecasts

I. Short-Term Cash Forecasts : Short-Term Cash forecasts which generally cover a period of with in 12 months. It is also called cash budgeting where short term financing requirement is focused.

II Long-Term Cash Forecasts : All the forecasts beyond one year come under this head. These forecasts are prepared to forecasts of long range investing and financing of a business interm of the strategic goals of an enterprise. The main purpose of long term forecast to meet specific requirements for say company's expansion, modernization and acquisition etc.

Methods of Cash Forecasts

I. For Short-Term Cash Forecast:

(a) Receipts and Payment Method (or) Cash Budget Method.

(b) Adjusted Net Income Method (or) Cash Flow Statement Method.

II. For Long Term Cash Forecast :

(a) Fund Flow Statement Analysis (or) Balance Sheet Forecast Method.

I. For Short-Term Budged

(a) Cash Budget (Receipts and Payment Method) : A cash budget is a summary statement of the firm's expected cash inflows and outflows over a projected time period.

In other words, this method used to show the short-term forecast of all cash receipts and payments for limited periods such as week or a month. Forecasts of cash receipts and payments are made according to requirements of the individual cash budget is also called cash flow analysis. Cash budget, under the conditions of certainty, while controlling the inflow and outflow of cash to satisfy the following objections :

(1) To know in advance the periods in which there would be deficit or surplus of funds.

(2) To find out whether the shortage or excess of funds is temporary or permanent.

(3) To reduce the carrying costs of cash.

Difference between Cash Forecast and Cash Budgets

Both cash budgets and cash forecasts are refer to the anticipated actions and events. But still there are wide differences between cash budgets and cash forecasts as given below :

Cash Forecasts	*Cash Budgets*
(1) Cash forecasts are mainly concerned with anticipated or probable events.	(1) Cash budget is related to planned events.
(2) Cash forecasts may be done on short-term or long term basis.	(2) Cash budget is planned or prepared for a shorter period to anticipate short term financing.
(3) Cash forecast is only a tentative estimate.	(3) Cash budget is a target fixed for period.
(4) Cash forecast result in planning.	(4) Result of financial planning is cash budgeting.
(5) The function of cash forecast ends with the cash forecast of likely events.	(5) The process of cash budget starts where cash forecast ends and converted into a cash budget.
(6) It is usually covers a specific business function.	(6) It helps to determine operating cash requirements.
(7) It does not act as a tool of controlling measurement.	(7) It is used as a effective tool of cash planning and control.

Factors Determining Cash Budgets

While preparing the cash budgets, the following factors to be considered carefully :

(1) Operating Decisions.

(2) Capital expenditure decisions or plans.

(3) Accounts receivable and Inventory targets.

(4) Customer credit decisions.

(5) Supplier credit decisions.

(6) Tax on profit.

(7) Financial obligations.

(8) Financing decisions.

(9) Degree of liquidity.

(10) Availability of financial resources.

(11) Profit plan.

(12) Statement of financial position at the start of the period.

(13) Debt repayment and Dividend plans.

(14) Selling and distribution expenses to incurred during the budget period.

(15) The amount of salaries and wages to be paid.

(16) Overhead expenses to be incurred.

Basis For Estimation of Cash Receipts and Cash Payments

In order to prepare a effective cash budget, it is essential to consider the items of cash receipts and cash payments are estimated on suitable basis.

Items of Cash Receipts and Cash Payments	*Basis of Estimation*
(1) Cash purchases of raw materials consumable items.	(1) Value of estimated total purchases (or) Average value of cash and credit purchases and terms of credit purchases.
(2) Payment for purchases (Payment to sundry creditor or suppliers).	(2) do.
(3) Cash sales of finished goods.	(3) Value of estimated total sales or Average value of cash and credit sales and Terms of credit sales.
(4) Collection of accounts receivable (Collections from sundry debtors).	(4) do.
(5) Interest received.	(5) Short term or long term investment in Securities/Debentures etc.
(6) Commission received.	(6) Sale or Non-Trading activities.
(7) Dividend received.	(7) Firm's portfolio securities/shares.
(8) Raising loans, marketable securities and issue of shares and debenture.	(8) Financial plan.
(9) Sale of Assets.	(9) Proposed sale of redundant assets.
(10) Wages and salaries.	(10) No. of employees in each department or manpower planning.
(11) Manufacturing expenses.	(11) Production plan.
(12) Office & Administrative expenses.	(12) Administration and sales personnel and proposed sales.
(13) Selling Expenses.	(13) Estimated sales.
(14) Purchase of capital assets.	(14) Value of estimated capital assets.

Purposes or Uses of Cash Budget

The following are the important purposes of cash budget :

(1) Cash budget used as a tool of cash planning and control.

(2) It facilitate to co-ordination of total working capital sale, investment and credit.

(3) Cash budget is a pre-determined statement that gives the estimating cash income and cash expenditure over a some period of time.

(4) It is prepared to identifying the excess cash or shortage of cash in a definite future period.

(5) It helps to utilize the excess cash in a profitable manner.

(6) It guides the financial management to formulate investment plans and dividend policy.

(7) Cash budget act as a tool to measure the effective utilization of cash.

(8) It gives necessary information to the management for decision making.

(9) It ensures adequate or sufficient cash for smooth and effective operation of the business.

(10) It helps to take advantage of cash discounts on accounts payable.

(11) Cash budgets helps to estimate cash requirements of the business during the budget period.

(12) It proposes arrangements to be made overdraft to meet any shortage of cash.

(13) It reveals the surplus amount, and the effect of the seasonal fluctuations on cash position.

Steps in Cash Budget

The following steps are involved in preparing cash budget. It is to be assumed in this exercise that there would not be any additional finance :

(1) Estimating the timing and amount of cash.

(2) Estimating the expenditure involving cash and its timing.

(3) Controlling cash receipts with expenditure.

(4) Findout or forecasting the requirements of additional finance or funds and its timing or when there would be deficit of cash.

Accuracy of cash budget depends upon

(1) Accuracy of other budget like sales budget, production budget, purchase budget etc.

(2) Utilization of current assets indicated by rate of rotation of accounts receivable, inventories etc.

(3) Estimate of contingency cash required to be mentioned at all times.

Items of Cash Receipts and Cash Payments

The major financial and operating items affecting the cash flows are shown in the given table :

Cash Receipts	*Cash Payments*
Cash Sales Payments by Sundry Debtors Bills Receivable **Non-Trading Incomes :** Capital Grants Sales of fixed assets Proceeds of New Shares Debenture issues Income from sale of investment Raising loans Dividend received Interest & received Rent received Commission received Any other income from non-trading operations	Wages and Salaries Advance payments to creditors or supplies Payment of rent, rates, electricity, Telex, Telephones, Maintenance, heating, lighting, cleaning, Insurance premium etc. Payments relating to selling expenses Payments relating to distribution expenses Any other payments relate to operating nature of revenue and capital expenditure **Non-Trading Payments :** Bank charges Tax payments Dividend payments Interest payment Capital expenditure Debenture / loan repayments Leasing & hire purchase payments.

Illustration: 1

A company is expecting to have s.2,50,000 cash in hand on 1st April 2003 and it require you to prepare an estimate of cash poison during the three months. April to June 2003

	Sales	*Purchase*	*Wages*	*Expenses*
	Rs.	Rs.	Rs.	Rs.
February	7,00,000	4,00,000	80,000	60,000
March	8,00,000	5,00,000	80,000	70,000
April	9,20,000	5,20,000	90,000	70,000
May	10,00,000	6,00,000	1,00,000	80,000
June	12,00,000	5,00,000	1,20,000	90,000

Additional Information

(a) Period of credit allowed by suppliers two months.

(b) 25% of sale is for cash and the period of credit allowed to customer for credit sa one month.

(c) Delay in payment of wages and expenses one month.

(d) Income Tax Rs. 2,50,000 is to be paid in June 2004.

Solution:

Cash Budget

Particulars	April Rs.	May Rs.	June Rs.	Total Rs.
Opening balance of cash	2,50,000	5,30,000	8,10,000	15,90,000
Cash Respects :				
Cash Sales	2,30,000	2,50,000	3,00,000	7,80,000
Debtors	6,00,000	6,90,000	7,50,000	20,40,000
Total Cash Receipts –1	10,80,000	14,70,000	18,60,000	44,16,000
Cash Payments :				
Creditors	4,00,000	5,00,000	5,20,000	14,20,000
Wages	80,000	90,000	1,00,000	2,70,000
Expenses	70,000	70,000	80,000	2,20,000
Income tax	—	—	2,50,000	2,50,000
Total Payment – 2	5,50,000	6,60,000	9,50,000	21,60,000
Closing Balance of Cash (1–2)	5,30,000	8,10,000	9,10,000	22,50,000

llustration: 2

Prasad & Co wishes to prepare cash budget from January. Prepare a cash budget for the irst six months from the following estimated revenue and expenses.

Month	*Total Sales Rs.*	*Materials Rs.*	*Wages Rs.*	*Production Overheads Rs.*	*Selling and Distribution Overheads Rs.*
January	1,00,000	1,00,000	20,000	16,000	4,000
February	1,10,000	70,000	22,000	16,500	4,500
March	1,40,000	70,000	23,000	17,000	4,500
April	1,80,000	1,10,000	23,000	17,500	5,000
May	1,50,000	1,00,000	20,000	16,000	4,500
June	2,00,000	1,25,000	25,000	18,000	6,000

Additional Information

(1) Cash balance on 1st January was Rs. 50,000. A new machinery is to be installed at Rs.1,00,000 on credit, to be repaid by two equal installments in March and April.

(2) Sales commission @ 5% on total sales is to be paid with in a month of following actual sales.

(3) Rs. 50,000 being the amount of 2nd call may be received in March. Share Premium amounting to Rs. 10,000 is also obtainable with the 2nd call.

(4) Period of credit allowed by suppliers—2 months.

(5) Period of credit allowed to customers—1 month.

(6) Delay in payment of overheads—1 month.

(7) Delay in payment of wages—½ month.

(8) Assume cash sales to be 50% of total sales.

Solution:

Cash Budget From January to June

Particular	*January* Rs.	*February* Rs.	*March* Rs.	*April* Rs.	*May* Rs.	*June* Rs.
Opening Balance	50,000	90,000	1,49,000	1,35,000	1,23,500	1,65,500
Estimated Cash Receipts :						
Cash Sales	50,000	55,000	70,000	90,000	75,000	1,00,000
Credit Sales	—	50,000	55,000	70,000	90,000	75,000
Second Call	—	—	50,000	—	—	—
Share Premium	—	—	10,000	—	—	—
Total Cash Receipts (A)	1,00,000	1,95,000	3,34,000	2,95,000	2,88,500	3,40,500
Estimated Cash Payments :						
Materials	—	—	1,00,000	70,000	70,000	1,10,000
Wages	10,000	21,000	22,500	23,000	21,500	22,500
Production Overheads	—	16,000	16,500	17,000	17,500	16,000
Selling & Distribution Overheads	—	4,000	4,500	4,500	5,000	4,500
Sales Commission	—	5,000	5,500	7,000	9,000	7,500
Purchase of Machinery	—	—	50,000	50,000	—	—
Total Cash Payment (B)	10,000	46,000	1,99,000	1,71,500	1,23,000	1,60,500
Closing Balance (A – B)	90,000	1,49,000	1,35,000	1,23,500	1,65,500	1,80,000

Illustration: 3

From the following data, forecast the cash position at the end of April, May and June 2003.

Month	*Sales Rs.*	*Purchase Rs.*	*Wages Rs.*	*Miscellaneous Rs.*
February	6,00,000	4,20,000	50,000	35,000
March	6,50,000	5,00,000	60,000	40,000
April	4,00,000	5,20,000	40,000	30,000
May	5,80,000	5,30,000	50,000	60,000
June	4,40,000	4,00,000	40,000	30,000

Additional Informations

(1) Sales : 10% realized in the month of sales; balance realized equally in two subsequent months.

(2) Purchases : There are paid in the month following the month of supply.

(3) Wages : 10% Paid in arrears following month.

(4) Miscellaneous expenses : Paid a month in arrears.

(5) Rent : Rs. 5,000 pe month paid Quarterly in advance due in April.

(6) Income Tax : First installment of advance tax Rs.1,50,000 due on or before 15th June.

(7) Income from Investment : Rs.30,000 received quarterly in April, July etc.

(8) Cash in hand : Rs.30,000 on 1st April 2004.

Solution:

Cash Budget for the month of April, May and June

Particulars	*April Rs.*	*May Rs.*	*June Rs.*
Opening Balance of Cash	30,000	75,500	7,000
Add : Cash Receipts :			
Cash Sales	40,000	58,000	44,000
Receipts from Debtors (Credit Sales) :			
Collection in 1st month	2,92,500	1,80,000	1,98,000
Collection in 2nd month	2,70,000	2,92,500	1,80,000
Income from Investment	30,000	—	—
Total Cash Receipts (1)	6,62,500	6,06,000	4,29,000
Less : Cash Payments :			
Creditors for Purchases	5,00,000	5,20,000	5,30,000
Wages : Current (90%)	36,000	45,000	36,000
Arrears (10%)	6,000	4,000	5,000
Rent	5,000	—	—
Miscellaneous Expenses	40,000	30,000	60,000
Income Tax	—	—	15,000
Total Payments (2)	5,87,000	5,99,000	7,81,000
Closing Balance of Cash (1 – 2)	75,500	7,000	(-) 3,52,000

Working Notes

(1) Out of total sales, 10% are cash sales. Balance 90% are credit sales. In any given month 50% of credit sale of the previous two months are collected (See W.N).

(2) In any given month, 90% of the wages of the same month and 10% of previous month's wages are paid.

(3) Working Notes for collections of cash from Debtors and Sales :

Particulars	*February* *Rs.*	*March* *Rs.*	*April* *Rs.*	*May* *Rs.*	*June* *Rs.*
Total Sales	6,00,000	6,50,000	4,00,000	5,80,000	4,40,000
Less : Cash Sales (10%)	60,000	65,000	40,000	58,000	44,000
Credit Sales	5,40,000	5,85,000	3,60,000	5,22,000	3,96,000
Collection in 1st month after Credit Sales	—	2,70,000	2,92,500	1,80,000	1,98,000
Collection 2nd month after Credit Sales	—	—	2,70,000	2,92,500	1,80,000
Total Credit			5,62,500	4,72,500	3,78,000

Illustration: 4

From the following forecasts of income and expenditure, you are required to prepare cash budget for the month of January to April 2004:

Months	*Sales (credit) Rs.*	*Purchases (credit) Rs.*	*Wages Expenses Rs.*	*Manufacturing Rs.*	*Administrative Expenses Rs.*	*Selling Expenses Rs.*
2003 Nov.	60,000	30,000	6,000	2,300	2,120	1,000
Dec.	70,000	40,000	6,400	2,450	2,080	1,100
2004 Jan.	50,000	30,000	5,000	1,980	2,200	1,200
Feb.	60,000	40,000	6,000	2,100	2,300	1,240
March.	70,000	45,000	4,800	2,200	2,440	1,140
April	80,000	50,000	5,200	2,400	2,360	1,420

Additional information is as follows

(1) The customers are allowed a credit period of 2 months.

(2) The dividend of Rs. 20,000 is payable in April.

(3) Capital expenditure incurred : Plant purchased on 15th January for Rs. 10,000 Building has been purchased on 1st march and the payment are to be made in monthly installments of Rs. 4000 each.

(4) The creditors are allowing a credit of 2 months.

(5) Wages are paid on the 1st of the next month.

(6) Lag in payment of other expenses is one month.

(7) Balance of cash in hand on 1st January 2004 is Rs. 30,000.

Solution:

Cash Budget (for the months from January to April 2004)

Particulars	*January* *Rs.*	*February* *Rs.*	*March* *Rs.*	*April* *Rs.*
Cash Receipts :				
Opening Balance	30,000	37,970	57,590	61,950
Cash received from Debtors	60,000	70,000	50,000	60,000
Total Cash Receipts	90,000	1,07,970	1,07,590	1,21,950
Cash Payments :				
Payment for credit purchases	30,000	40,000	30,000	40,000
Wages	6,400	5,000	6,000	4,800
Manufacturing Expenses	2,450	1,980	2,100	2,200
Administrative Expenses	2,080	2,200	2,300	2,440
Selling Expenses	1,100	1,200	1,240	1,140
Payment of Dividend	—	—	—	20,000
Purchase of Plant	5,000	—	—	—
Installment of Building loan	—	—	4,000	4,000
Total Cash payments	52,030	50,380	45,640	74,580
Closing Balance of Cash	37,970	57,590	61,950	47,370

Illustration: 5

X Y Z Ltd, has given the forecast sales for January 2000 to July 2004 and actual sales for November and December 2004 as under with other particulars given prepare a cash budget for the five months *i.e.*, from January to May 2004.

			Rs.
(i) Sales	2003	November	3,20,000
		December	2,80,000
	2004	January	3,20,000
		February	4,00,000
		March	3,20,000
		April	4,00,000
		May	3,60,000
		June	4,80,000
		July	4,00,000

(ii) Sales 20% cash and 80% credit payable in the third month (January sales in March).

(iii) Variable expenses 5% on turnover, time lag half month.

(iv) Commission 5% on credit sales payable in the third month.

(v) Purchases 60% of the sales of the third month, payment will be made in 3rd month of purchases.

(vi) Rent and other expenses Rs.12,000 paid every month.

(vii) Other payments :

Fixed Assets Purchases—March Rs. 2,00,000

Taxes—April Rs. 80,000.

(viii) Opening cash balances Rs. 1,00,000.

Solution:

Working Notes :

(i) Realization from Sales :

	Nov. *Rs.*	*Dec.* *Rs.*	*Jan.* *Rs.*	*Feb.* *Rs.*	*Mar.* *Rs.*	*April* *Rs.*	*May* *Rs.*
Sales	3,20,000	2,80,000	3,20,000	4,00,000	3,20,000	4,00,000	3,60,000
Cash sales 20%			64,000 (Jan)	80,000 (Feb)	64,000 (Mar)	80,000 (April)	72,000 (May)
Credit Sales 80%			2,56,000 (Nov)	2,24,000 (Dec)	2,56,000 (Jan)	3,20,000 (Feb)	2,56,000 (Mar)
Total			3,20,000	3,04,000	3,20,000	4,00,000	3,28,000

(ii) Creditors for goods :

	Nov. *Rs.*	*Dec.* *Rs.*	*Jan.* *Rs.*	*Feb.* *Rs.*	*Mar.* *Rs.*	*April* *Rs.*	*May* *Rs.*
Purchase 60% of sales of	1,92,000 (Jan)	2,40,000 (Feb)	1,92,000 (Mar)	2,40,000 (April)	2,16,000 (May)	2,88,000 (June)	2,40,000 (July)
Payment to Creditors			1,92,000 (Nov)	2,40,000 (Dec)	1,92,000 (Jan)	2,40,000 (Feb)	2,16,000 (Mar)
Commission 5% on Credit Sales			38,000 (Nov)	11,200 (Dec)	38,000 (Jan)	1,600 (Feb)	38,000 (Mar)

Cash Budget (January to May 2004)

Particular	*January* *Rs.*	*February* *Rs.*	*March* *Rs.*	*April* *Rs.*	*May* *Rs.*
Cash Receipts :					
Opening Balance	1,00,000	1,88,200	3,11,000	196,200	2,30,200
Realization from sales	3,20,000	3,04,000	3,20,000	4,00,000	3,28,000
Total Cash Receipts (A)	4,20,000	5,92,200	6,31,000	5,96,200	5,58,200
Cash Payments :					
Payment for goods purchase	1,92,000	2,40,000	1,92,000	2,40,000	2,16,000
Variable Expenses	15,000	18,000	18,000	18,000	19,000
Commission	12,800	11,200	12,800	16.000	12,800
Rent & Other Expenses	12,000	12,000	12,000	12,000	12,000
Additional Fixed Assets	—	—	2,00,000	—	—
Taxes	—	—	—	80,000	—
Total Cash Payments	2,31,800	2,81,200	4,34,800	3,66,000	2,59,800
Closing Balance of Cash	1,88,200	3,11,000	196,200	2,30,200	2,98,400

Illustration: 6

ABC Ltd, furnishes the following forecast for the quarter ending 31st March 2004.

Sales : January Rs. 12,00,000

February Rs. 11,00,000

March Rs. 14,00,000

During the month of December last the company made a sale of Rs.10,00,000 and computed the cost of sales as under :

Raw material Rs. 3,50,000

Wages (variable) Rs. 1,75,000

Overheads (variable) Rs. 1,75,000

Overheads (fixed) Rs. 1,50,000

The fixed overheads include depreciation of Rs. 40,000.

One-fifth of sales is for cash on which a cash discount of 1.5% is allowed. Of the remaining portion 50% is collected in the same month and the balance in the next month. Raw material suppliers allow a credit of one month. Wages are paid on the last working day of the month to which they relate. While variable overheads are paid in the next month, fixed overhead expenses are met in the same month.

The percentage of contribution to sales as obtained in December last is expected to be maintained during the forthcoming quarter also. The cash balance on 1st January 2004 is Rs. 50,000. The company has to pay a sum of Rs. 60,000 as installment of arrears of wages in March 2004 and the bank will debit quarterly interest of Rs. 4,00,000 on drawings in March 2004.

Prepare a cash budget showing the cash position for each of the three months of the quarter ending March 2004.

Solution:

Particulars	*Dec. 2003 Rs.*	*Jan. 2004 Rs.*	*Feb. 2004 Rs.*	*Mar. 2004 Rs.*
Sales and Cost of Sales :				
Cash Sales	2,00,000	2,40,000	2,20,000	2,80,000
Credit Sales	8,00,000	9,60,000	8,80,000	11,20,000
Total Sales	10,00,000	12,00,000	11,00,000	14,00,000
Cost of Sales :				
Raw Materials	3,50,000	4,20,000	3,85,000	4,90,000
Wages	1,75,000	2,10,000	1,95,000	2,45,000
Overheads Variable	1,75,000	2,10,000	1,92,000	2,45,000
Depreciation	40,000	40,000	40,000	40,000
Overheads Fixed	1,10,000	1,10,000	1,10,000	1,10,000

Cash Budget

Particulars	*Jan. 2004 Rs.*	*Feb. 2004 Rs.*	*Mar. 2004 Rs.*
Cash Receipts :			
Opening balance	50,000	(-) 28,600	1,75,600
Debtors (for last month)	4,00,000	4,80,000	4,40,000
Debtors (for this month)	4,80,000	4,40,000	5,60,000
Cash sales less discount	2,36,400	2,16,700	2,75,800
Total Cash Receipts (A)	11,66,400	11,08,100	14,51,400
Cash Payments :			
Raw materials	3,50,000	4,20,000	3,85,000
Wages	2,10,000	1,92,500	2,45,000
Overhead variable	1,75,000	2,10,000	1,92,500
Overheads fixed	1,10,000	1,10,000	1,10,000
Arrears of wages	—	—	60,000
Interest on term loan	3,50,000	—	—
Bank interest	—	—	4,00,000
Total Cash Payments (B)	11,95,000	9,32,500	13,92,500
Deficit (carried over) to be met by loan or overdraft) (A – B)	(–) 28,600	—	—
Surplus carried over (after liquidation of loan or overdraft (A–B)	—	1,75,600	58,900

In framing the cash budget, a provision will be made for meeting the deficit in January 2004 to the extent of Rs.28,600 by loan or over draft. If we assume that the loan/draft is paid back in February 2004, the closing balances at the end of February and March 2004, will be Rs.1,75,000 and Rs.58,900 respectively 2004.

Illustration: 7

Based on the following information prepare a Cash Budget for PPP Ltd.

Particulars	*1st Qtr. Rs.*	*2nd Qtr. Rs.*	*3rd Qtr. Rs.*	*4th Qtr. Rs.*
Opening Cash Balance	10,000	—	—	—
Collection from Customers	1,25,000	1,50,000	1,60,000	2,21,000
Payment :				
Purchase of Materials	20,000	35,000	35,000	54,200
Other Expenses	25,000	20,000	20,000	17,000
Salary and Wages	90,000	95,000	95,000	1,09,200
Income Tax	5,000	—	—	—
Purchase of Machinery	—	—	—	20,000

The company desired to maintain a cash a balance of Rs.15,000 at the end of each quarter. Cash can be borrowed or repaid in multiples of Rs.500 at an interest of 10% per annum. Management does not want to borrow cash more than what is necessary and wants to repay as early as possible. In any event, loans cannot be extended beyond four quarters. Interest is computed and paid when the principal is repaid. Assume that borrowings take place at the beginning and repayments are made at the end of the quarters.

Solution:

PPP Ltd.

Cash Budget

Particulars	*1st Qtr.* *Rs.*	*2nd Qtr.* *Rs.*	*3rd Qtr.* *Rs.*	*4th Qtr.* *Rs.*
Cash Receipts :				
Opening Cash Balance	10,000	15,000	15,000	15,325
Add : Collections from Customers	1,25,000	1,50,000	1,60,000	2,21,000
Total Cash Receipts (A)	1,35,000	1,65,000	1,75,000	2,46,325
Cash Payments :				
Purchase of Materials	20,000	35,000	35,000	54,400
Other Expenses	25,000	20,000	20,000	17,000
Salary and Wages	90,000	95,000	95,000	1,09,000
Income Tax	5,000	—	—	—
Purchase of Machinery	—	—	—	20,000
Total Cash Payments (B)	1,40,000	1,50,000	1,50,000	2,00,400
Minimum Cash Balance required	15,000	15,000	15,000	15,000
Total Cash Required	1,55,000	1,65,000	1,65,000	2,15,400
Excess (Deficit) (A) – (B)	(20,000)	—	10,000	30,925
Financing :				
Borrowing	20,000	—	—	—
(Repayment)	—	—	(9000)	(11000)
Interest Payment	—	—	(675)	(1100)
Total effect of financing (C)	20,000	—	(9,675)	(12,100)
Closing Cash Balance (A + C – B)	15,000	15,000	15,325	23,825

QUESTIONS

(1) What you understand by cash management?

(2) Define Cash.

(3) Explain the important motives for holding cash.

(4) Explain the objectives of cash management.

(5) Briefly discuss the factors determining the amount of cash requirements of a firm.

(6) What are the advantages of maintaining optimum cash?

(7) Explain the important issues in cash management.

(8) How can a firm avoiding the cash deficit?

(9) What are ways for utilization of cash surplus

(10) Explain the different types of marketable securities

(11) Write short notes on :

(1) Commercial Paper

(2) Global Depository Receipts

(3) Factoring

(4) Treasury Securities

(5) Banker's Acceptance

(12) What do you understand by cash cycle?

(13) Explain the different stages in cash cycle model.

(14) Discuss in details about the functions of cash management.

(15) Explain the different methods of controlling inflow of cash.

(16) What do you understand by Accelerating Collection?

(17) Brief note on Concentration Banking.

(18) Explain the method of Lock-box agreement in accelerating flow of funds.

(19) Explain the term 'Float'. What are its different kinds?

(20) What are the important cash management model?

(21) Discuss in details about William J. Baumal's Mathematical Model.

(22) Briefly explain the Miller—Orr Cash Management Model.

(23) What do you understand by Cash Forecast?

(24) Explain the types of cash forecast.

(25) Define cash budget.

(26) What are difference between cash forecasts and cash budgets?

(27) Explain the basis for estimation of cash receipts and cash payments.

(28) What are the factors determining cash budgets?

(29) Explain the uses or purposes of cash budget.

(30) What are the important components of cash budget?

METHODS OF CASH FORECAST

I. For Short-Term Forecast—Cash Flow Statement Analysis

II. For Long-Term Cash Forecast—Fund Flow Statement Analysis

I. Cash Flow Statement : (For Short-Term Cash Forecast)

Introduction

Cash Flow is the life blood of a business which plays a vital role in an entire economic life. The word fund is used in a narrower sense refers to cash. When cash is used as 'fund' the analysis relates to movement of cash. Cash flows refer to the actual movement of cash into and out of an organization. In other words, the movement of cash inclusive of inflow of cash and out flow of cash. When the cash flows into the organization, it represents 'Inflow of Cash'. Similarly, when the cash flows out of the business concern, it called as "Cash Outflow".

In order to ensure cash flows are adequate to meet current liabilities such as tax payments, wages, amounts due to trade creditors, it is essential to prepare a statement of changes in the financial position of a firm on cash basis is called as "Cash Flow Statement". This statement depicting movement of cash position from one period to another.

Uses of Cash Flow Statement

Cash Flow Statement is a useful tool to the management for taking important financial decision making. The following are the uses of this statement :

(1) This Statement is the most useful to the management to prepare dividend and retention policies.

(2) It guides the management to evaluate the changes cash position.

(3) It presents in brief to the management about the financial consequences of operational, financial and investment.

(4) It helps to know how the movement of cash took place and the factors which caused the changes in cash flows.

(5) It guides the management in order to take decisions about short term obligations.

(6) It also presents the details about the sources of cash and applications of cash during the particular period.

Limitations of Cash Flow Statement

(1) Cash Flow Statement has limited scope as it compares with Fund flow statement. Because it discloses inflows and outflows of cash alone. It does not reveal the over all financial position of the concern.

(2) Cash Flow Statement can not provide a comprehensive picture of a financial position because non-cash items of expenses and incomes are excluded.

(3) The balances as disclosed by the cash flow statement may not treated the actual liquid position of a concern since it can not be easily influenced by postponing purchases and other payments.

Preparation of Cash Flow Statement

Cash Flow Statement is prepared like Fund Flow Statement. The movement of cash may be an actual inflow of cash or outflow of cash. If any transactions result in increase the cash position is refer to Inflow of Cash or Sources of Cash. Similarly if any transaction results in decrease the cash position is said to be decrease in cash position does not result in any actual flow of cash, it is known as No Flow of Cash. While preparing a cash flow statement it starts with an opening balance of cash in hand and cash at bank, all the sources of cash are added to an opening balance and all the applications of cash are deducted. The balance represents cash and bank balances at the end of accounting period.

SOURCES AND APPLICATIONS OF CASH

Sources of Cash (Inflow of Cash)

The following are the main sources of cash such as :

(1) Cash From Operations or Trading Profit
(2) Sale of Fixed Assets for Cash
(3) Sale of Investments for Cash
(4) Raising Long Term Loans from Banks and Financial Institutions
(5) Issue of Shares and Debentures for Cash

Application of Cash (Outflow of Cash)

Application of cash can be involve in the following forms :

(1) Cash Lost in Operations or Trading Losses
(2) Redemption of Shares and Debentures by Cash
(3) Purchase of Fixed Assets
(4) Repayment of Long Term Loans

Computation of Cash Flow Statement

A comprehensive Cash Flow Statement is ascertained in two stages:

I. Cash From Operations *i.e.*, internal sources of cash calculated by preparing combined statements of adjusted and loss account.

II. External Sources and Applications of Cash *i.e.*, Flow of Cash involves in non-current items ascertained by the Statement of Sources and Applications of Cash.

Diagram of Sources and Applications of Cash

The summary of sources and applications of cash is presented in the chart give below :

Sources of Cash (Inflow of Cash)	*Applications of Cash (Outflow of Cash)*
Cash From Operations	Cash Lost in Operations
Sale of Fixed Assets	Purchase of Fixed Assets
Sale of Investments	Purchase of Investment
Issue of Shares	Redemption of Preference Shares
Issue of Debentures	Redemption of Debentures
Raising Long Term Loans	Repayment of Long Term Loans
Increase in any Liabilities	Decrease in any liability
Decrease in any Assets	Decrease in any Assets

I. Cash From Operations

Cash from operations is the main source of inflow of cash. The Net Profit or Net Loss is the net effect of business transactions shown by the profit and loss account. In order to find out the actual movement of cash from trading operations, it is essential to ascertaining cash from operations. It can be calculated under the following situations.

(a) When All Transactions Are Cash Transactions .

(b) When All Transactions Are Not Cash Transactions.

(a) When All Transactions Are Cash Transactions : It assumes that where all the expenses and losses, incomes and gains are paid or received in cash during the particular period. The Net Profit or Net Loss shown by the profit and loss account is taken as the amount of cash from operations. Thus, Net Profit or Net Loss is equal to cash from operations. When Net Profit made by a firm represents Cash Inflow or Cash Profit From Operations. Similarly the Net Loss shown by the profit and loss account refers to Cash Outflow From Operations.

(b) When All Transactions Are Not Cash Transactions : In actual practice, in business transactions are made either on cash basis or credit basis. For example goods purchased or sold on cash as well as on credit. Certain expenses are always outstanding and some of the incomes are not immediately realized under such circumstances, the net profit made by a firm can not generate equivalent amount of cash. Therefore, the charging of non-fund or non-cash items such as outstanding expenses, incomes received in advances, prepaid expenses and outstanding incomes etc. to profit and loss account should be readjusted. In such circumstances the actual cash from operations can be calculated by preparing adjusted profit and loss account.

Calculation of Cash From Operations : Cash From Operations can be calculated by either of the following two methods.

(A) Cash From Operations calculated with the help of Adjusted Profit and Loss Account. Under this method, all non-fund or non-operations items should be readjusted to cash profit from operations. The specimen form of cash from operations is given below :

Cash From Operations

(Adjusted Profit and Loss Account)

Particulars	*Rs.*	*Particulars*	*Rs.*
To Depreciation on Fixed Assets		By Balance b/d	
To Transfer to General Reserve		(Opening Balance of P & L A/c)	
To Loss on Sale of Fixed Assets		By Profit on Sale of Fixed Assets	
To Increase in Outstanding Expenses		By Profit on Sale of Investments	
To Decrease in Prepaid Expenses		By Decrease in Outstanding Expenses	
To Preliminary Expenses written off		By Increase in Prepaid Expenses	
To Balance c/d		By Cash From Operations	
(Closing Balance of P & L A/c)		(Balancing figure)	
	* * *		* * *

(B) Cash From Operations can also be calculated on the basis of current assets and current liabilities. Under this method, the amount of changes in the various items of current assets and current liabilities other than cash and bank balances should be adjusted with the help of Adjusted Profit and Loss Account. It may be noted that, as compared to above this method any increase or decrease in items of creditors, stocks, debtors, bills receivable and bills payable are not adjusted while calculating cash profit from operations and they may be directly taken as an Sources (inflow) of Cash or Application (outflow) of Cash. This method is generally adopted in practice.

While applying this method, the following general principles may be taken for measuring cash from operations :

Increase in Current Assets	⟶	Decrease in Cash
Decrease in Current Assets	⟶	Increase in Cash
Increase in Current Liability	⟶	Increase in Cash
Decrease in Current Liability	⟶	Decrease in Cash

Specimen From

The specimen form for computation of Cash From Operations is given below :

Calculation of Cash From Operations :

(Combining Current Assets & Current Liabilities & Non—Cash & Non—Operating Items)

Particulars	*Rs.*	*Rs.*
Net Profit		
(Closing Balance of Profit & Loss A/c)		***
Add:		
Depreciation on Fixed Assets	***	
Transfer to General Reserve		
Loss on Sale of Fixed Assets		
Loss on Sale of Investments		
Goodwill Written off		
Increase in Outstanding Expenses		
Decrease in Prepaid Expenses		
Decrease in Current Assets		
(Other than Cash and Bank)		
Increase in Current Liabilities		
Preliminary Expenses Written off	***	***
Less :		***
Profit on Sale of Fixed Assets	***	
Profit On Sale of Investments		
Decrease in Outstanding Expenses		
Increase in Prepaid Expenses		
Increase in Current Assets		
(Other than Cash and Bank)		
Increase in Current Liabilities		
Opening Balance of Profit & Loss A/c	***	***
Cash From Operations		***

lustration: (1)

rom the following Balance Sheet of ABC Ltd, you are required to calculate Cash From perations.

Particulars	*2002 Rs.*	*2003 Rs.*
Capital and Liabilities :		
Share Capital	2,00,000	2,00,000
Profit made during the year	1,41,000	1,73,000
Provision for Depreciation	10,000	14,000
Long Term Loans	20,000	30,000
Trade Creditors	64,500	53,000
Outstanding Expenses	8,500	1,500
	4,44,000	4,71,500
Assets :		
Plant and Machinery	2,85,000	3,00,000
Stocks	98,000	1,13,000
Trade Debtors	39,500	28,500
Cash Balances	21,500	30,000
	4,44,000	4,71,500

olution:

Calculation of Cash From Operations

Particulars	*2002 Rs.*	*2003 Rs.*
Profit made during the year (Closing Balance of P & L A/c)		1,73,000
Add :		
Provision for Depreciation	4,000	
Decrease in Debtors	11,000	15,000
		1,88,000
Less :		
Decrease in Creditors	11,500	
Decrease in Outstanding Expenses	7,000	
Increase in Stock	15,000	
Net Profit (Opening Balance of P & L A/c)	1,41,000	1,74,500
Cash From Operations		13,500

Illustration: (2)

From the following balance you are required to calculate cash from operations

Particulars	*2003* *Rs.*	*2004* *Rs.*
Trade Debtors	10,00,000	9,40,000
Bills Receivable	2,00,000	2,50,000
Trade Creditors	4,00,000	5,00,000
Bills Payable	1,60,000	1,20,000
Outstanding Expenses	20,000	24,000
Prepaid Expenses	16,000	14,000
Accrued Income	12,000	15,000
Income Received in Advance	6,000	5,000
Profit made during the year	—	26,00,000

Solution:

Calculation of Cash From Operations

Particulars	*Rs.*	*Rs.*
Net Profit (Closing Balance)		26,00,000
Add :		
Decrease in Debtors	60,000	
Increase in Creditors	1,00,000	
Increase in Outstanding Expenses	4,000	
Decrease in Prepaid Expenses	2,000	1,66,000
		27,66,000
Less :		
Increase in Bills Receivable	50,000	
Decrease in Bills Payable	40,000	
Increase in Accrued Income	3,000	
Decrease in Income Received in Advance	1,000	94,000
Cash From Operations		26,72,000

Illustration: 3

From the following informations given by RR Ltd you are required to prepare Cash From Operations.

Particulars	*2004* *Rs.*	*2004* *Rs.*
Bills Payable	1,00,000	1,60,000
Trade Creditors	2,40,000	3,20,000

Outstanding Expenses	40,000	20,000
Bills Receivable	4,00,000	3,60,000
Trade Debtors	8,00,000	12,00,000
Prepaid Expenses	40,000	60,000
Accrued Incomes	1,00,000	1,60,000
Incomes Received in Advance	40,000	20,000

dditional Informations

Ltd., earned profit of Rs.40,00,000 after charging or crediting the following items to its ofit and loss account during the year 2003 :

(1) Profit on Sale of Investments Rs. 8,0000.

(2) Loss on Sale of Building Rs. 1,80,000.

(3) Depreciation on Fixed Assets Rs. 1,40,000.

(4) Good will written off Rs. 40,000.

lution:

Calculation of Cash From Operations

Particulars	*Rs.*	*Rs.*
et Profit during the year		40,00,000
dd :		
oss on Sale of Building	1,80,000	
epreciation on Fixed Assets	1,40,000	
ood will Written off	40,000	
ncrease in Bills Payable	60,000	
ncrease in Trade Creditors	80,000	
ecrease in Bills Receivable	40,000	5,40,000
		45,40,000
ess :		
rofit on Sale of Investments	80,000	
ecrease in Outstanding Expenses	20,000	
ecrease in Income Received in Advance	20,000	
ncrease in Trade Debtors	4,00,000	
ncrease in Prepaid Expenses	20,000	
ncrease in Accrued Income	60,000	6,00,000
ash From Operations		39,40,000

II. EXTERNAL SOURCES AND APPLICATIONS OF CASH

ternal Sources of Cash

following are the external sources of cash such as :

(1) Fresh Issue of Shares : Cash is received by issue of fresh shares to the publi after deducting necessary expenses and discount on issue of shares will be treated a sources of cash.

(2) Issue of Debentures : The Net Cash is received by the issue of debentures sources of cash.

(3) Raising Long-Term Borrowings : Lon term loans received from banks and financi institutions are refer to inflow of cash.

(4) Sale of Fixed Assets & Investments : Net cash received from the sale of permane assets and investments are treated as sources of cash.

APPLICATIONS OF CASH

Applications of cash or cash outflows or uses of cash may take any of the following form

(1) Redemption of Shares and Debentures : When redeemable preference shar and debentures are redeemed by paid in cash. It refers to as application or outflow cash.

(2) Purchase of Fixed Assets : Cash used for purchase of plant and machinery, la and building, furniture & fixtures etc., or renewals and replacement of fixed assets a to be treated as outflow of cash.

(3) Payment of Long-Term Loans : The repayment or discharge of long term loa received from banks and financial institutions results in outflow of cash.

Specimen From of Cash Flow of Statement : Cash Flow Statement is prepared any one of the following two ways :

(1) Account Form

(2) Report Form

(1) Account Form

CASH FLOW STATEMENT

Sources or Inflow of Cash	*Rs.*	*Applications or Outflow of Cash*	*Rs*
Opening Balances :		Cash Lost in Operations	
Cash		Redemption of Preference Shares	
Bank		Redemption of Debentures	
Fresh Issue of Shares		Repayment of Long Term Loans	
Issue of Debentures		Purchase of Fixed Assets	
Raising Long Term Loans		Purchase of Investments	
Sale of Fixed Assets		Tax Paid	
Sale of Investments		Dividend Paid	
Dividends Received		Closing Balance :	
Cash From Operations		Cash	
		Bank	
	***		*

(2) Report Form

CASH FLOW STATEMENT

Particulars	*Rs.*	*Rs.*
Opening Balances :		
Cash		***
Bank		***
Add : Sources of Cash :		
Fresh Issue of Shares	***	
Issue of Debentures		
Long Term Loans from Bank & Financial Institutions		
Sale of Fixed Assets		
Sale of Investments		
Dividends Received	***	
Cash From Operations		***
Total Inflow of Cash (A)		***
Less : Applications of Cash :		
Redemption of Preference Shares	***	
Redemption of Debentures		
Repayment of Long Term Loans		
Purchase of Fixed Assets		
Payment of Dividends		
Payment of Tax		
Cash Lost of in Operations	***	***
Total Outflow of Cash (B)		***
Closing Balance of Cash and Bank		***

Illustration: 4

From the following Balance sheets of ABC Ltd, you are required to prepare a Cash Flow Statement.

Balance Sheet

Liabilities	*2003 Rs.*	*2004 Rs.*	*Assets*	*2003 Rs.*	*2004 Rs.*
Share Capital	2,00,000	3,00,000	Fixed Assets	2,00,000	3,00,000
Profit & Loss A/c	1,00,000	1,60,000	Good will	1,00,000	80,000
General Reserve	60,000	80,000	Stock	1,00,000	1,60,000
Debenture	1,00,000	1,20,000	Trade Debtors	1,00,000	1,60,000
Trade Creditors	60,000	80,000	Bills Receivable	20,000	40,000
Outstanding Expenses	20,000	30,000	Bank Balance	20,000	30,000
	5,40,000	7,70,000		5,40,000	7,70,000

Solution:

Calculation of Cash From Operations

Particulars	*Rs.*	*Rs.*
Net Profit during the year		
(Closing Balance of Profit & Loss A/c)		1,60,000
Add :		
General Reserve (60,000 – 80,000)	20,000	
Good will Written off (1,00,000 – 80,000)	20,000	
Increase in Outstanding Expenses	10,000	
Increase in Trade Creditors	20,000	70,000
		2,30,000
Less :		
Increase in Stock (1,00,000 – 1,60,000)	60,000	
Increase in Debtors (1,00,000 – 1,60,000)	60,000	
Increase in Bills Receivable	20,000	
Opening Balance of P & L A/c	1,00,000	2,40,000
Cash Lost in Operations		(–10,000)

Cash Flow Statement

Sources of Cash	*Rs.*	*Application of Cash*	*Rs.*
Opening Balances :		Purchase of Fixed Assets	1,00,000
Cash at Bank	20,000	Cash lost in Operations	10,000
Add :		Closing Balance :	
Issue of Shares	1,00,000	Cash at Bank	30,000
Issue of Debenture	20,000		
	1,40,000		1,40,000

Illustration: 5

From the following informations, Prepare Cash From Operations and Cash Flow Statement :

Particulars	*Rs.*	*Rs.*
Assets :		
Cash Balances	50,000	35,000
Trade Debtors	1,50,000	2,50,000
Stock	1,75,000	1,25,000
Machinery	4,00,000	2,75,000
Land	2,00,000	2,50,000
Building	1,75,000	3,00,000
	11,50,000	12,35,000

Capital and Liabilities :		
Capital	6,25,000	7,65,000
Long Term Loans	2,00,000	2,50,000
Mortgage Loans	1,25,000	—
Trade Creditors	2,00,000	2,20,000
	11,50,000	12,35,000

Additional Informations

(1) During the year a machine costing Rs. 50,000 (accumulated depreciation Rs. 15,000) was sold for Rs. 25,000

(2) The provision for depreciation against machinery during the year 2002 was Rs. 1,25,000 and Rs. 2,00,000 in 2003

(3) Net Profit earned during the year 2003 was Rs. 2,25,000

Solution:

Cash Flow Statement

Sources of Cash	*Rs.*	*Applications of Cash*	*Rs.*
Opening Balances :		Purchase of land	50,000
Cash at Bank	50,000	Purchase of Building	1,25,000
Add :		Mortgage loan repaid	1,25,000
Long-Term Loans	50,000	Drawings	85,000
Sale of Machinery	25,000	Closing Balances :	
Cash From Operations	2,95,000	Cash at Bank	35,000
	4,20,000		4,20,000

Working Note: (1)

Calculation of Cash From Operations

Particulars	*Rs.*	*Rs.*
Net Profit during the year		2,25,000
Add :		
Depreciation on Machinery	90,000	
Loss on Sale of Machinery	10,000	
Decrease in Stock	50,000	
Increase in Creditors	20,000	1,70,000
		3,95,000
Less :		
Decrease in Creditors	1,00,000	1,00,000
Cash From Operations		2,95,000

(2) **Machinery Account**

Particulars	*Rs.*	*Particulars*	*Rs.*
To Balance b/d	5,25,000	By Bank	25,000
		By Loss on sale of machinery	10,000
		By Provision for depreciation	15,000
		By Balance c/d (40,000 + 5000 + 2500)	4,75,000
	5,25,000		5,25,000

(3) **Provision For Depreciation**

Particulars	*Rs.*	*Particulars*	*Rs.*
To Machinery A/c	15,000	By Balance b/d	1,25,000
To Balance c/d	2,00,000	By P & L A/c (Depreciation Charged – Balancing Figure)	90,000
	2,15,000		2,15,000

(4) Capital Account :

	Rs.
Opening Balance of Capital	6,25,000
Add : Profit	2,25,000
	8,50,000
Less : Closing Balance of Capital	7,65,000
Drawings	85,000

Illustration: 6

The summarized balance sheet of William & Co Ltd, you are required to prepare a Cash Flow Statement.

Balance Sheet

Liabilities	*2002 Rs.*	*2003 Rs.*	*Assets*	*2002 Rs.*	*2003 Rs.*
Share Capital	9,00,000	9,00,000	Fixed Assets	8,00,000	6,40,000
General Reserve	6,00,000	6,20,000	Investments	1,00,000	1,20,000
Profit & Loss A/c	1,12,000	1,36,000	Stock	4,80,000	4,20,000
Creditors	3,36,000	2,68,000	Debtors	4,20,000	9,10,000
Provision for Tax	1,50,000	20,000	Bank	2,98,000	3,94,000
Mortgage Loan	—	5,40,000			
	20,98,000	24,84,000		20,98,000	24,84,000

Additional Informations

(1) Investments costing Rs. 16,000 were sold during the year 2003 for Rs. 17,000.

(2) Provision for tax made during the year was Rs. 18,000.

(3) During the year part of the fixed assets costing Rs. 2,0000 was sold for Rs. 24,000 and the profit was included in profit and loss account.

(4) Dividend paid during the year amounted to Rs. 8,000.

Solution:

Calculation of Cash From Operations

Particulars	*Rs.*	*Rs.*
Net Profit during the year (1,36,000 – 1,12,000)		24,000
Add :		
Transfer to General Reserve	20,000	
Provision for Tax	18,000	
Dividend	80,000	
Depreciation	1,40,000	
Decrease in Stock	60,000	3,18,000
		3,42,000
Less :		
Profit on Sale of Investments	1,000	
Profit on Sale of Fixed Assets	4,000	
Increase in Debtors	4,90,000	
Decrease in Creditors	68,000	5,63,000
Fund Lost in Operations		2,21,000

Solution:

Cash Flow Statement

Sources of Cash	*Rs.*	*Applications of Cash*	*Rs.*
Opening Balances :		Cash Lost in Operations	2,21,000
Cash at Bank	2,98,000	Payment of Tax	1,48,000
Add :		Payment of Dividend	80,000
Sale of Investments	17,000	Purchase of Investment	36,000
Sale of Fixed Assets	24,000	Closing Balances :	
Mortgage Loan	5,40,000	Cash at Bank	3,94,000
	8,79,000		8,79,000

Working Note:

Provision For Tax Account

To Bank (Balancing Figure)	1,48,000	By Balance b/d (Opening Balance)	1,50,000
To Balance c/d (Closing Balance)	20,000	By P & L A/c (Provision for 2003)	18,000
	1,68,000		1,68,000

Investment Account

To Balance b/d	1,00,000	By Cash A/c (Sold during the year)	16,000
To Bank (Purchased of Investments - Balancing Figure)	36,000	By Balance c/d)	1,20,000
	1,36,000		1,36,000

Illustration: 7

From the following informations, prepare

(a) Cash From Operations (b) Cash Flow Statement

Balance Sheet

Particulars	*2003 Rs.*	*2002 Rs.*
Assets :		
Furniture and Fittings	1,17,000	1,30,000
Motor Vans	1,54,000	80,000
Long Tem Investments	3,00,000	2,60,000
Stock	8,29,000	8,00,000
Trade Debtors	90,000	1,09,000
Cash at Bank	1,43,000	1,40,000
Preliminary Expenses	10,000	15,000
	16,43,000	15,34,000
Capital and Liabilities :		
Equity Share Capital	9,00,000	6,00,000
Preference Share Capital	—	2,00,000
Profit & Loss Account	1,10,000	75,000
Debentures	2,50,000	3,00,000
Bank Loan	75,000	1,00,000
Bills Payable	45,000	40,000
Trade Creditors	1,50,000	1,15,000
Outstanding Expenses	18,000	19,000
Provision for Taxation	95,000	85,000
	16,43,000	15,34,000

Solution:

Cash Flow Statement

Sources of Cash	Rs.	*Applications of Cash*	Rs.
Opening Balances :		Redemption of Preference Shares	2,00,000
Cash at Bank	1,40,000	Redemption of Debenture	50,000
Add :		Repayment of Bank Loan	25,000
Cash From Operations	35,000	Purchase of Motor Vans	74,000
Depreciation on Furniture	13,000	Purchase of Long Term Investments	40,000
Preliminary Expenses written off	5,000	Increase in Stock	29,000
Issue of Share Capital	3,00,000	Decrease in Outstanding Expenses	1,000
Decrease in Debtors	19,000	Closing Balances :	
Increase in Bills Payable	5,000	Cash at Bank	1,43,000
Increase in Trade Creditors	35,000		
Increase in Provision Tax	10,000		
	5,62,000		5,62,000

Note : While preparing Cash Flow Statement, increase or decrease in the various items of current assets and current liabilities are taken as Sources of Cash or Applications of Cash. Here they are not adjusted while computing Cash from Operations.

Cash Flow Statement

Sources of Cash	Rs.	*Applications of Cash*	Rs.
Fund From Operations	53,000	Redemption of preference shares	2,00,000
Issue of Equity Shares	3,00,000	Redemption of Shares	50,000
Decrease in Working Capital	36,000	Repayment of Bank Loan	25,000
		Purchase of Motor Vans	74,000
		Purchase of Long Term Investments	40,000
	3,89,000		3,89,000

Calculation of Cash From Operations
(Adjusted Profit and Loss Account)

Particulars	Rs.	*Particulars*	Rs.
To Depreciation on Furniture & Fixtures	13,000	By Opening Balance of Profit & Loss A/c	75,000
To Preliminary Expenses written off	5,000	By Cash From operations (Balancing figure)	53,000
To Closing Balance of Profit and Loss A/c	1,10,000		
	1,28,000		1,28,000

Illustration: 8

From the following Balance sheet of Brard Well & Co Ltd, make out the statement of Cash Flow

Particulars	*2002* *Rs.*	*2003* *Rs.*
Assets :		
Good Will	57,500	45,000
Land & Buildings	1,00,000	85,000
Machinery	40,000	1,00,000
Trade Debtors	80,000	1,00,000
Stock	38,500	54,500
Bills Receivable	10,000	15,000
Cash in Hand	7,500	5,000
Cash at Bank	5,000	4,000
	3,38,500	4,08,500
Capital & Liabiiities :		
Equity Share Capital	1,50,000	2,00,000
Preference Share Capital	75,000	50,000
General Reserve	20,000	35,000
Profit and Loss A/c	15,000	24,000
Proposed Dividend	21,000	25,000
Trade Creditors	27,500	41,500
Bills Payable	10,000	8,000
Provision for Taxations	20,000	25,000
	3,38,500	4,08,500

Additional Information :

(1) Depreciation on Machinery of Rs.5,000 during the year 2003.

(2) Depreciation on Land and Building of Rs.10,000 during the year 2003.

(3) An interim dividend of Rs.10,000 was paid during the year 2003.

(4) Income Tax Rs.17,500 was paid during the year 2003.

Solution:

Cash Flow Statement

Sources of Cash	*Rs.*	*Applications of Cash*	*Rs.*
Opening Balances :		Redemption of Preference Shares	25,000
Cash in Hand	7,500	Machinery Purchased	65,000
Cash at Bank	5,000	Interim Dividend Paid	10,000
Add :		Proposed Dividend of 2002 paid	21,000
Cash From Operations	80,000	Tax Paid	17,500
Issue of Equity Shares	50,000	Closing Balances :	
Sale of Buildings	5,000	Cash in Hand	5,000
		Cash at Bank	4,000
	1,47,500		1,47,500

Calculation of Cash From Operations

Particulars	*Rs.*	*Rs.*
Net Profit during the year (Rs.24,000 – Rs.15,000)		9,000
Add :		
Depreciation on Machinery	5,000	
Depreciation on Land & Buildings	10,000	
Transfer to General Reserve	15,000	
Interim Dividend	10,000	
Proposed Dividend	25,000	
Provision for Tax	22,500	
Good will written off	12,500	
Increase in Creditors	14,000	1,14,000
		1,23,000
Less :		
Increase in Debtors	20,000	
Decrease in Bills Payable	2,000	
Increase in Stock	16,000	
Increase in Bills Receivable	5,000	43,000
Cash From Operations		80,000

Note : Provision for Tax and Dividend are treated as Non-current items.

Provision For Taxation Account

To Bank (Tax Paid)	17,500	By Balance b/d	20,000
To Balance c/d	25,000	(Opening Balance)	
(Closing Balance)		By Profit & Loss A/c	22,500
	42,500		42,500

Machinery Account

To Balance b/d	40,000	By Depreciation	5,000
To Bank (Purchases)	65,000	By Balance c/d	1,00,000
(Balancing Figure)		(Provision for 2003)	
	1,05,000		1,05,000

Land and Buildings Account

To Balance b/d	1,00,000	By Depreciation	10,000
(Opening Balance)		By Bank (Sale) (Balancing Figure)	5,000
		By Balance c/d (Closing Balance)	85,000
	1,00,000		1,00,000

Note : Balancing figure in Land and Buildings is treated as sale of building because closing balance of depreciation on Land and Buildings already given in the problem (Rs. 1,00,000 – Rs. 85,000 = Rs. 15,000).

QUESTIONS

(1) What is meant by Cash Flow Statement?

(2) Explain briefly the uses of Cash Flow Statement.

(3) What are the differences between Cash Flow Statement and Fund Flow Statement?

(4) What are the limitations of Cash Flow Statement?

(5) Explain the procedure for preparing a Cash Flow Statement.

(6) What are the components of Sources and Applications of Cash?

Particulars Problems

(1) From the following Balance sheet of Gupta & Co, Ltd, as on 31st Dec.2002 and 2003, you are required to prepare Cash Flow Statement.

Particulars	*2002 Rs.*	*2003 Rs.*
Capital and Liabilities :		
Equity Share Capital	2,30,000	2,30,000
General Reserve	60,000	60,000
Profit and Loss Account	16,000	23,000
Debenture	90,000	70,000
Bills Payable	1,03,000	96,000
Outstanding Salary	13,000	12,000
Depreciation Fund	40,000	44,000
	5,52,000	5,35,000
Assets :		
Cash Balances	90,000	90,000
Trade Debtors	67,000	43,000
Bills Receivable	1,10,000	74,000
Stock	82,000	1,06,000
Prepaid Expenses	1,000	2,000
Land & Building	1,50,000	1,50,000
Machinery	52,000	70,000
	5,52,000	5,35,000

Additional Informations

(1) Now machinery for Rs. 30,000 was purchased but old machinery costing Rs. 6,000 was sold for Rs. 4,000; accumulated depreciation was Rs. 6,000.

(2) Rs. 20,000, 8% Debenture were redeemed by purchase from open market @ Rs. 96 for a debenture of Rs. 100.

(3) Rs. 36,000 investments were sold at book value.

(4) 10% dividend was paid in cash.

(Ans : Cash From Operations Rs. 54,200 ; Cash Flow statement Rs. 2,08,200)

(2) The summarized Balance sheet of X Y Ltd as on 31st December 2002 & 2003 you are required to prepare (a) Cash From Operations and (b) Cash Flow Statements.

Particulars	*2002 Rs.*	*2003 Rs.*
Assets :		
Plant and Machinery	1,00,000	1,00,000
Land and Buildings	2,00,000	1,50,000
Furniture and Fixtures	1,00,000	1,30,000
Investments	50,000	60,000
Stock	2,00,000	2,00,000
Bills Receivable	1,40,000	1,10,000
Trade Debtors	1,10,000	2,95,000
Bank Balances	1,49,000	1,97,000
	10,49,000	12,42,000
Capital and Liabilities :		
Equity Share Capital	2,00,000	2,00,000
Preference Share Capital	2,50,000	4,50,000
General Reserve	3,00,000	3,10,000
Profit and Loss A/c	56,000	68,000
Bills Payable	1,20,000	1,10,000
Trade Creditors	48,000	24,000
Tax Provisions	75,000	10,000
Long Term Loans	—	70,000
	10,49,000	12,42,000

Additional Information

(1) Tax Provision made during the year was Rs. 9,000.

(2) Investment costing Rs. 8000 was sold for Rs. 8,500.

(3) A part of the land and building costing Rs. 10,000 was sold for Rs. 12000 and the profit was included in profit and loss A/c.

(Ans : Cash lost in operations Rs. 1,50,500
Cash flow statements Rs. 4,39,500)

(3) The financial position of RX Ltd as on 31st December 2002 and 2003, you are required to prepare the Cash Flow Statement.

Particulars	*2002 Rs.*	*2003 Rs.*
Assets :		
Cash in hand	10,000	15,000
Cast at Bank	30,000	21,000
Trade Debtors	3,50,000	3,84,000
Bills Receivable	1,50,000	1,30,000
Stock	1,00,000	90,000
Land	2,00,000	3,00,000
Buildings	5,00,000	5,50,000
Machinery	8,00,000	8,60,000
	21,40,000	23,50,000
Capital and Liabilities :		
Trade Creditors	2,80,000	3,00,000
Bills Receivable	80,000	1,10,000
Long Term Loans	—	2,00,000
Short Term Loans	3,00,000	2,50,000
Capital and Reserves	14,80,000	14,90,000
	21,40,000	23,50,000

Additional Information

(1) Dividend of Rs. 2,60,000 was paid during the year.

(2) The provision for depreciation against machinery of Rs. 2,70,000 was made during the year 2002 and Rs. 3,60,000 was during the year 2003.

Ans : (a) Cash From Operations Rs.3,60,000
(b) Cash Flow Statement Rs.6,80,000
(Total Figure)

(4) The following are the summarized Balance sheet of PH & Co Ltd, you are required to prepare the Cash Flow Statement.

Particulars	*2002 Rs.*	*2003 Rs.*
Assets :		
Land and Buildings	10,00,000	9,50,000
Machinery	7,50,000	8,45,000
Stock	5,00,000	3,70,000
Sundry Debtors	4,00,000	3,21,000
Cash Balances	2,500	3,000
Bank Balances	—	40,000
Good will	—	25,000
	26,52,500	25,54,000

Capital & Liabilities :		
Share Capital	10,00,000	12,50,000
General Reserve	2,50,000	3,00,000
Profit and Loss A/c	1,52,500	1,53,000
Long Term Loan	3,50,000	—
Trade Creditors	7,50,000	6,75,000
Provision for Taxation	1,50,000	1,75,000
	26,52,500	25,54,000

Additional Informations

During the year ended 31st December 2003.

(1) Dividend of Rs.1,15,000 was paid.

(2) Assets of another company are purchased for a consideration Rs.2,50,000 payable in shares.

(3) Purchase of Stock Rs.1,00,000.

(4) Purchase of Machinery Rs.1,25,000 on shares.

(5) Machinery was further purchased for Rs.40,000 for cash.

(6) Depreciatic written off of machinery Rs.60,000.

(7) Income tax provided during the year Rs.1,65,000.

(8) Loss on sale of machinery Rs.1,000 was written off to General Reserve.

(Ans : Cash From Operations Rs.4,41,500; Cash Flow Statement Rs.6,88,000)

(5) From the following Balance Sheet of Ram & Co Ltd, you are required to prepare Cash Flow Statement

Particulars	*2002* *Rs.*	*2003* *Rs.*
Assets :		
Good will	2,00,000	1,00,000
Land & Buildings	4,00,000	8,12,000
Stock	9,84,000	8,54,000
Trade Debtors	2,98,000	3,54,000
Bank Balances	1,80,000	—
	20,62,000	21,20,000
Capital and Liabilities :		
Share Capital	14,00,000	14,80,000
Debentures	2,40,000	1,20,000
Trade Creditors	2,07,200	2,36,800
Profit and Loss A/c	2,00,800	2,11,200
Provision for doubtful Debts	14,000	16,000
Bank overdraft	—	56,000
	20,62,000	21,20,000

Additional Information

(1) During the year a building costing of Rs. 4,12,000 was purchased in.

(2) Good will written off Rs. 1,00,000.

(3) Dividend of Rs. 70,000 has been paid during the year 2003.

(4) Debenture loan of Rs. 12,000 was repaid during the year 2003.

(5) An overdraft of Rs. 56,000 availed during the year 2003.

(Ans : Cash From Operations Rs. 1,82,400.
Cash Flow Statement Rs. 6,58,000.)

(6) The Balance Sheet of Nair & Co Ltd, as on 31st Dec. 2002 and 2003, you are required to prepare a Cash Flow Statement.

Balance Sheet

Liabilities	*2002 Rs.*	*2003 Rs.*	*Assets*	*2002 Rs.*	*2003 Rs.*
Share Capital	2,00,000	3,20,000	Fixed Assets	3,04,000	4,00,000
Profit & Loss A/c	1,40,500	1,70,600	Stock	1,86,800	1,78,400
Accumulated Depreciation	1,20,000	80,000	Trade Debtors	61,600	42,200
			Prepaid Expenses	7,900	6,000
Debenture	1,00,000	—	Bank Balances	56,200	40,000
Trade Debtors	56,000	96,000			
	6,16,500	6,66,600		6,16,500	6,66,600

Additional Information

(1) Profit earned during the year was Rs. 54,100.

(2) Depreciation charge Rs. 20,000.

(3) Cash dividend declared during the year Rs. 24,000.

(4) An addition to the building was made during the year at cost of Rs. 1,56,000 and fully depreciated equipment costing Rs. 60000 was discarded as no salvage being realized.

(Ans :
(1) Cash From Operations Rs.82,000
(2) Closing Balance of Cash Rs.40,000)

(7) From the following Balance sheet of Ratha & Co Ltd, as on 31st December 2003, you are required to prepare a Cash Flow Statement.

Balance sheet

Particulars	2002 Rs.	2003 Rs.
Assets :		
Land and Buildings	3,20,000	3,82,000
Plant and Machinery	1,80,000	2,76,000
Stock	60,000	80,000
Trade Debtors	1,20,000	1,60,000
Bills Receivable	20,000	28,000
Cash Balances	40,000	60,000
	7,40,000	9,86,000
Capital and Liabilities :		
Share Capital	4,00,000	5,60,000
Bank Overdraft	2,40,000	3,20,000
Bills Payable	28,000	32,000
Sundry Creditors	68,000	68,000
Outstanding Wages	4,000	6,000
	7,40,000	9,86,000

dditional Information

(1) Profit earned during the year was Rs. 1,60,000.

(2) A machine costing Rs. 40,000 included in the plant and machinery was sold at Rs. 30,000.

(3) The depreciation so charged on it up to the date of sale was Rs. 6,000.

(4) Accumulated Balance of depreciation on Plant and Machinery during the year 2002 was Rs. 60,000 and Rs. 80,000 was in 2003.

) From the following Balance sheet as at 31st December 2002 and 31st December 2003, you are required to prepare a Cash Flow Statement.

Balance Sheet

Liabilities	2002 Rs.	2003 Rs.	Assets	2002 Rs.	2003 Rs.
Share Capital	1,00,000	1,50,000	Fixed Assets	1,00,000	1,50,000
Profit & Loss A/c	50,000	80,000	Goodwill	50,000	40,000
General Reserve	30,000	40,000	Inventories	50,000	80,000
12% Bonds	50,000	60,000	Debtors	50,000	80,000
Sundry Creditors	30,000	40,000	Bills Receivable	10,000	20,000
Outstanding Expenses	10,000	15,000	Bank Balance	10,000	15,000
	2,70,000	3,85,000		2,70,000	3,85,000

ns : Cash from Operations Rs.5,000; Total Cash Flow Statements Rs.60,000)

(9) Prepare Cash Flow Statement of Rajan & Co Ltd from the following information

Balance Sheet

Liabilities	*2002* Rs.	*2003* Rs.	*Assets*	*2002* Rs.	*2003* Rs.
Share Capital	1,00,000	4,00,000	Goodwill	—	20,000
8% Debentures	—	2,00,000	Machinery	1,25,000	4,75,000
Retained Earnings	60,000	90,000	Stock	20,000	80,000
Sundry Creditors	40,000	1,00,000	Sundry Debtors	30,000	1,00,000
Bills Payable	20,000	40,000	Cash at Bank	50,000	1,50,000
Provision for Tax	30,000	40,000	Cash in hand	25,000	45,000
	2,50,000	8,70,000		2,50,000	8,70,000

Additional Informations

(1) Depreciation charge on Machinery was Rs. 30,000.

(2) The debenture were issued at a premium of 5% which is included in the retaine earnings.

(3) Provision for tax charged in 2003 was Rs. 35,000.

(4) During 2003, the business of a firm was purchased by issuing shares for Rs 2,00,000. The assets acquired from the firm were; Goodwill Rs. 20,000; Machiner Rs. 1,00,000; Stock Rs. 50,000 and Debtors Rs. 30,000.

(Ans : Cash From Operations Rs. 1,15,000; Total of Cash Flow Statements Rs. 5,00,000

(10) From the following Balance sheet of Patil & Co Ltd on 31st December 2002 and 2003 you are required to prepare a Cash Flow Statements.

Balance Sheet

Liabilities	*2002* Rs.	*2003* Rs.	*Assets*	*2002* Rs.	*2003* Rs.
Equity Share (Rs. 100 each)	10,00,000	15,00,000	Plant & Machinery (at Cost)	15,00,000	18,00,000
Redeemable Preference Shares (Rs. 100 each Rs. 50 Paid)	5,00,000	—	Inventory	6,00,000	3,00,000
Share Premium	25,000	—	Sundry Debtors	15,00,000	10,00,000
Capital Redemption Reserve	—	5,00,000	Cash at Bank	2,00,000	5,00,000
General Reserve	10,00,000	7,00,000			
Profit & Loss A/c	2,75,000	3,00,000			
Current Liabilities	10,00,000	6,00,000			
	38,00,000	36,00,000		38,00,000	36,00,000

Additional Informations

(1) During the year the company paid Rs. 2,00,000 as equity dividend and Rs. 56,2 as preference dividend

(2) The company redeemed the preference shares at a premium of 5% after making a call of Rs. 50 per shares to make the shares fully paid.

(3) During the year one plant, the book value of which was Rs. 1,00,000, was sold at Rs. 25,000 and the company purchased plant for Rs. 6,00,000.

(Ans : Cash From Operation Rs. 7,56,250; Total of Cash Flow Statement Rs. 27,81,000)

(11) Mohan & Co Ltd gives you the following balance sheet as at 31st December 2002 and 2003

Balance Sheet

Liabilities	*2002* Rs.	*2003* Rs.	*Assets*	*2002* Rs.	*2003* Rs.
Equity Share Capital	50,000	60,000	Fixed Assets	85,000	1,04,000
8% Redeemable Preference Shares	20,000	—	Investments	10,000	8,000
Capital Redemption reserve	—	10,000	Preliminary Expenses	4,000	3,000
Share Premium	5,000	5,000	Stock	20,000	28,000
Profit and Loss A/c	14,000	27,000	Sundry Debtors	18,000	17,000
General Reserve	10,000	13,000	Cash balances	6,000	11,000
Taxation Reserve	7,000	9,000			
Proposed Dividend	5,000	6,000			
Sundry Creditors	14,000	18,000			
Provision for Depreciation	18,000	23,000			
	1,43,000	1,71,000		1,43,000	1,71,000

Additional Informations

(1) During 2003 the proposed dividend was paid in addition to the preference dividend up to 30th June, 2003 on which date the preference shares were reduced at a percent of 5%. The premium had been provided out of share premium account.

(2) Tax liability in respect of 2002 came to Rs. 5,500, the balance in the Taxation reserve as on 31st December 2002 was transferred to general reserve.

(3) During the year a fixed costing Rs. 3,000 (depreciation provided for Rs. 1,600) was sold for Rs. 1,000.

(4) Investment—costing Rs. 2,000 were realized for Rs. 1,600. These matters have been adjusted in the profit and loss account. Prepare a statement showing the source and application of cash during 2003.

(Ans: Cash from operations Rs. 48,700; Total of cash flow statement Rs. 73,300)

II. FOR LONG-TERM CASH FORECAST

Fund Flow Statement Method

Introduction

The purpose of measuring trading performance, operational efficiency, profitability and financial position of a concern revealed by Trading, Profit and Loss Account and Balance Sheet. These financial statements are prepared to find out the Gross Profit or Gross Loss, Net Profit or Net Loss and financial soundness of a firm as a whole for a particular period of time. From the management point of view, the usefulness of information's provided by these income statements functions effectively and efficiently. In the true sense they do not disclose the nature of all transactions. Management, Creditors and Investors etc. want to determining or evaluating the sources and application of funds employed by the firm for the future course of action. Based on these backgrounds, it is essential to analyze the movement of assets, liabilities, funds from operations and capital between the components of two years financial statements. The analysis of financial statements helps to the management by providing additional informations in a meaningful manner.

Meaning of Fund

The term "Fund" refers to Cash, to Cash Equivalents or to Working Capital and all financial resources which are used in business. These total resources of a concern whether in the form of men, materials, money, plant and equipments and others.

In a broader meaning the word "Fund" refers to Working Capital. The Working Capital indicates the difference between current assets and current liabilities. The term working capital may be :

(a) Gross Working Capital and

(b) Net Working Capital

"Gross Working Capital" represents total all Current Assets.

"Net Working Capital" refers to excess of Current Assets over Current Liabilities.

In a narrow sense the word "Fund" denotes cash or to cash equivalents.

Meaning of Flow of Funds

The term "Flow of Funds" refer to changes or movement of funds or changes in working capital in the normal course of business transactions takes place. The changes in working capital may be in the form of inflow of working capital or outflow of working capital. In other words, any increase or decrease in working capital when the transactions takes place is called as "Flow of Funds". If the components of working capital results in increase the fund is known as Inflow of Fund or Sources of Fund. Similarly if the components of working capital effects in decreasing the financial position is treated as Outflow of Fund. For example, If the fund raised by way of issue of shares will be taken as a source of fund or inflow of fund. This transaction results in increase the financial position. Like this if the fund used for the purchase of machinery will be taken as application or use of fund or outflow of fund. Because it stands to reduce the fund position.

The following chart shows the movement of funds :

Movement of Funds

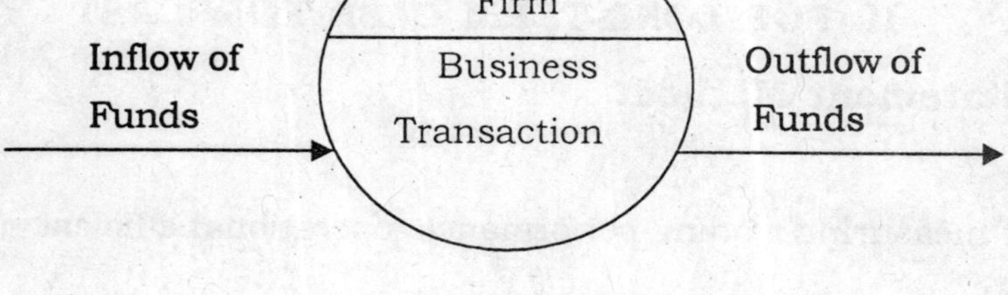

Firm

Inflow of Funds → Business Transaction → Outflow of Funds

No Flow of Funds

Some transactions may not make any movement or changes in the fund position. Such transactions are involved with in the business concern. If the transaction which involve both between current assets and current liabilities or between non-current assets and non-current liabilities and hence do not result in the flow of funds. For example, conversion of shares in to debenture. Such transaction involve between non-current account only and this activity do not effect in increase or decrease the working capital position.

Statement of Changes in Financial Position

It is a statement prepared on the basis of all financial resources *i.e.*, assets, liabilities and capital. This statement is attempt to measures changes in both current and non-current accounts. The changes in financial position may occurs in deal with following transactions.

(a) Involves between current assets and non-current assets (fixed assets or permanent assets).

(b) Involves between current liabilities and non-current assets.

(c) Involves between current assets and non-current liabilities (long term liabilities and capital).

(d) Involves between current liabilities and non-current liabilities.

The following chart explains the flow of funds when transaction involves between current and non-current accounts:

Flow of Funds Chart

Transaction involves between

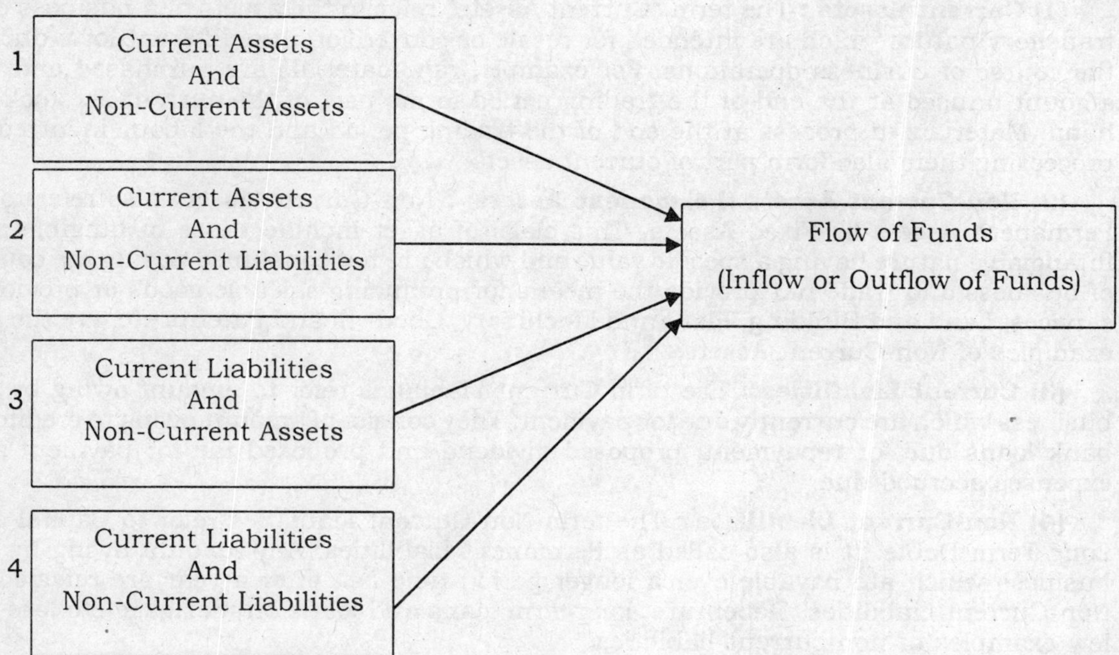

When the transaction involves between non-current account and between current account it does not movement of funds. The following chart shows the no flow of funds :

No Flow of Funds Chart

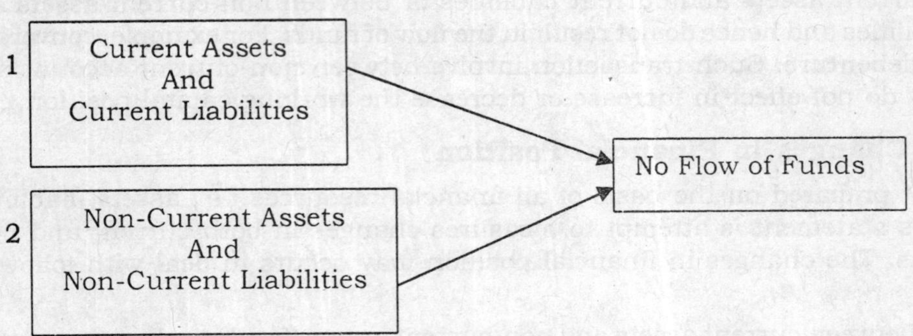

Components of Flow of Funds

In order to analyse the sources and application of funds, it is essential to know the meaning and components of flow of funds given below :

(1) Current Assets
(2) Non-Current Assets (Fixed or Permanent Assets)
(3) Current Liabilities
(4) Non-Current Liabilities (Capital & Long Term Liabilities)
(5) Provision for Tax
(6) Proposed Dividend

(1) Current Assets : The term "Current Assets" refer to the assets of a business of a transitory nature which are intended for resale or conversion into different form during the course of business operations. For example, raw materials are purchased and the amount unused at the end of the trading period forms part of the current as stock on hand. Materials in process at the end of the trading period and the labour incurred in processing them also form part of current assets.

(2) Non-Current Assets (Permanent Assets) : Non-Current Assets also refer to as Permanent Assets or Fixed Assets. This class of asset include those of tangible and intangiable nature having a specific value and which are not consumed during the course of business and trade but provide the means for producing saleable goods or providing services. Land and Building, Plant and Machinery, Goodwill and Patents etc. are the few examples of Non-Current Assets.

(3) Current Liabilities : The term Current Liabilities refer to amount owing by the business which are currently due for payment. They consist of amount owing to creditors, bank loans due for repayment, proposed dividend and proposed tax for payment and expenses accrued due.

(4) Non-Current Liabilities : The term Non-Current Liabilities refer to Capital and Long Term Debts. It is also called as Permanent Liabilities. Any amount owing by the business which are payable over a longer period time *i.e.*, after a year are referred as Non-Current Liabilities. Debenture, long term loans and loans on mortgage etc. are the few examples of non-current liabilities.

(5) Provision for Taxation : Provision for taxation may be treated as a current liability or an appropriation of profit. When it is made during the year is not used for adjusting the net profit, it is advisable to treate the same as current liability. Any amount of tax paid during the year is to be treated as application of funds or non-current liability. Because it is used for adjusting the net profit made during the year.

(6) Proposed Dividend : Like provision for taxation, it is also treated as a current liability and non-current liability. When dividend may be considered as being declared. And thus, it will not be used for adjusting the net profit made during the year. If it is treated as an appropriation *i.e.*, an non-current liability when the dividend paid during the year.

(7) Provisions Against Current Assets and Current Liabilities : Provision for bad and doubtful debts, provision for loss on inventories, provision for discount on creditors and provision made against investment etc. are made during the year, they may be treated separately as current assets or current liabilities or reduce the same from the respective gross value of the assets or liabilities.

The list of Current Accounts and Non-Current Accounts are given below :

Current Accounts

Current Liabilities	*Current Assets*
(1) Bills Payable	(1) Cash in hand
(2) Sundry Creditors	(2) Cash at Bank
(3) Outstanding Expenses	(3) Bills Receivable
(4) Dividends Payable	(4) Sundry Debtors
(5) Bank Overdraft	(5) Short Term Investments
(6) Short Term Loans	(6) Marketable Securities
(7) Provisions against Current Assets	(7) Stock of Raw Materials, Work in Progress & Finished Goods
(8) Provision for taxation	(8) Prepaid Expenses
(9) Proposed Dividend (May be Current or Non-Current Liabilities)	(9) Accrued Incomes

Non-Current Accounts

Non -Current or Permanent Liabilities	*Non -Current or Permanent Assets*
(1) Equity Share Capital	(1) Good will
(2) Preference Share Capital	(2) Land
(3) Debentures	(3) Building
(4) Long Term Loans	(4) Plant and Machinery
(5) Share Premium	(5) Furniture and Fittings
(6) Share forfeited	(6) Trade Marks
(7) Profit and Loss Account	(7) Patent Rights
(8) Capital Reserve	(8) Long Term Investments
(9) Capital Redemption Reserve	(9) Discount on Issue of Shares and Debentures
	(10) Preliminary Expenses
	(11) Other Deferred Expenses

Fund Flow Statement

It is a statement summarizing the significant financial changes in items of financial position which have occurred between the two different balance sheet dates. This statement is prepared on the basis of "Working Çapital" concept of funds. Fund flow Statement helps to measure the different sources of funds and application of funds from transactions involves during the course of business.

The fund flow statement also termed as Statement of Sources and Application of Fund, Where Got and Where Gone Out Statement, Inflow of Fund or Outflow of Fund Statement.

Importance or Uses of Fund Flow Statement

Fund Flow Statement are prepared for financial analysis in order to meet the needs of people serving the following purposes.

(1) It highlights the different sources and application or uses of funds between the two accounting period.

(2) It brings into light about financial strength and weakness of a concern.

(3) It acts as a effective tool to measure the causes of changes in working capital.

(4) It helps to the management to take corrective actions while deviations between two balance sheet figures.

(5) It is an instrument used by the investors for effective decisions at the time of their investment proposals.

(6) It also presents detailed information's about profitability, operational efficiency and financial affairs of a concern.

(7) It serves as a guide to the management to formulate its dividend policy, retention policy and investment policy etc.

(8) It helps to evoluate the financial consequences of business transactions involves in operational financial and investment.

(9) It gives the detailed explanation about movement of funds from different sources or uses of funds during a particular accounting period.

Difference between Fund Flow Statement and Income Statement

Fund Flow Statement	*Income Statement*
(1) It explains the different sources and uses of funds during the particular period.	(1) It reveals the net profit or net loss in a particular period of time.
(2) No standard format is required for preparation of fund flow statement.	(2) As per the double entry book keeping, prescribed format is used for preparation of income statement.
(3) Fund Flow Statement considers both capital and revenue nature of income and expenditure.	(3) It considers only revenue nature of income and expenditure.
(4) It disclosed the exact flow of funds from operations. Thus, it is complementary to income statement.	(4) It is prepared not for fund flow statement.

Difference between Fund Flow Statement and Balance Sheet

Fund Flow Statement	*Balance Sheet*
(1) It presents significant financial changes between two balance sheet.	(1) It is a statement that incorporate of assets and liabilities prepare at the end of accounting period.
(2) It is prepared on the basis Trading, Profit & Loss account and Balance sheet.	(2) It is prepared on the basis of Trial Balance.
(3) It provides additional informations to the management for discharge its functions effectively.	(3) It explains the financial position of a concern as a whole in a particular period.
(4) Fund from operation, schedule of changes in working capital has to be required for preparation of fund flow statement.	(4) It is prepared after the Trading, Profit and Loss Account is completed.

Difference between Fund Flow Statement and Cash Flow Statement

Fund Flow Statement and Cash Flow Statement are the two useful tools of financial analysis in order to determining Long-term and Short-term cash forecast respectively. But at the same time both the statements are differ from other in the following manner.

(1) Fund Flow Statement helps to measure the causes of changes in working capital where as cash flow statement focus on the causes for the movement of cash during a particular period

(2) Fund Flow Statement is prepared on the basis of fund or all financial resources while cash flow statement is based on cash basis of accounting

(3) Cash Flow Statement guides to the management for short-term financial planning while Fund flow analysis helps to the management for intermediate and long term financial planning

(4) Statement of changes in working capital is required for the preparation of fund flow statement while for cash flow statement no such statement is required

Limitations of Fund Flow Statement

Fund Flow Statement has suffered with the following limitations :

(1) It is prepared on the basis of informations related to historical in nature. It ignores to project future operations.

(2) This statement does not focus on transactions involves in non-fund items.

(3) It is also ignores when transactions involves between current accounts or non-current accounts.

(4) It does not provide any additional informations to the management because financial statements are simply rearranged and presented.

Preparation of Fund Flow Statement

Fund flow analysis involves the following important three statements such as :

I. Fund From Operations

II. Statement of Changes in Working Capital

III. Fund Flow Statement

I. Fund From Operations : Fund From Operation is to be determined on the basis of Profit and Loss Account. The operating profit revealed by Profit and Loss Account is represent the excess of sales revenue over cost of goods sold. In the true sense, it does not reflect the exact flow of funds caused by business operations. Because the revenue earned and expenses incurred are not in confirmity with the flow of funds. For example depreciations charges on fixed assets, write up of fixed assets or fictious assets any appropriations etc. which they do not cause a actual flow of funds. Because they have already been charged to such profits. Hence, fund from operation is prepared to find out exact inflow or outflow of funds from the regular operations on the basis of items which have readjusted to the current profit or loss. The balancing amount of adjusted profit and loss account is described as fund from operations.

Calculation of Fund From Operations : Fund from operations is calculated with help of following adjustments are to be made. The adjustments may be shown in the specimen proforma of profit and loss account is given below :

Particulars	*Amount Rs.*	*Amount Rs.*
Net Profit or Retained Earnings		* * *
(Closing balance of P & L A/c as given in the Balance Sheet)		
Add : Non-Fund and Non-Operating items which have already been debited to P & L A/c :		
(1) Depreciation and Depletion	* * *	
(2) Amortization of Fictious and Intangible Assets etc.		
(a) Good will, Patents written off		
(b) Discount on Issue of shares written off		
(c) Preliminary Expenses written off		
(d) Premium on redemption of debenture		
(3) Appropriation of Retained Earnings :		
Profit transfer to General Reserve	* * *	
Profit transfer to Sinking Fund		
Profit transfer to Contingency		
Provision for Taxation (not taken as current liability)		
Provision for Proposed Dividend (not taken as current liability)		
Loss on Sale of Fixed Assets		
Loss on Sale of Plant and Machinery		
Loss on Sales of Land and Building		
Loss on Sale of Furniture and Fixtures	* * *	* * *
Total (A)	* * *	* * *

Particulars	Amount Rs.	Amount Rs.
Less : Non-Fund and Non-Operating items which have already been credited to P & L A/c :		
(1) Profit on sale of Fixed Assets	* * *	
Profit on sale of Land & Building		
Profit on sale of Plant & Machinery		
Profit on sale of Furniture & Fixtures		
(2) Appreciation or Revaluation of fixed assets	* * *	
(3) Dividend received on investment	* * *	
(4) Profit on redemption of Shares and Debentures	* * *	
(5) Excess provisions written back	* * *	
(6) Any other non trading items already credited to P & L A/c	* * *	
(7) Net Profit or Retained Earnings (Opening balance of P & L A/c)	* * *	
Total (B)	* * *	* * *
Fund From Operations (Total A—B)		* * *

Alternative Specimen Format : The following is the specimen of adjusted profit and loss account to calculate fund from operations :

ADJUSTED PROFIT AND LOSS ACCOUNT

Particulars	Amount Rs.	Particulars	Amount Rs.
To Depreciation on Fixed Assets		By Opening Balance of P & L A/c	
To Loss on Sale of Fixed Assets		By Profit on Sale of Fixed Assets	
To Loss on Sale Investments		By Excess provision written back	
To Goodwill written off		By Dividend received on investment	
To Discount on shares written off		By Revaluation of fixed assets	
To Transfer to reserve		By Fund From Operations (Balancing Figure)	
To Preliminary expenses written off			
To Provision for Tax			
To Proposed Dividend			
To Closing Balance of P & L A/c			
	* * *		* * *

Illustration: 1

From the following Profit and Loss Account, Calculation fun from operation :

Profit and Loss Account

Particulars	*Rs.*	*Particulars*	*Rs.*
To Rent	60,000	By Gross Profit b/d	5,00,000
To Salaries	1,40,000	By Transfers to General Reserve	70,000
To Advertisement	30,000	By Preliminary Expenses	10,000
To Office Expenses	20,000	By Profit on Sale of Investment	20,000
To Depreciation on Plant	50,000		
To Good will written off	30,000		
To Loss on Sales of Plant	20,000		
To Provision for Tax	40,000		
To Interim Dividend	30,000		
To Net Profit	1,80,000		
	6,00,000		6,00,000

Solution:

Calculation of Fund From Operations

Particulars	*Amount Rs.*	*Amount Rs.*
Net Profit or Retained Earnings (Closing Balance of P & L A/c)		1,80,000
Add : Non-Fund or Non-Trading items already debited to P & L A/c :		
Depreciation on Plant	50,000	
Good will written off	30,000	
Loss on Sale of Plant	20,000	
Provision for Tax	40,000	
Interim Dividend	30,000	
Preliminary Expenses	10,000	
Transfer to General Reserve	70,000	2,50,000
		4,30,000
Less : Non-Fund or Non-Trading items already Credited to P & L A/c :		
Profit on Sale of Investments	20,000	20,000
Fund From Operations		4,10,000

Note : Provision for tax and Interim Dividend are not treated as current liability.

Alternatively

Adjusted Profit And Loss Account

To Depreciation on Plant	50,000	By Profit on sale of Investment	20,000
To Goodwill written off	30,000	By Fund Form Operations	4,10,000
To Loss on Sale of Plant	20,000	(Balancing figure)	
To Provision for Tax	40,000		
To Interim Dividend	30,000		
To Preliminary Expenses	10,000		
To Transfer General Reserve	70,000		
To Net Profit (Closing Balance of P & L A/c)	1,80,000		
	4,30,000		4,30,000

Illustration: 2

Calculate fund from operations from the following Profit and Loss Account

To Salaries	4,50,000	By Gross Profit b/d	20,00,000
To Rent & Rates	1,50,000	By Profit on Sale of Plant	1,00,000
To Office Expenses	1,50,000	By Dividend received on Investment	40,000
To Administrative Expenses	2,00,000		
To General Expenses	50,000	By Preliminary Expenses	20,000
To Depreciation on Machinery	2,50,000	By Transfer to General Reserve	40,000
To Depletion of natural resources	1,00,000		
To Depreciation on Building	50,000		
To Loss on Sale of Building	1,00,000		
To Good will written off	1,00,000		
To Discount written off	30,000		
To Advertisement written off	50,000		
To Net Profit	5,20,000		
	22,00,000		22,00,000

Solution:

Calculation of Fund From Operations

Particulars	*Amount Rs.*	*Amount Rs.*
Net Profit or Retained Earnings (Closing balance of Profit & Loss A/c)		5,20,000
Add : Non-fund or Non-Trading items already debited to P & L A/c :		
Depreciation on Plant & Machinery	2,50,000	
Depreciation on Building	50,000	
Depletion of natural resources	1,00,000	
Loss on Sale of building	1,00,000	
Good will written off	1,00,000	
Discount written off	30,000	
Advertisement Written off	50,000	
Preliminary Expenses	20,000	7,00,000
		12,20,000
Less : Non-Fund or Non-Operating items already credited to P & L A/c :		
Profit on Sale of Plant	1,00,000	
Dividend received on Investment	40,000	
Transfer to General Reserve	40,000	1,80,000
Fund From Operations		10,40,000

Alternatively

Solution:

Adjusted Profit & Loss Account

Particulars	*Amount Rs.*	*Particulars*	*Amount Rs.*
To Depreciation on Plant and Machinery	2,50,000	By Profit on Sale of Plant	1,00,000
To Depreciation on Building	50,000	By Dividend received on Investment	40,000
To Depletion of natural resources	1,00,000	By Transfer to General Reserve	40,000
To Loss on Sale of Building	1,00,000	By Fund From Operations (Balancing figure)	10,40,000
To Good will written off	1,00,000		
To Discount written off	30,000		
To Advertisement written off	50,000		
To Preliminary Expenses	20,000		
To Net Profit (Closing Balance)	5,20,000		
	12,20,000		12,20,000

I. Statement of Changes in Working Capital

t is also termed as Statement of Changes in Working Capital. Before preparation of fund low statement, it is essential to prepare first the schedule of changes in working capital nd fund from operations. Statement of changes in working capital is prepared on the asis of items in current assets and current liabilities of between two balance sheet. 'his statement helps to measure the movement or changes of working capital during a articular period. The term working capital refers to excess of current assets over current iabilities. The working capital may be "Increase in working capital" or "Decrease in vorking capital". An increase in the amount of an item of current assets in the current 'ear as compared to the previous year represents to an increase in working capital. imilarly, a decrease in the amount of an item of current assets in the current year as ompared to the previous year would represent decrease in working capital. In the same vay over all changes in working capital is calculated and presented in the schedule of hanges in working capital. The final result of Net Decrease in Working Capital refers to ource of Funds or Inflow of Funds. Like this, Net Increase in Working Capital represent pplication of Fund or Uses of Funds.

rinciple or Rules for Preparation of Working Capital Statement

'he following rules may be kept in mind while preparing working capital statement.

(1) Increase in Current Asset ⟶ Increases Working Capital

(2) Decrease in Current Asset ⟶ Decreases Working Capital

(3) Increase in Current Liability ⟶ Decreases Working Capital

(4) Decrease in Current Liability ⟶ Increases Working Capital

Specimen Form of Schedule of Changes in Working Capital :

The following is a specimen form may be used for preparation of schedule of changes n working capital.

Schedule of Changes in Working Capital
(or)
Statement of Changes in Working Capital

Particulars	*Previous Year Rs.*	*Current Year Rs.*	*Effect on Working Capital*	
			Increase	*Decrease*
Current Assets :				
Cash in Hand	***	***	***	—
Cash at Bank				
Sundry Debtors				
Bills Receivable				
Short Term Investments				
Stock				
Prepaid Expenses				
Outstanding Incomes	***	***	—	***
Total Current Assets (A)	***	***		

Current Liabilities :				
Sundry Creditors	***	***	***	—
Bills Payable				
Bank Overdraft				
Outstanding Expenses				
Short Term Loans	***	***	—	***
Total Current Liabilities (B)	***	***		
Working Capital (A—B)	***	***		
Net Increase / Decrease In Working Capital	***	—		***
Total	***	***	***	***

Illustration: 3

From the following Balance Sheet of Gupta Ltd, Prepare Schedule of Changes in Working Capital.

Balance Sheet

Liabilities	*2003 Rs.*	*2004 Rs.*	*Assets*	*2003 Rs.*	*2004 Rs.*
Creditors	55,000	83,000	Cash in hand	15,000	10,000
Bills Payable	20,000	16,000	Cash at bank	10,000	8,000
Share Capital	1,00,000	1,50,000	Debtors	1,60,000	2,00,000
General Reserve	7,000	8,000	Stock	77,000	1,09,000
Debenture	1,00,000	1,00,000	Bills Receivable	20,000	30,000
	2,82,000	3,57,000		2,82,000	3,57,000

Solution:

Schedule of Changes in Working Capital

Particulars	*2003 Rs.*	*2004 Rs.*	*Changes in Working Capital*	
			Increase	*Decrease*
Current Assets :				
Cash in hand	15,000	10,000	—	5,000
Cash at Bank	10,000	8,000	—	2,000
Debtors	1,60,000	2,00,000	40,000	—
Stock	77,000	1,09,000	32,000	—
Bills Receivable	20,000	30,000	10,000	—
Total (A)	2,82,000	3,57,000		

Current Liabilities :				
Creditors	55,000	83,000	—	28,000
Bills Payable	20,000	16,000	4,000	—
Total (B)	75,000	99,000		
Working Capital (A—B)	2,07,000	2,58,000		
Net Increase in Working Capital	51,000	—	—	51,000
	2,58,000	2,58,000	86,000	86,000

Illustration: 4

You are required to prepare a Schedule of changes in working capital from the following Balance sheet of Nancy Ltd, at the end of 2003 and 2004.

Balance Sheet

Liabilities	*2003 Rs.*	*2004 Rs.*	*Assets*	*2003 Rs.*	*2004 Rs.*
Share Capital	50,000	75,000	Cash at bank	15,000	25,000
General Reserve	25,000	30,000	Plant	50,000	70,000
Bill Payable	10,000	15,000	Building	50,000	60,000
Debenture	30,000	50,000	Stock	30,000	35,000
Trade Creditors	40,000	50,000	Bills Receivable	25,000	40,000
Short Term Loans	30,000	40,000	Trade Debtors	15,000	30,000
	1,85,000	2,60,000		1,85,000	2,60,000

Solution:

Schedule of Changes in Working Capital

Particulars	*2003 Rs.*	*2004 Rs.*	*Changes in Working Capital*	
			Increase	*Decrease*
Current Assets :				
Cash at Bank	15,000	25,000	10,000	—
Stock	30,000	35,000	5,000	—
Bills Receivable	25,000	40,000	15,000	—
Trade Debtors	15,000	30,000	15,000	—
Total (A)	85,000	1,30,000		
Current Liabilities :				
Bills Payable	10,000	15,000	—	5,000
Trade Creditors	40,000	50,000	—	10,000
Short Term Loans	30,000	40,000	—	10,000
Total (B)	80,000	1,05,000		
Working Capital (Total A – B)	5,000	25,000		
Net Increase in Working Capital	20,000	—	—	20,000
	25,000	25,000	45,000	45,000

Illustration: 5

From the following Balance Sheet of John Ltd, Prepare a Schedule of changes in working capital

Balance Sheet

Particulars	*2003 Rs.*	*2004 Rs.*
Assets :		
Cash Balances	30,000	40,000
Debtors	60,000	56,000
Stock	1,10,000	1,44,000
Building	1,60,000	2,00,000
Machinery	30,000	20,000
	3,90,000	4,60,000
Liabilities :		
Capital	1,26,000	2,00,000
Long Term Loans	1,00,000	1,20,000
Sundry Creditors	84,000	78,000
Bank Overdraft	70,000	50,000
Outstanding Expenses	10,000	12,000
	3,90,000	4,60,000

Solution:

Schedule of Changes in Working Capital

Particulars	*2003 Rs.*	*2004 Rs.*	*Changes in Working Capital*	
			Increase	*Decrease*
Current Assets :				
Cash Balances	30,000	40,000	10,000	—
Debtors	60,000	56,000	—	4,000
Stock	1,10,000	1,44,000	34,000	—
Total (A)	2,00,000	2,40,000		
Current Liabilities :				
Sundry Creditors	84,000	78,000	6,000	—
Bank Overdraft	70,000	50,000	20,000	—
Outstanding Expenses	10,000	12,000	—	2,000
Total (B)	1,64,000	1,40,000		
Working Capital (Total A—B)	36,000	1,00,000		
Net Increase in Working Capital	64,000	—	—	64,000
	1,00,000	1,00,000	70,000	70,000

Fund Flow Statement

In the analysis and interpretation of financial statements fund flow statement is one of the important technique. The statement of changes in working capital is prepared with the help of current assets and current liabilities. Similarly, fund from operation is prepared on the basis of profit and loss account to find out the exact movement of funds in different operations. After preparing schedule of changes in working capital and fund from operations, at the last stage a comprehensive fund flow statement can be prepared on the basis of component of non-current assets, non-current liabilities of balance sheet and relavent information. In other words, this statement is prepared with the help of the changes in non-current assets and non-current liabilities of balance sheet.

Components of Sources and Application of Funds

The following are the components different sources and applications of funds presented below :

Components of Sources of Funds

(1) Fresh Issue of Equity Share Capital
(2) Fresh Issue of Preference Share Capital
(3) Issue of Debentures and Bonds
(4) Long Term Loans raised from bank, financial institutions and public
(5) Long Term Loans on Mortgage
(6) Sale of Fixed Assets
(7) Sale of Long Term Investments
(8) Non-Trading Incomes
(9) Fund From Operations
(10) Net Decrease in Working Capital (as per schedule of changes in working capital)

Components of Applications of Funds

Generated funds from various sources may be utilized this funds in the following ways for meeting the future productive programmes of the business.

(1) Redemption of Shares and Debentures
(2) Repayment of Loans raised from bank, financial institutions and public
(3) Purchase of Fixed Assets
(4) Purchase of Long Term Investments
(5) Non-Trading Expenditure
Payment of Tax
Payment of Dividend
(6) Fund Lost in Operations
(7) Net Increase in Working Capital (as per schedule of changing in working capital)

Specimen form of Fund Flow Statement

The following are the two usual formats for preparation of Sources and Application of Fund is presented below.

(1) Statement Form
(2) Account Form

(1) Statement Form

Fund Flow Statement

Particulars	*Amount Rs.*	*Amount Rs.*
Sources of Funds :		
Fund Form Operations	***	
Issue of Share Capital		
Issue of Debentures		
Long Term Loans		
Sale of Fixed Assets		
Sale of Investments		
Non-Trading Incomes		
Decrease in Working Capital (as per schedule of changes in working capital)	***	***
Total Sources (or) Total Inflows (A)		***
Application or Uses of Funds :		
Fund Lost in Operations	***	
Redemption of Shares		
Redemption of Debentures		
Purchase of Fixed Assets		
Repayment of Long Term Investments		
Non-Trading Expenditure		
Payment of Tax		
Payment of dividend		
Increase in Working Capital (as per schedule of changes in working capital)	***	***
Total Application or Total Outflows (B)		***

(2) Account Form

Fund Flow Statement

Sources of Funds	*Amount Rs.*	*Application of Funds*	*Amount Rs.*
Fund From Operations	***	Fund Lost in Operations	***
Issue of Share Capital		Redemption of Shares	
Issue of Debentures		Redemption of Debenture	
Long Term Loans		Purchase of Fixed Assets	
Sale of Fixed Assets		Repayment of Long Term Loans	
Sale of Investments		Non-Trading Expenditure	

Non-Trading Incomes Decrease in Working Capital (As per schedule of changes in working capital)	***	Payment of Tax Payment of Dividend Increase in Working Capital (as per schedule of changes in working capital)	***
Total Inflow	***	Total Outflow	***

Illustration: 6

From the following Balance sheet of William & Co Ltd, you are required to prepare a Schedule of Changes in Working Capital and Statement of Sources and Application of Funds.

Balance sheet

Liabilities	*2003 Rs.*	*2004 Rs.*	*Assets*	*2003 Rs.*	*2004 Rs.*
Capital	8,00,000	8,50,000	Cash in hand	40,000	90,000
P & L A/c	1,45,000	2,45,000	Sundry Debtors	1,65,000	1,95,000
Sundry Creditors	90,000	50,000	Stock	90,000	70,000
Long Term Loans	—	50,000	Machinery	2,40,000	3,40,000
			Building	5,00,000	5,00,000
	10,35,000	11,95,000		10,35,000	11,95,000

Solution:

Schedule of Changes in Working Capital

Particulars	*2003 Rs.*	*2004 Rs.*	*Effect on Working Capital*	
			Increase	*Decrease*
Current Assets :				
Cash at Bank	40,000	90,000	50,000	—
Sundry Debtors	1,65,000	1,95,000	30,000	—
Stock	90,000	70,000	—	20,000
Total (A)	2,95,000	3,55,000		
Current Liabilities :				
Sundry Creditors	90,000	50,000	40,000	—
Total (B)	90,000	50,000		
Working Capital (Total A – B)	2,05,000	3,05,000		
Net Increase in Working Capital	1,00,000	—	—	1,00,000
	3,05,000	3,05,000	1,20,000	1,20,000

Fund Flow Statement

Sources of Fund	*Rs.*	*Application of Fund*	*Rs.*
Issue of Capital (8,00,000 – 8,50,000)	50,000	Purchase of Machinery (24,000 – 34,000)	1,00,000
Long Term Loans	50,000	Net Increase in Working Capital	1,00,000
Fund From Operations (1,45,000 – 2,45,000)	1,00,000		
	2,00,000		2,00,000

Illustration: 7

From the following Balance sheet of RR & Co Ltd, you are required to prepare (a) Schedule of Changes in Working Capital (b) Fund Flow Statement and (c) Fund From Operations.

Balance Sheet

Liabilities	*2003 Rs.*	*2004 Rs.*	*Assets*	*2003 Rs.*	*2004 Rs.*
Equity Capital	10,00,000	10,00,000	Good will	60,000	60,000
General Reserve	1,40,000	1,80,000	Patents	60,000	60,000
Profit & Loss A/c	1,60,000	1,30,000	Building	5,00,000	4,60,000
Bank Overdraft	30,000	20,000	Machinery	2,70,000	2,60,000
Sundry Creditors	50,000	34,000	Investments	1,00,000	1,10,000
Bills Payable	12,000	8,000	Stock	2,00,000	1,34,000
Provision for Taxation	1,00,000	1,10,000	Bills Receivable	1,20,000	1,32,000
Proposed Dividend	60,000	70,000	Debtors	1,80,000	1,90,000
Provision for Doubtful Debts	4,000	6,000	Cash at Bank	66,000	1,52,000
	15,56,000	15,58,000		15,56,000	15,58,000

Additional Informations

(1) Depreciation Charged on Machinery Rs. 40,000 and on Building Rs. 40,000.

(2) Provision for Taxation of Rs. 1,90,000 was made during the year 2004.

(3) Interim Dividend of Rs. 80,000 was Paid during the year 2004.

Solution:

Calculation of Fund from Operations

Particulars	*Amount*	*Amount*
Profit and Loss A/c (Closing Balance of 2004)		1,30,000
Add : Non-Fund or Non-Trading items already Debited to P&L A/c :		
Depreciation on Machinery	40,000	
Depreciation on Building	40,000	
Interim Dividend Paid	80,000	
Transfer to General Reserve	40,000	
Provision for Tax (See Note 1)	1,90,000	
Proposed Dividend	10,000	4,00,000
		5,30,000
Less : Non –Fund or Non-Trading items already Credited to P&L A/c :		
Profit and Loss A/c (Opening balance as per 2003)		1,60,000
Fund From Operations		3,70,000

Schedule of Changes in Working Capital

Particulars	*2003*	*2004*	*Changes in Working Capital*	
	Rs.	*Rs.*	*Increase*	*Decrease*
Current Assets :				
Cash at Bank	66,000	1,52,000	86,000	—
Debtors	1,80,000	1,90,000	10,000	—
Stock	2,00,000	1,34,000	—	66,000
Bills Receivable	1,20,000	1,32,000	12,000	—
Total (A)	5,66,000	6,08,000		
Current Liabilities :				
Bank Overdraft	30,000	20,000	10,000	—
Sundry Creditors	50,000	34,000	16,000	—
Prevention for Doubtful Debits	4,000	6,000	—	2,000
Bills Payable	12,000	8,000	4,000	—
Total (B)	96,000	68,000		
Working Capital (Total A – B)	4,70,000	5,40,000		
Net Increase in Working Capital	70,000	—	—	70,000
	5,40,000	5,40,000	1,38,000	1,38,000

Fund Flow Statement

Sources of Fund	*Rs.*	*Application of Fund*	*Rs.*
Fund From Operations	3,70,000	Purchase of Machinery	30,000
		Tax Paid (see Note 3)	1,80,000
		Investment Purchased (1,00,000 – 1,10,000)	10,000
		Interim Dividend Paid	80,000
		Net Increase in Working Capital	70,000
	3,70,000		3,70,000

Machinery Account

To Balance b/d	2,70,000	By Depreciation	40,000
To Bank (Purchase of Machinery Balancing figure)	30,000	By Balance c/d	2,60,000
	3,00,000		3,00,000

Building Account

To Balance b/d	5,00,000	By Depreciation	40,000
		By Balance c/d	4,60,000
	5,00,000		5,00,000

Provision for Taxation

To Bank (By Balancing figure)	1,80,000	By Balance b/d	1,00,000
To Balance c/d	1,10,000	By Provision for Taxation	1,90,000
	2,90,000		2,90,000

Illustration: 8

From the following are the comparative Balance sheet of Gupta & Co, you are required to prepare (a) Schedule of Changes in Working Capital (b) Fund Flow Statement and (c) Fund From Operations.

Balance Sheet

Liabilities	*2002* *Rs.*	*2003* *Rs.*	*Assets*	*2002* *Rs.*	*2003* *Rs.*
Share Capital	9,00,000	10,00,000	Good will	1,20,000	1,00,000
General Reserve	1,40,000	1,80,000	Buildings	4,00,000	3,60,000
Profit & Loss A/c	1,95,000	1,20,000	Machinery	3,70,000	3,60,000
Provision for Taxation	1,60,000	1,70,000	Stock	3,00,000	2,54,000
Sundry Creditors	80,000	54,000	Sundry Debtors	2,00,000	2,22,000
Bills Payable	62,000	13,000	Cash at Bank	66,000	1,52,000
Provision for Doubtful Debts	19,000	21,000	Investments	1,00,000	1,10,000
	15,56,000	15,58,000		15,56,000	15,58,000

Addition Information

(1) Depreciation Charged on Machinery was Rs. 40,000 and on building of Rs. 40,000.

(2) Interim Dividend paid during 2003 was Rs. 75,000.

(3) Provision of Rs. 50,000 was made taxation during the 2003.

Solution:

Calculation of Fund From Operations

Particulars	*Rs.*	*Rs.*
Net Profit (Closing Balance)		1,20,000
Add : Non-fund or Non-operating items		
Which already Debited to P & L A/c :		
Good will written off	20,000	
Depreciation on Machinery	40,000	
Depreciation on Building	40,000	
Interim Dividend Paid	75,000	
Transfer to General Reserve	40.000	2,15,000
		3,35,000
Less : Non-Fund or Non-Operating items		
already Credited to P & L A/c :		
Net Profit (Opening Balance)		1,95,000
Fund From Operations		1,40,000

Schedule of Changes in Working Capital

Particulars	*2002* *Rs.*	*2003* *Rs.*	*Changes in Working Capital*	
			Increase	*Decrease*
Current Assets :				
Stock	3,00,000	2,54,000	—	46,000
Sundry Debtors (Less Provision For Doubtful Debts)	1,81,000	2,01,000	20,000	—
Cash Balances	66,000	1,52,000	86,000	—
Total (A)	5,47,000	6,07,000		
Current Liabilities :				
Sundry Creditors	80,000	54,000	26,000	—
Bills Payable	62,000	13,000	49,000	—
Prevention for Tax	1,60,000	1,70,000	—	10,000
Total (B)	3,02,000	2,37,000		
Working Capital (Total A – B)	2,45,000	3,70,000		
Net Increase in Working Capital	1,25,000	—	—	1,25,000
	3,70,000	3,70,000	1,81,000	1,81,000

Fund Flow Statement

Sources of Fund	*Rs.*	*Application of Fund*	*Rs.*
Issue of Share Capital (9,00,000 – 10,00,000)	1,00,000	Purchase of Machinery	30,000
		Purchase of Investments	10,000
Funds From Operations	1,40,000	Interim Dividend Paid	75,000
		Net Increase in Working Capital	1,25,000
	2,40,000		2,40,000

Machinery Account

To Balance b/d	3,70,000	By Depreciation	40,000
To Bank (Purchase of Machinery Balancing figure)	30,000	By Balance c/d	3,60,000
	4,00,000		4,00,000

Building Account

To Balance b/d	4,00,000	By Depreciation	40,000
		By Balance c/d	3,60,000
	4,00,000		4,00,000

Illustration: 9

From the following Balance sheet of X Y Z Ltd, on 31st Dec.2002 and 2003, you are required to prepare (a) Fund From Operations (b) Schedule of Changes in Working Capital and (c) Fund Flow Statement.

Balance Sheet

Liabilities	*2002 Rs.*	*2003 Rs.*	*Assets*	*2002 Rs.*	*2003 Rs.*
Bills Payable	2,00,000	2,20,000	Cash Balances	1,00,000	70,000
Creditors	2,00,000	2,20,000	Debtors	2,00,000	2,00,000
Ramesh's Loan	2,50,000	—	Bills Payable	1,00,000	3,00,000
Loan from Kannan	4,00,000	5,00,000	Stock	3,50,000	2,50,000
Equity Share Capital	10,00,000	10,00,000	Machinery	8,00,000	5,50,000
Preference Share Capital	2,50,000	5,30,000	Land	4,00,000	5,00,000
			Building	3,50,000	6,00,000
	23,00,000	24,70,000		23,00,000	24,70,000

Addition Information

(1) During the year machine costing Rs. 1,00,000 (accumulated depreciation Rs. 30,000) was sold for Rs. 50,000.

(2) The provision for depreciation against machinery on 1st Jan.2003 was Rs. 2,50,000 and on 31st December was Rs. 4,00,000.

(3) Net profit for the year 2003 amounted to Rs. 4,50,000.

Solution:

Calculation of Fund From Operations

Particulars	*Rs.*	*Rs.*
Net Profit (Closing Balance P & L A/c)		4,50,000
Add : Non-Fund or Non-Operating items already debited to P & L A/c		
Loss on sale of machinery (see note –1)	20,000	
Depreciation on machinery	1,80,000	2,00,000
		6,50,000
Less : Fund or Non-Operating items already credited to P & L A/c	—	—
Fund From Operations		6,50,000

Schedule of Changes in Working Capital

Particulars	*2002* *Rs.*	*2003* *Rs.*	*Effects on Working Capital* *Increase*	*Decrease*
Current Assets :				
Cash Balances	1,00,000	70,000	—	30,000
Bills Payable	1,00,000	3,00,000	2,00,000	—
Stock	3,50,000	2,50,000	—	1,00,000
Total (A)	5,50,000	6,20,000		
Current Liabilities :				
Bills Payable	2,00,000	2,20,000	—	20,000
Creditors	2,00,000	2,20,000	—	20,000
Total (B)	4,00,000	4,40,000		
Working Capital (Total A – B)	1,50,000	1,80,000		
Net Increase in Working Capital	30,000	—	—	30,000
	1,80,000	1,80,000	2,00,000	2,00,000

Fund Flow Statement

Sources of Fund	*Rs.*	*Application of Fund*	*Rs.*
Fund from Operations	6,50,000	Ramesh Loan Repaid	2,50,000
Loan From Kannan	1,00,000	Drawings	1,70,000
Sale of Machinery	50,000	Purchase of Land	1,00,000
(See Note)		Purchase of Building	2,50,000
		Net Increase in Working Capital	30,000
	8,00,000		8,00,000

Machinery Account

To Balance b/d	10,50,000	By Provision for depreciation on machinery sold	30,000
		By Bank	50,000
		By Loss on sale of machinery	20,000
		By Balance c/d	9,50,000
	10,50,000		10,50,000

Provision for Depreciation on Machinery

To Machinery A/c	30,000	By Balance b/d	2,50,000
To Balance c/d	4,00,000	By P & L (depreciation Provided during the year—balancing figure)	1,80,000
	4,30,000		4,30,000

Capital Account

Opening Balance of Equity Share Capital	10,00,000
Opening Balance of Preference Share Capital	2,50,000
Net Profit during the year 2003	4,50,000
	17,00,000
Less : Closing Balance of Equity Share Capital & Preference Share Capital	15,30,000
Drawing (10,00,000 + 5,30,000)	1,70,000

Illustration: 10

The following summarized balance sheet are give to you by Pilh & Co Ltd.

Balance Sheet

Liabilities	*2002* Rs.	*2003* Rs.	*Assets*	*2002* Rs.	*2003* Rs.
Share Capital	10,00,000	11,00,000	Fixed Assets		
Reserve	3,50,000	3,00,000	Less : Depreciation	11,70,000	16,90,000
Profit & Loss A/c	80,000	70,000	Investments	2,00,000	2,50,000
Loans @ 10%	6,00,000	8,00,000	Sundry Debtors	5,00,000	4,50,000
Provision for tax	2,10,000	2,40,000	Stock in Trade	4,50,000	3,90,000
Provision for Doubtful debts	30,000	20,000	Cash at Bank	90,000	60,000
			Goodwill	2,70,000	2,00,000
Sundry Creditors	3,10,000	2,90,000			
Proposed Dividend	1,00,000	1,20,000			
	26,80,000	29,40,000		26,80,000	29,40,000

Additional Information

(1) Investments were sold during 2003 at a loss of 20% on the cost.

(2) An item of fixed assets, cost Rs. 70,000, depreciation provided for Rs. 66,000 had to be discarded in 2003 without any scrap value.

(3) Depreciation provided during 2003 came to Rs. 1,80,000.

(4) The increase in share capital was because of issue of bonus shared out of reserves Prepare the fund flow statement for the year ended 31st December 2003.

Solution:

Statement of Changes in Working Capital

Particulars	*2002* *Rs.*	*2003* *Rs.*	*Changes in Working Capital*	
			Increase	*Decrease*
Current Assets :				
Sundry Debtors	5,00,000	4,50,000	—	50,000
Stock in Trade	4,50,000	3,90,000	—	60,000
Cash at Bank	90,000	60,000	—	30,000
Total Current Assets (A)	10,40,000	9,00,000		
Current Liabilities :				
Sundry Creditors	3,10,000	2,90,000	20,000	—
Provision for Taxation	2,10,000	2,40,000	—	30,000
Provision for doubtful debts	30,000	20,000	10,000	—
Total Current Liabilities (B)	5,50,000	5,50,000		
Working Capital (A – B)	4,90,000	3,50,000		
Net Decrease in Working Capital	—	1,40,000	1,40,000	—
	4,90,000	4,90,000	1,70,000	1,70,000

Fund Flow Statements

Particulars	*Amount Rs.*	*Particulars*	*Amount Rs.*
New Loan raised (8,00,000 – 6,00,000)	2,00,000	Fixed Assets acquired	7,04,000
Sale of Investments	40,000	Dividend Paid	1,00,000
Net Decrease in Working Capital	1,40,000		
Fund From Operations	4,24,000		
	8,04,000		8,04,000

Calculation of Fund From Operations

Particulars	*Amount Rs.*	*Amount Rs.*
Profit & Loss A/c (Closing Balance)		70,000
Add : Non-fund or Non-Operating items which have already been debited to P & L A/c		
Proposed dividend for 2003	1,20,000	
Loss on investment 20% of Rs. 50,000	10,000	

Loss on fixed assets scraped	4,000	
Depreciation provided	1,80,000	
Goodwill Written off	70,000	
Transfer to reserves	50,000	4,34,000
		5,04,000
ess : Non-fund and Non-operating items which have already been credited to P & L A/c	—	
Profit & Loss A/c (opening balance)	80,000	80,000
Fund From Operations		4,24,000

Fixed Assets Account

Particulars	*Amount Rs.*	*Particulars*	*Amount Rs.*
o Balance b/d	11,70,000	By Book Value of item Scraped	4,000
o Bank A/c	7,04,000	By Depreciation	1,80,000
Purchase of new assets)		By Balance c/d	16,90,000
	18,74,000		18,74,000

ovement of Reserves :

	Rs.
Opening Balance of Reserves	3,50,000
Less : Utilized for bonus shares	1,00,000
	2,50,000
Closing Balance of Reserves	3,00,000
Addition during the year	50,000

ustration: 11

om the following Balance sheet of Mohan & Co Ltd. as on 31st December 2002 and 03, you are required to prepare (a) Fund From Operations (b) A Schedule of Changes in orking Capital and (c) A Fund Flow Statements.

Balance Sheet

Liabilities	*2002 Rs.*	*2003 Rs.*	*Assets*	*2002 Rs.*	*2003 Rs.*
undry Creditors	5,00,000	4,80,000	Cash in hand	2,50,000	2,20,000
ills Payable	4,00,000	3,90,000	Cash at Bank	2,50,000	1,80,000
ank Overdraft	1,30,000	90,000	Sundry Debtors	3,00,000	2,80,000
utstanding Expenses	1,30,000	2,20,000	Bills Receivable	4,70,000	4,50,000
5% Debentures	9,00,000	7,00,000	Short Term		
epreciation Fund	4,00,000	4,40,000	Investments	11,00,000	8,40,000

General Reserve	6,00,000	5,00,000	Prepaid Expenses	10,000	20,00
Profit and Loss A/c	1,60,000	2,30,000	Inventories	9,20,000	10,60,0
Equity Share Capital	10,00,000	10,00,000	Land & Buildings	5,00,000	5,00,0
Preference Share Capital	8,00,000	8,00,000	Furniture	5,00,000	5,00,0
			Plant & Machinery	7,20,000	8,00,0
	50,20,000	48,50,000		50,20,000	48,50,0

Additional Informations

(1) Dividend was paid in cash was Rs. 1,80,000.

(2) New machinery for Rs. 2,00,000 was purchased but old machinery costing 1,20,000 was sold for Rs. 40,000, accumulated depreciation was Rs. 60,000.

(3) Rs. 2,00,000 15% debentures were redeemed by purchase from open mark Rs. 96.

(4) Rs. 1,00,000 was debited to General reserve for settlement of previous tax liabi

(5) Rs. 2,60,000 investments were sold at book value.

Solution:

Statement of Changes in Working Capital

Particulars	*2002*	*2003*	*Changes in Working Capi*	
	Rs.	*Rs.*	*Increase*	*Decrease*
Current Assets :				
Cash in hand	2,50,000	2,20,000	—	30,000
Cash at Bank	2,50,000	1,80,000	—	70,000
Sundry Debtors	3,00,000	2,80,000	—	20,000
Bills Receivable	4,70,000	4,50,000	—	20,000
Short Term Investment	11,00,000	8,40,000	—	2,60,000
Prepaid Expenses	10,000	20,000	10,000	—
Inventories	9,20,000	10,60,000	1,40,000	—
Total Current Assets (A)	33,00,000	30,50,000		
Current Liabilities :				
Sundry Creditors	5,00,000	4,80,000	20,000	—
Bills Payable	4,00,000	3,90,000	10,000	—
Bank Overdraft	1,30,000	90,000	40,000	—
Outstanding Expenses	1,30,000	2,20,000	—	90,000
Total Current Liabilities (B)	11,60,000	11,80,000	—	
Working Capital (A – B)	21,40,000	18,70,000	—	
Net Decrease in Working Capital	—	2,70,000	2,70,000	
	21,40,000	2,14,000	4,80,000	4,80,000

Calculation of Fund From Operations

Particulars	Amount Rs.	Amount Rs.
rofit & Loss A/c (Closing Balance)		
dd : Non-fund or Non-Operating items already been debited to P & L A/c		2,30,000
epreciation on Machinery	1,00,000	
oss on Sale of Machinery	20,000	
ividend Paid	1,80,000	3,00,000
		5,30,000
ess : Non-Fund and Non-Operating items Already been credited to P & L A/c		
rofit on redemption of debentures	8,000	
rofit and Loss A/c (Opening balance)	1,60,000	1,68,000
Fund From Operations		3,62,000

r. **Fund Flow Statement** Cr.

Sources of Fund	Amount Rs.	Application of Funds	Amount Rs.
ale of Machinery	40,000	Dividends Paid	1,80,000
und From Operations	3,62,000	Purchase of Machinery	2,00,000
et Decrease in Working Capital	2,70,000	Tax Paid	1,00,000
		Debenture Redeemed	1,92,000
	6,72,000		6,72,000

r. **Machinery Account** Cr.

Particulars	Amount Rs.	Particulars	Amount Rs.
ɔ Balance b/d	7,20,000	By Bank (Sold)	40,000
ɔ Bank (New Machinery)	2,00,000	By Depreciation Fund (A/c)	60,000
		By Profit & Loss A/c (Loss) (60,000 + 40,000 – 1,20,000)	
		By Balance c/d	8,00,000
	9,20,000		9,20,000

Dr. **Depreciation Fund Account** Cr.

Particulars	*Amount* Rs.	*Particulars*	*Amount* Rs.
To Machinery A/c	60,000	By Balance b/d	4,00,000
To Balance c/d	4,40,000	By Profit & Loss A/c	
		(Depreciation)	1,00,000
	5,00,000		5,00,000

Illustration: 12

From the following Balance sheet of Hari & Co Ltd as on 31st December 2002 and 200: you are required to prepare (a) Fund From operations (b) Schedule of Changes in Workin Capital and (c) Fund Flow Statement.

Balance Sheet

Liabilities	*2002* Rs.	*2003* Rs.	*Assets*	*2002* Rs.	*2003* Rs.
Equity Share Capital	2,00,000	2,00,000	Fixed Assets at Cost	10,00,000	10,00,000
7% Preference Share			Less : Depreciation	2,60,000	3,10,000
Capital	2,00,000	3,00,000		7,40,000	6,90,000
Capital Reserve	—	20,000	Trade Investments	1,10,000	90,000
General Reserve	1,80,000	2,10,000	Sundry Debtors	1,50,000	2,00,000
Debenture	3,00,000	2,00,000	Bills Receivable	1,70,000	2,50,000
Profit and Loss A/c	70,000	90,000	Preliminary Expenses	30,000	20,000
Sundry Creditors	50,000	50,000			
Bills Payable	30,000	20,000			
Bank Overdraft	50,000	50,000			
Provision for Income Tax	80,000	60,000			
Proposed Dividend	40,000	50,000			
	12,00,000	12,50,000		12,00,000	12,50,000

Additional Informations

(1) During the year 2003 depreciation provided for Rs. 1,00,000.

(2) Redeemed the debentures at Rs. 1,05,000.

(3) Sold one machine for Rs. 40,000 the cost of the machine was Rs. 80,000 and th depreciation provided for it amounted to Rs. 30,000.

(4) Sold some trade investments at profit which was credited to capital reserve.

(5) Decided to value the stock at cost where as previously the practice was valu stock at cost less 10%. The opening stock according to books was Rs. 63,000. Th stock on 31st December 2003 was correctly valued at cost.

Solution:

Schedule of Changes in Working Capital

Particulars	*2002*	*2003*	*Changes in Working Capital*	
	Rs.	*Rs.*	*Increase*	*Decrease*
Current Assets :				
Sundry Debtors	1,50,000	2,00,000	50,000	—
Bills Receivable	1,70,000	2,50,000	80,000	—
Inventory	7,000	—	—	7,000
Total Current Assets (A)	3,27,000	4,50,000		
Current Liabilities :				
Sundry Creditors	50,000	50,000	—	—
Bills Payable	30,000	20,000	10,000	—
Bank Overdraft	50,000	50,000	—	—
Total Current Liabilities (B)	1,30,000	1,20,000		
Working Capital (A – B)	1,97,000	3,30,000	—	1,33,000
Net Increase in Working Capital	1,33,000	—	1,40,000	1,40,000

Calculation of Fund From Operations

Particulars	*Rs.*	*Rs.*
Net Profit (Closing Balance)		90,000
Add : Net-fund and Non-operating items which already been debited to profit and loss A/c		
Loss on sale of machinery	10,000	
Loss on redemption of debenture	5,000	
Depreciation provided	1,00,000	
Preliminary expenses (Rs. 30,000 – Rs. 20,000)	10,000	
Proposed dividend	50,000	
Transfer to General Reserve (Rs. 2,10,000 – Rs. 1,80,000)	30,000	
Provision for income	60,000	2,65,000
		3,55,000
Less: Non—Fund and Non—Operating items which already credited to Profit and Loss A/c	—	
Opening Stock Written off	7,000	
Net Profit (Opening balance)	70,000	77,000
Fund From Operations		2,78,000

Fund Flow Statement

Sources of Funds	*Rs.*	*Application of Funs*	*Rs.*
Equity Share Capital	—	Purchase of Fixed Assets	1,00,000
7% Preference Share Capital (2,00,000 – 3,00,000)	1,00,000	Redemption of Debenture	1,05,000
Sale of Trade Investments (Rs. 1,10,000 + 20,000 – 90,000)	40,000	Proposed Dividend for 2002 (Assumed to be paid)	40,000
Sale of Machine	40,000	Provision for Taxation for (2002 assumed to be paid)	80,000
Fund From Operations	2,78,000	Net Increase in Working Capital	1,33,000
	4,58,000		4,58,000

Fixed Assets Account

Particulars	*Amount Rs.*	*Particulars*	*Amount Rs.*
To Balance b/d	10,00,000	By Cash (Sale)	40,000
To Cash (Purchase) Balancing figure	1,00,000	By Accumulated depreciation	30,000
		By Adjusted P & L (Loss on Sale)	10,000
		By Accumulated depreciation (Fixed Asset Written off)	20,000
		By Balance c/d	10,00,000
	11,00,000		11,00,000

Debenture Account

Particulars	*Amount Rs.*	*Particulars*	*Amount Rs.*
To Bank	1,05,000	By Balance b/d	3,00,000
To Balance c/d	2,00,000	By Adjusted P & L A/c (Loss on redeemed)	5,000
	3,05,000		3,05,000

Accumulated Depreciation Account

Particulars	*Amount Rs.*	*Particulars*	*Amount Rs.*
To Fixed Assets (Depreciation on Machinery Sold)	30,000	By Balance B/d	2,60,000
To Fixed Assets Written off (50,000 – 30,000)	20,000	By Adjusted P & L A/c (Depreciation during the year)	1,00,000
To Balance c/d	3,10,000		
	3,60,000		3,60,000

QUESTIONS

(1) What is mean by Fund Flow Statement?

(2) Explain the Changes of Financial Position.

(3) Briefly explain the Flow of funds and No Flow of Funds. Illustrate with a numerical examples.

(4) What are the components of Flow of Fund?

(5) What do you understand by Fund Flow Statement? How is it Prepared?

(6) Explain the importance of Fund Flow Statement.

(7) Distinguish between.

(a) Fund Flow Statement and Income Statement.

(b) Fund Flow Statement and Balance Sheet.

(8) Explain the limitations of Fund Flow Statement.

(9) Explain the procedure for preparation of Fund Flow Statement.

(10) What do you understand by Fund From Operations?

(11) What is meant by Schedule of Changes in Working Capital. How is it prepared?

Practical Problems

(1) From the following Balance sheet of X Y & Co as on 31st Dec.2002 and 2003, you are required to prepare Statement of Changes in Working Capital.

Balance Sheet

Liabilities	*2002* Rs.	*2003* Rs.	*Assets*	*2002* Rs.	*2003* Rs.
Equity Share Capital	1,00,000	1,25,000	Cash Balances	30,000	47,000
Preference Share Capital	1,00,000	1,25,000	Debtors	60,000	60,000
Creditors	40,000	20,000	Bills Payable	60,000	55,000
Bills Payable	30,000	25,000	Stock	40,000	45,000
Retained Earnings	10,000	23,000	Short Term Loan	40,000	45,000
			Building	50,000	66,000
	2,80,000	3,18,000		2,80,000	3,18,000

[Ans : Net Increase in working capital Rs.47,000]

(2) From the following information, you are required to prepare (a) Fund From Operations (b) Statement of Changes in Working Capital and (c) Fund Flow Statement.

Comparative Balance Sheet

Particulars	*2002 Rs.*	*2003 Rs.*
Liabilities and Capital :		
Share Capital	5,00,000	4,00,000
Reserve and Surplus	1,50,000	50,000
Secured Loans	3,50,000	4,00,000
Current Liabilities	5,00,000	6,00,000
Total Liabilities and Capital	15,00,000	14,50,000
Assets :		
Fixed Assets	3,10,000	3,00,000
Investments	15,000	—
Cash Balances	25,000	12,500
Stock	7,50,000	7,87,500
Sundry Debtors	4,00,000	3,50,000
Total Assets	15,00,000	14,50,000

Additional Information

(a) The net profit for the year after adjustments Rs. 10,00,000.

(b) Additional fixed assets during the year Rs. 40,000 and depreciation for the year Rs. 30,000.

[Ans : (a) Fund From Operations Rs. 13,00,000

(b) Statement of changes in working capital Rs. 1,25,000 (Net Increase in Working Capital)

(c) Fund Flow Statement Rs. 2,30,000]

(3) From the following particulars, you are required to prepare Schedule of Changes in Working Capital.

Particulars	*2002 Rs.*	*2003 Rs.*
Capital and Liabilities :		
Share Capital	1,50,000	1,87,500
Trade Creditors	53,000	35,000
Profit and Loss A/c	7,000	15,500
Total Liabilities	2,10,000	2,38,000
Assets :		
Plant and Machinery	35,000	50,000
Bills Payable	60,500	68,000
Trade Debtors	90,500	85,000
Cash Balances	24,000	35,000
Total Assets	2,10,000	2,38,000

[Ans : Increase in Working Capital Rs. 31,000)

(4) Calculate funds from operations from the following Particulars

	Rs.
Transfer to General Reserve	50,000
Loss on Sale of Investments	50,000
Depreciation on Machinery	1,00,000
Depreciation on Building	40,000
Discount on Issue of Debenture	1,50,000
Provision for Taxation	1,00,000
Proposed Dividend	2,00,000
Closing Balance of P & L A/c	3,06,000
Opening Balance of P & L A/c	3,05,000

[Ans : Funds From Operations Rs. 6,91,000]

(5) The following Balance Sheets of X and Y Ltd for the year 2002 and 2003, you are required to prepare (a) Funds Form Operations (b) Statement of Changes in Working Capital and (c) Funds Flow Statement.

Balance Sheet

Liabilities	*2002 Rs.*	*2003 Rs.*	*Assets*	*2002 Rs.*	*2003 Rs.*
Share Capital	5,00,000	5,00,000	Good will	60,000	60,000
General Reserve	70,000	90,000	Buildings	2,00,000	1,80,000
Profit & Loss A/c	80,000	65,000	Machinery	1,85,000	1,80,000
Trade Creditors	40,000	27,000	Investments	50,000	55,000
Bills Payable	6,000	4,000	Stock	1,50,000	1,17,000
Provision for Taxation	80,000	90,000	Bills Receivable	10,000	16,000
Provision for Doubtful Debts	2,000	3,000	Trade Debtors	90,000	95,000
			Cash Balance	33,000	76,000
	7,78,000	7,79,000		7,78,000	7,79,000

Additional Information

(1) Depreciation charged on machinery was Rs. 20,000 and on Building was Rs. 20,000.

(2) Provision for taxation of Rs. 95,000 was made during the year 2003.

(3) Interim dividend of Rs. 40,000 was paid during the year 2003.

[Ans : Funds From Operations Rs. 1,80,000

Statement of Changes in Working Capital Rs. 35,000

Fund Flow Statements Rs. 1,80,000]

(6) Following are the summarized Balance sheet of ABC Ltd as on 31st December 2002 and 2003.

Balance Sheet

Liabilities	*2002 Rs.*	*2003 Rs.*	*Assets*	*2002 Rs.*	*2003 Rs.*
Share Capital	2,00,000	2,50,000	Land & Buildings	2,00,000	1,90,000
General Reserves	50,000	60,000	Machinery & Plant	1,50,000	1,69,000
Profit & Loss A/c	30,500	30,600	Stock	1,00,000	74,000
Bank Loan	70,000	—	Sundry Debtors	80,000	64,200
Sundry Creditors	1,50,000	1,35,200	Cash	500	600
Provision for taxation	30,000	35,000	Bank	—	8,000
			Goodwill	—	5,000
	5,30,500	5,10,800		5,30,500	5,10,800

Additional Informations

(1) During the year ended 31st December 2003

(a) Dividend was paid Rs. 23,000.

(b) Assets of another company were purchased for a consideration of Rs. 50,000 payable in shares. The following assets were purchased; stock Rs. 20,000 machinery Rs. 25,000.

(c) Machinery was purchased for Rs. 8,000.

(d) Depreciation written off; Building Rs. 10,000; Machinery Rs. 14,000.

(e) Income Tax paid during the year Rs. 28,000; provision of Rs. 33,000 was charged to profit and loss A/c.

Prepare a statement of sources and application of funds for the year ended 31st December 2003.

(Ans : Fund From Operations Rs. 90,100;
Decrease in Working Capital Rs. 18,900
Sources and Applications of fund Rs. 1,29,000)

(7) The Balance sheet of Jai & Co Ltd as at 31st December 2002 and 2003 are given below :

Balance Sheet

Liabilities	*2002 Rs.*	*2003 Rs.*	*Assets*	*2002 Rs.*	*2003 Rs.*
Share Capital	1,00,000	1,50,000	Freehold Land	1,00,000	1,00,000
Share Premium	—	5,000	Plant at Cost	1,04,000	1,00,000
General Reserve	50,000	60,600	Furniture at Cost	7,000	9,000
Profit & Loss A/c	10,000	17,000	Investment at Cost	60,000	80,000
6% Debentures	70,000	50,000	Sundry Debtors	30,000	70,000
Provision for Depreciation on Plant	50,000	56,000	Stock	60,000	65,000
			Cash at Bank	30,000	45,000
Provision for Depreciation on furniture	5,000	6,000			
Provision for taxation	20,000	30,000			
Sundry Creditors	86,000	95,000			
	3,91,000	4,69,000		3,91,000	4,69,000

A plant purchased for Rs. 40,000 (Depreciation Rs. 2,000) was sold for cash Rs. 800 on 30th September 2003. On 30th June 2003 an item of furniture was purchased for Rs. 2,000. There the only transactions concerning fixed assets during 2003.

Depreciation was provided on plant at 8% on cost (the sold out item is not taken in to consideration) and on furniture at 12 ½ % on average cost. A dividend of 22 ½ % on original shares was paid.

Prepare a schedule of changes in working capital and also a statement of sources and application of funds during 2003.

(Ans : Net increase in Working Capital Rs. 41,000
Fund From Operations Rs. 49,700
Sources and Application of fund Rs. 1,05,500)

(8) From the following Balance sheet of XY & Co Ltd as on 31st December 2002 and 2003, you are required to prepare a funds flow statement showing change in working capital.

Balance Sheet

Liabilities	*2002* Rs.	*2003* Rs.	*Assets*	*2002* Rs.	*2003* Rs.
Equity Share Capital	3,00,000	4,00,000	Buildings	2,50,000	3,00,000
Preference Share Capital	2,00,000	—	Machinery	3,00,000	3,20,000
Capital Redemption Reserve	—	1,00,000	Furniture	20,000	18,000
			Investments	1,00,000	1,50,000
General Reserve	2,00,000	1,20,000	Stock	3,00,000	2,50,000
Share Premium	30,000	30,000	Debtors	1,40,000	2,00,000
Profit and Loss A/c	1,20,000	1,80,000	Cash at Bank	20,000	32,000
10% Debenture	2,00,000	3,00,000			
Creditors	80,000	1,40,000			
	11,30,000	12,70,000		11,30,000	12,70,000

Additional Informations

(1) Preference share were redeemed at 10% premium.

(2) Rs. 20,000 was transferred to reserve fund from profit and loss account.

(3) Investment (book value Rs. 40,000) were sold for Rs. 70,000.

(4) Depreciation provided on building, machinery and furniture Rs. 20,000, Rs. 30,000 and Rs. 2,000 respectively.

(5) Depreciation paid Rs. 50,000 and income tax paid Rs. 45,000.

(Ans : Net Decrease in Working Capital Rs. 38,000
Fund From Operations Rs. 2,17,000
Sources and Application Funds Rs. 5,25,000)

(9) From the following Balance sheet of Saxena & Co Ltd as on 31st December 2002 and 2003, you are required to prepare the Fund Flow Statement.

Balance Sheet

Liabilities	*2002 Rs.*	*2003 Rs.*	*Assets*	*2002 Rs.*	*2003 Rs.*
Share Capital	10,00,000	10,00,000	Land & Building at Cost	6,00,000	6,00,000
Capital Reserve	50,000	50,000			
Long Term Loans	5,00,000	6,50,000	Plant & Machinery at Cost	3,30,000	4,50,000
Sundry Creditors	6,00,000	7,85,000			
			Furniture at Cost	3,00,000	3,00,000
			Stock in Trade	4,10,000	5,60,000
			Sundry Debtors	3,40,000	2,10,000
			Cash at Bank	20,000	5,000
			Profit & Loss A/c	1,50,000	3,60,000
	21,50,000	24,85,000		21,50,000	24,85,000

Additional Informations

During the year 2003 Depreciation provided on Land and Building was Rs. 50,000; Plant and Machinery was Rs. 50,000 and Furniture was Rs. 15,000.

(10) The following are the summarized Balance sheet of Gupta & Co Ltd as at 31st December 2002 and 2003, you are required to prepare a statement showing the sources and application of funds for the year 2003 and a schedule setting out changes in working capital.

Balance Sheet

Liabilities	*2002 Rs.*	*2003 Rs.*	*Assets*	*2002 Rs.*	*2003 Rs.*
Share Capital	2,00,000	2,60,000	Goodwill	—	20,000
Profit & Loss A/c	39,690	41,220	Plant & Machinery	1,12,950	1,16,200
General Reserve	50,000	50,000	Buildings	1,48,500	1,44,250
Tax Provision	40,000	50,000	Stock	1,11,040	97,370
Bank Overdraft	59,560	—	Sundry Debtors	87,490	73,360
Bills Payable	33,780	11,525	Cash at Bank	2,500	2,700
Sundry Creditors	39,550	41,135			
	4,62,480	4,53,880		4,62,480	4,53,880

Additional Informations

(1) During the year 2003 an interim dividend of Rs. 26,000 was paid.

(2) The assets of another company were purchased for Rs. 60,000 payable in fully paid share of Gupta & Co Ltd. These assets include stock Rs. 22,000 and machinery Rs. 18,000 p.a. In addition sundry machinery amounted to Rs. 5,600.

(3) Income tax paid during the year for Rs. 25,000.

(4) Net profit for the year before tax was Rs. 62,530.

(Ans : Increase in Working Capital Rs. 42,530
Fund From Operations Rs. 77,130
Total Fund Flow Statement Rs. 1,37,130)

(11) The summarized balance sheet of Karunya & Co Ltd as at 31st December 2002 and 2003, you are required to prepare a statement of sources and application of funds.

Balance Sheet

Liabilities	2002 Rs.	2003 Rs.	Assets	2002 Rs.	2003 Rs.
Share Capital	4,50,000	4,50,000	Land & Building	2,00,000	1,00,000
General Reserve	3,00,000	3,10,000	Plant & Machinery	2,00,000	1,20,000
Profit & Loss A/c	56,000	68,000	Investments	50,000	60,000
Sundry Creditors	1,68,000	1,34,000	Stock	2,40,000	2,10,000
Provision for Taxation	75,000	10,000	Sundry Debtors	2,10,000	4,55,000
Mortgage Loan	—	2,70,000	Bank Balances	1,49,000	1,97,000
	10,49,000	12,42,000		10,49,000	12,42,000

Additional Informations

(1) Investment costing Rs. 8,000 were sold during the years 2003 for Rs. 8,500.

(2) Provision for tax made during the year was Rs. 9,000.

(3) During the year part of the land and buildings costing Rs. 10,000 were sold for Rs. 12,000 and the profit was included in profit and loss account and.

(4) Dividend paid during the year announced to Rs. 40,000.

(Ans : Fund From Operations Rs. 1,38,500
Total Sources Rs. 4,29,000
Applications Rs. 1,32,000)

12) From the following Balance sheet of Ramasamy & Co Ltd as on 31st December 2003 you are required to prepare a Fund Flow Statement.

Balance Sheet

Liabilities	2002 Rs.	2003 Rs.	Assets	2002 Rs.	2003 Rs.
Equity Share Capital	3,00,000	3,50,000	Fixed Assets	5,10,000	6,20,000
Preference Share Capital	2,00,000	1,00,000	Investments	30,000	80,000
10% Debenture	1,00,000	2,00,000	Sundry Creditors	40,000	75,000
Reserves	1,10,000	2,70,000	Stock	1,00,000	2,00,000
Provision for Doubtful Debts	10,000	15,000	Bills Receivable	1,00,000	1,00,000
Sundry Creditors	35,000	45,000	Discount on Debenture	10,000	5,000
Bills Payable	35,000	1,00,000			
	7,90,000	10,80,000		7,90,000	10,80,000

Additional Informations

(1) Provision for depreciation stood at Rs. 1,50,000 on 31st December 2002 and at Rs 1,90,000 on 31st December 2003.

(2) During the year 2003, a machine costing Rs. 70,000 (book value Rs. 40,000) wa disposed off for Rs. 25,000.

(3) Preference share redemption was carried out at a premium of 5% on 1st Januar 2003 and.

(4) Dividend @ 15% was paid on equity shares for the year 2002.

(Ans : Fund From Operations Rs. 2,34,000

Net Increase in Working Capital Rs. 55,000

Total Flow of Funds Rs. 4,84,000)

INVENTORY MANAGEMENT

Introduction

Inventory, as a current assets which firms store as inventory comprises raw materials, work-in-progress maintence materials, consumable stores, component parts, tools and packing materials and finished goods. Each business unit is to maintain a considerable volume of inventory in response to the conditions in which the business operates. The raw material inventory contains items that are purchased by the firm from suppliers and are converted into finished goods through the manufacturing process. They are an important input of the final product. The work-in-progress inventory consists of items currently being used in the production process. They are normally partially or semi-finished goods that are at various stages of production in a multi-stage production process. Finished goods represent final or completed products which are available for sale. As such a large quantum of fund is necessary to finance the required volume of inventory. As a mater of fact, inventories are very important to the management of an enterprise as they have direct impact on the firm's profit. The financial manager has the responsibility to ensure that inventories are properly monitored and effectively controlled. In order to achieve this, it is necessary to consider the following aspects of inventory management :

(a) Meaning and definition of inventories

(b) Motives or need for holding inventories

(c) Cost of holding inventory

(d) Techniques of inventory management

(e) Order quantity—EOQ model

(f) Determination of stock levels

(g) Pricing of raw materials and valuation of stock

(h) Monitoring and control of inventories

(i) ABC analysis

(j) Perpetual inventory system

Meaning and Definition of Inventories

The term 'inventory' is used in day to day life as a manpower inventory, equipment inventory, inventory documents, inventory of raw materials, inventory of spare parts, inventory of semi-finished items, inventory of finished goods, inventory of vehicles etc. as the dictionary the world as "Stock of goods" or "Item in stock."

Broadly, inventory means the aggregate investment of items of tangible personal property that (i) are held for sale in ordinary course of business (ii) are in the process of production for sale or (iii) are to be currently consumed in the production of goods or services to be available for sales.

Inventory may be defined as the physical stock of items that a business or production organization keeps in hand for efficient running of affairs of its production. Inventories consists of raw materials, component part supplies and finished assemblies which an organization purchases from an outside source and parts, assemblies and finished products which the company manufactures itself.

Characteristics of Inventory

The following are the important charactertics of inventories, which are observed from the above said definitions :

(1) Inventory ensure to maintaining undisturbed production and employment rates.

(2) Inventories require valuable space and consumes taxation and insurance charges.

(3) Inventory provides production economics.

(4) Inventory as the physical stock of items of tangible assets.

(5) Inventories are the result of many interrelated decisions and policies with in an organization.

(6) Inventories are used in the production for sale in the ordinary course of business.

Types of Inventories

The various types of inventories for a manufacturing or Trading Organization are as classified as under :

(1) Raw materials and consumable stores

(2) Work-in-progress

(3) Finished goods inventories

(1) Raw materials and consumable stores : These materials refer to all commodities or components which are consumed in the process of manufacture. These items form part of the finished products. For example, cotton used in textile mills, timber used in furniture industries. Some materials indirectly used for conversion from raw materials into finished products. For example, oil, spare parts, nails etc. These items are to be purchased by the firm from suppliers or dealers and kept in stock before and during production of goods.

(2) Work-in-progress : Work-in-progress otherwise known as semi-finished goods or process inventories or convertible inventories. These are processed or semi-finished products manufactured at various stages during the production cycles. In other words, it consists of items which are currently used in the production process. For example, in a bicycle factory frames, pedals, rims, axles etc. these are semi-finished products that are held at various stages of production process.

(3) Finished goods Inventories : Finished goods inventories are final or completed products ready to sent away to the market or consumers. These products have been fabricated or manufactured or assembled from production and in process inventories.

Functions of Inventories

The following are the important functions of inventories :

(1) It ensure continuity of supply of uniform quality goods.

(2) Inventories help to prevent excessive investment in materials stock.

(3) It ensure continuous flow of production without interruptions.

(4) It provide maximum service and satisfaction to the customers with regard to fulfilling the due dates strictly as per orders.

(5) Inventories helps to achieve the overall company objectives.

(6) Inventories activise the market.

(7) Inventories helps in avoiding unnecessary wastage or losses.

(8) Inventories ensure optimum investment in materials.

(9) Inventories make sure of the availability of all types of materials.

(10) Proper inventory system provide necessary information to the management for effective decision making.

Need to hold Inventories

Inventories are typically not end in themselves. What are then the main purposes which they serve? There are three needs or motives for holding inventories.

(1) Transaction Motives

(2) Precautionary Motives

(3) Speculative Motives

(1) Transaction Motives : Transaction implies the total time of converting an intent into the material; after finalizing the order or processing the customer's order in a marketing situation or set up time in manufacturing situation, producing the item, transporting the item and inspecting the item before taking in to the warehouse. It is not generally possible to synchronise the inflow and outflow of the commodity in question completely. So inventories are held. In other words, it expresses the need to maintain inventories to facilitate production and sales operation smoothly. The cycle of production involves a steady and smooth flow of raw materials for conversion into finished product which is meant for sale and conversion in to cash.

(2) Precautionary Motives : Precaution means safety or minimum stock as commonly understood in the industry. Inventories are held due to the usual inability to predict demand exactly and the consequent need to maintain some kind of a safety margin. This occurs due to the inability to obtain instantaneous delivery of commodities without extra costs. In other words, it necessitates holding of inventories to guard against the risk of unpredictable change in demand and supply forces.

(3) Speculative Motives : The speculative element is more prominent in the case of sensitive commodities. Speculation could be due to non-availability of item as demand exceeds supply or fear of increase price levels in future, forcing the inventory controller to hoard the stock. And also, when prices are rising or when there are expected changes in costs, profits may be made by holding inventories at the lower price until the higher price obtains. In other words, it influences the decision to increase or reduce inventory levels to take advantages of price fluctuations.

Factors Affecting the Volume of Inventories

The quantity of inventory to be maintained is based on the following factors :

(a) Availability of Finance
(b) Quantity discounts allowed
(c) Storage space available
(d) Ordering cost
(e) Receiving cost
(f) Risk of loss due to price fluctuations
(g) Risk of loss due to evaporation, obsolescence theft, deterioration etc.
(h) Economic ordering quantity
(i) Time to obtain delivery or lead time

Advantages of Inventory

Both excessive and inadequate inventories are not desirable. They are two danger point within which the firm should operate. The below are the main advantages while adoptin optimum level of inventory in any manufacturing concern.

(1) It helps to avoid over investment or under investment in inventories.
(2) It helps to reducing carrying cost.
(3) It helps to maintain the optimum level of inventory investment.
(4) It ensures uninterrupted production.
(5) Effective material handing in possible.
(6) Lot of manual work may be eliminated.
(7) Effective material control is possible.
(8) Ensure minimum wastages.
(9) Facilitates prompt flow of finished goods for immediate sales.
(10) Effective utilization of floor space.
(11) Better forecasting is possible.
(12) Inventories reduce the risk of closing down the plant or keeping workers an machine idle.

Disadvantages of Excessive or Inadequate Inventories

The following are the disadvantages while the firm holding excessive or inadequa inventories.

(1) Excessive level of inventories consumes the funds of the firm, which can not b used for any other purpose.
(2) Increase cost of storage, materials handling, insurance and transportation ar inspection.
(3) Delay and inconvenience because of over crowding of materials.

(4) High risk of liquidity due to inadequate inventories.

(5) Inadequate inventories will affect continuous flow of production.

(6) Inadequate inventories failure to meet delivery commitments.

(7) Ineffective supervision of stores due to mishandling and improper storage facilities

(8) Losses, damages, deterioration of materials will be high while excessive inventories in storage.

(9) Failure to meet the demands of consumers needs due to inadequate finished goods inventories.

(10) Greater risk of loss due to devaluation through changes in price of production cost.

Meaning and Definition of Inventory Control

Inventory control may be defined "as the systematic control over the procurement, storage and usage of materials so as to maintain an even flow of materials and at the same time avoiding excessive investment in inventories".

According to Jhon L Burbridge "inventory control is, concerned with the control of quantities and/or monetary value of these items at predetermined level or within safe limits".

Inventory control means control over materials lying in store. Inventory control keeps continuous track of inventories. But it is not merely record keeping. Inventory control aims to achieve maximum possible inventory turnover.

Objectives of Inventory Control Management

Inventories often constitute a major element of the total working capital and hence it has been correctly observed, good inventory management is good financial management. The basic responsibility of the financial manager is to make sure that the firm's cash flow are managed efficiently. Efficient management of inventory should ultimately result in the maximization of the owner's wealth. The basic managerial objectives of inventory are two-fold (a) Operating objectives and (b) Financial objectives. Operating objectives aims at avoiding the possibility of delay in production. The financial objective of inventory management to secure many economics. The objectives and importance of inventory management may be discussed as follows :

(1) Availability of Materials : The first and for most objective of inventory control management is to ensure a continuous supply materials to facilitate uninterrupted production. It is, therefore, the inventory management keeping the stock of goods at the most appropriate level at all times so that the requirements of production department and sales deportment can be always fulfilled.

(2) Minimizing the Wastage : If a firm maintains adequate inventories it can be avoid losses and damages on account of theft, improper handling, pilferage, leakage, spoilage and unauthorized removal from the storage. Product deterioration due to holding a product for too long a period or improper storage conditions.

(3) Better Services to Customers : Inventory control aims at holding inventories to facilitate production and sales operation smoothly. In order to execute the orders of customers and efficient customer service, the inventory management to maintain sufficient finished goods inventory. If a firm maintains adequate inventories it can avoid losses on account of losing the customers for non-supply of goods in times.

(4) Increase operational Efficiency : The chief aims of inventory control management is to increase the operational efficiency of the concern as a whole. It is necessary for providing right type of materials for safety production and sales demands. It will increase the efficiency of production and workers.

(5) Achieving Efficient Production Levels : Maintaining sufficient stock of raw materials in periods of short supply and anticipate price changes helps to achieving efficient production levels. Production variations can be avoided by receiving and recording of all goods routed in the store and keeping up to date trace of every outgoing items.

(6) Optimum level of Inventories : Maintaining an inadequate level of inventories is also dangerous. Keeping the stock of raw materials, work-in-progress and finished goods inventories at the optimum level will result in sufficient to meet the requirements of continuous flow of production and demands of the customers regularly. The optimum level of inventory should be determined on the basis of the trade off between costs and benefits associated with the level of inventory.

(7) Economy in Purchasing : The inventory control management should help to secure economy in purchasing. The economics due to bulk purchases such as low freight, higher discount, low price, less clerical work etc.

(8) Optimum Level Investment in Raw Materials : The firm should always avoid a situation of over investment or under investment in inventories. All manufacturing companies are to carry certain stocks and kept in stores before issued to production. The investment in raw materials should be just sufficient at the optimum level. It is necessary to consider the following aspects before deciding the level of stock of raw materials to be maintained (a) Safety or buffer stock (b) Economy in purchases (c) Stock holding cost (d) Rate of production (e) Efficient reporting of stock level and (f) Cost and availability of fund.

(9) Optimum Level Investment in Work-in-Progress : The chief aims of inventory management should control investment in inventories to maximize profitability. The term work in progress include those materials which have been committed to production process but have not yet been completed. The investment in work-in-progress include raw materials cost transferred to work-in-progress (direct material), direct expenses and wages of employees engaged in the production process and overhead costs like heat power, lighting, maintenance cost and supervision etc. Obviously, the more lengthy is the production process, the more will be the value of work-in-progress. It thus, requires huge working capital investment in WIP. The management will have to be very vigil to see that the production process is made as short as possible.

(10) Optimum Level Investment in Finished Goods : The objective of inventory management is to maintaining sufficient stock of finished goods for smooth sales operations. The term finished goods refer to the final output of the production process in a manufacturing firm. The life of finished stock starts from the point of completion of work—in progress and end at the point of delivery to customers in the form of sales. Maintaining sufficient stock of finished goods in periods of high demand helps to achieving the profitability of organization. At the same time, the inventory management should avoid excessive investment in finished goods stock held for more time. If the period of holding in finished stock is more, the cost of holding will be more. This affect the level of profitability of the organization.

Inventory costs

These are four component costs involved in general inventory policies :

(1) Ordering Costs

(2) Inventory Carrying Costs

(3) Over Stock Costs

(4) Stock-Out Costs

(1) Ordering Costs : This cost includes the variable cost associated with placing an order for the materials. This includes office and administrative expenses of purchasing the materials, transportation cost, and inspection cost, etc. The following costs are the examples of ordering cost:

(a) Cost of staff posted in administration and purchasing department

(b) Cost of inspection section

(c) Rent for the space used by the purchase department

(d) Cost of stationery, postage and telephone charges

(e) Cost of floating tenders

(f) Cost of comparative evaluation of quotations

(g) Cost of accounting and making payments

(h) Travelling expenses

(i) Legal expenses in case of purchase disputes

(2) Inventory Carrying Cost : Inventory carrying cost includes the expenses in keeping the materials in stores. This cost includes:

(a) Cost of storage charges such as rent

(b) Interest on capital

(c) Cost of Insurance and Tax charges for fire and theft

(d) Cost of heating and lighting

(e) Expenses of storage staff

(f) Cost of maintaing materials

(g) Cost of spoilage in stores and handling

(h) Cost of deterioration and obsolescence

(i) Cost wastage and material losses due to theft damage and breakage

(j) Material losses due to pilferage and evaporation

(k) Cost of stores recording

(l) Cost of bins and racks that have to be provided for the storage of materials

(m) Cost of stationery, postage, telephone and other consumable used by the sotres

(3) Over Stock Cost : Another kind of cost associated with carrying inventory result when there is a stock left on hand after the demand for the item has terminated. This cost is called the overstock cost. Any over stock typically undergoes a drastic devaluation (loss of value) and this is measured by the overstock cost.

(4) Stock-Out Costs : This cost incurred when an item is out of stock is called the Out of stock cost or Stock-out cost. If a company is out of stock when an order received, and the extra cost per unit which might have to be paid for an emergency purchase. These include loss of sales if there were no stock of finished goods, cost of production stoppage for want of material and costs associated with placing urgent orders for replenishment.

Inventory Control Techniques

Inventory control refers to the regulation of the stock and flow of materials and stores in an efficient effective and economical manner to meet the needs of manufacturing and trading concerns. In order to achieve this, the following important inventory control techniques are to be applied.

(1) Economic Order Quantity

(2) Fixation of Stock Levels

(3) ABC Analysis

(4) Techniques of Codification

(5) Inventory Turnover Ratio

(6) Input Output Ratio Analysis

(7) Perpetual Inventory and Continuous stock taking

(8) Pricing of raw materials and Valuation of stock

(1) Economic Order Quantity (EOQ) : Economic Order Quantity (EOQ) is one of the important techniques used to determine the optimum quantity or number of orders to be placed from the suppliers. The main objective of economic order quantity is to minimizes the cost of ordering and cost of carrying materials and total cost of production. Ordering costs include cost of stationary, salaries to those engaged in receiving and inspecting, general office and administrative expenses of purchase departments. Carring costs are incurred on stationary, salaries, rent, materials handling cost, interest on capital, insurance cost, risk of obsolescence, deterioration and wastage of materials and evaporation.

The quantity to be ordered should be such which minimizes the carrying and ordering costs. The exact quantity to be ordered at a time so as to achieve this objective is known as Economic Order Quantity or Re-order Quantity or Economic Lot Size. The EOQ technique can be determined by (a) Tabular Method (b) Formula Method and (c) Graphic Method.

The formula for EOQ can also be used for determining the optimum ordering quantity as given below :

$$\text{Economic Order Quantity (EOQ)} = \sqrt{\frac{2AB}{CS}}$$

Where :

EOQ = Economic Order Quantity

A = Annual Consumption in Units

B = Buying Cost per order *i.e.*, Cost of ordering and receiving the goods per order

C = Cost per unit

S = Storage and carrying cost per annum *i.e.*, holding cost of Inventory per year.

For example, a unit of material X costs of Re.1 and the yearly consumption is 16000 units. The cost of placing one order including the cost of receiving the material is Rs.18 and the storage and carrying cost is 20% of average inventory. The optimum quantity for which order is to be placed is :

$$EOQ = \sqrt{\frac{2AB}{CS}}$$

$$= \sqrt{\frac{2 \times 16{,}000 \times 18}{1 \times 20}}$$

$$= \sqrt{\frac{2 \times 16{,}000 \times 18}{1 \times \frac{20}{100}}}$$

$$= \sqrt{\frac{2 \times 16{,}000 \times 18 \times 100}{1 \times 20\%}} = 1{,}700 \text{ units}$$

To sum up, Economic Order Quantity is determined keeping in view the ordering costs and carrying costs. With the interaction of these two costs, the economic ordering costs during that period and total cost to order and carry is the lowest as is made clear in the diagram given below :

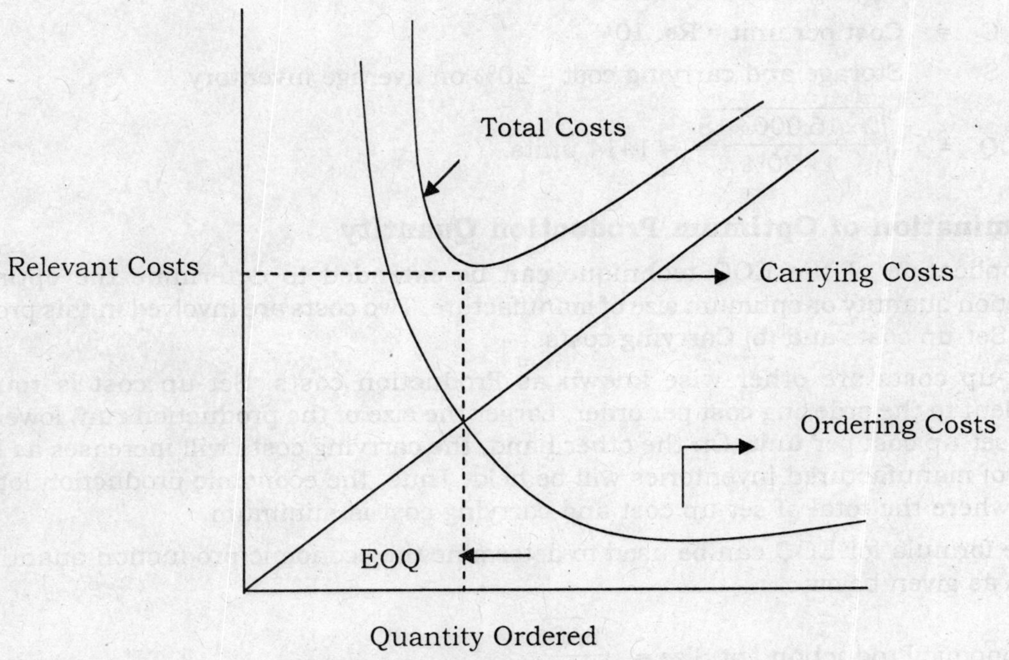

Fig 5.1 : Economic Order Quantity.

From the above diagram, it is clearly shows that the behaviour of the carrying cost, the ordering cost and the sum of these two costs. The carrying cost varies directly with the order size, where as the ordering cost varies inversely with the order size.

Assumption of the EOQ Technique

The calculation of the economic order quantity is based on the following assumptions :

(1) Ordering and carrying costs are constant per unit.

(2) The anticipated consumption of materials during a particular period is known.

(3) Cost per order is constant.

(4) The forcast usage of materials for a given period usually one year.

Illustration: 1

A company uses a particular material in a factory is 20,000 units per year. The cost per unit of material is Rs.10. The cost of placing one order is Rs.100 and the inventory carrying cost 20% on average inventory. From the above information calculate Economic Order Quantity.

Solution:

Determination of Economic Order Quantity

$$EOQ = \sqrt{\frac{2AB}{CS}}$$

Where :

A = Annual Consumption = 20,000 units

B = Buying Cost per Order = Rs. 100

C = Cost per unit = Rs. 10

S = Storage and carrying cost – 20% on average inventory

$$EOQ = \sqrt{\frac{2 \times 16{,}000 \times 18}{1 \times 20\%}} = 1414 \text{ units.}$$

Determination of Optimum Production Quantity

The application of the EOQ technique can be extended to determine the optimum production quantity or optimum size of manufacture. Two costs are involved in this process are (a) Set-up costs and (b) Carrying costs.

Set-up costs are other wise known as Production costs. Set-up cost is roughly equivalent to the ordering cost per order. Larger the size of the production run, lower will be the set-up cost per unit. On the other hand, the carrying costs will increases as large stocks of manufactured inventories will be held. Thus, the economic production lot size is one where the total of set-up cost and carrying cost is minimum.

The formula for EOQ can be used to determine the economic production quantity or lot size as given below :

$$\text{Economic Production Lot Size (EPLS)} = \sqrt{\frac{2AS}{C}}$$

Where :

EPLS = Economic Production Lot Size

A = Total Estimated Production or Output

S = Set-up cost per production

C = Cost of carrying cost per year

For example, the estimated annual production for the next year is 2,00,000 units and set-up cost per production run is Rs. 200 and the carrying cost per unit per year is Rs.5, the optimum production. Lot size can be determined by applying the EOQ formula

Economic Production Lot Size (E P L S) = $\sqrt{\frac{2AS}{C}}$

Where :

A = Annual Estimated Production 2,00,000 units

S = Set-up cost Per Production run Rs. 200

C = Carrying Cost Per unit per year Rs. 5

Economic Production Lot Size (E P L S) $= \sqrt{\frac{2AS}{C}}$

$= \sqrt{\frac{2 \times 2,00,000 \times 200}{5}}$

$= \sqrt{1,60,00,000}$

= 4,000 units per production run

Illustration: 2

Find out the Economic Order Quantity and order schedule of raw materials and packing materials with the following data given to you.

(1) Cost of Ordering :

Raw Materials = Rs. 1,000 per order

Packing Materials = Rs. 5,000 per order

(2) Cost of holding Inventory :

Raw Materials = 1 Paise per unit per month

Packing materials = 5 Paise per unit per month

(3) Production rate :

2,00,000 Units per month

Solution:

Calculation of Economic Order Quantity :

$$E\,OQ = \sqrt{\frac{2AS}{CS}}$$

Where :

EOQ = Economic Order Quantity

A = Units Consumed in a month

B = Buying Cost per order

C = Cost per unit

S = Inventory Carrying Cost per month

(a) Raw Materials :

$$EOQ = \sqrt{\frac{2 \times 2,00,000 \times 1000}{0.01}}$$

$$= \sqrt{40,00,00,00,000}$$

$$= 2,00,000 \text{ units}$$

Thus one order for 2,00,000 units each month.

(b) Packaging Materials :

$$EOQ = \sqrt{\frac{2 \times 2,00,000 \times 5000}{0.05}}$$

$$= \sqrt{40,00,00,00,000}$$

$$= 2,00,000 \text{ units}$$

Thus one order for 2,00,000 units per month.

Illustration: 3

A Ltd. is committed to supply 24000 bearings per annum to B Ltd. on a steady bases. It is estimated that it costs 10 paise as inventory holding cost per bearing per month and that the set up cost per run of bearing manufacture is Rs. 324.

(1) What should be the optimum run size for bearing manufacture?

(2) What would be the interval between two consecutive optimum runs?

(3) Find out the minimum inventory cost per annum?

Solution:

(1) Economic batch or run size

$$EOQ = \sqrt{\frac{2AS}{CS}}$$

Where :

A = Annual consumptions

B = Buying cost or set up cost

C = Cost per unit

S = Carrying cost or Holding cost per unit

$$= \sqrt{\frac{2 \times 324 \times 24,000}{10}} = 3,600 \text{ units}$$

Alternative Solution

The economic batch size figure can also be obtained by taking monthly figure as follows:

$$= \sqrt{\frac{2 \times 2,000 \text{ units} \times \text{Rs. } 324}{0.10}}$$

$$= 3600 \text{ units}$$

(2) Number of set up per annum :

$$\text{Number of set up per annum} = \frac{\text{Annual Production}}{\text{Economic run size}}$$

$$= \frac{24,000}{3,600}$$

$$= 6\frac{2}{3} \text{ times}$$

Interval between two consecutive optimum runs $= \frac{12}{\frac{20}{3}} = \frac{12 \times 3}{20} = \frac{36}{20}$ 1.8 months

(3) Minimum Inventory cost per year :

$$= \frac{24,000}{3,600} \times 324 + \frac{3,600}{2} \times 1.2$$

$$= \text{Rs. } 2,160 + \text{Rs. } 2,160 = \text{Rs. } 4320$$

Illustration: 4

A company manufactures a product from a raw material which is purchased at Rs. 60 per kg. The company incures a handling cost of Rs. 360 plus freight of Rs. 390 per order. The incremental carrying cost of inventory of raw material is Re. 0.50 per kg. per month. In addition, the cost of working capital finance on the investment in inventory of raw material is Rs. 9 per kg. per annum. The annual production of the product is 1,00,000 units and 2.5 units are obtained from one kg. of raw material.

Required :

(1) Calculate the Economic Order Quantity of raw materials.

(2) Advise, how frequently should order for procurement be placed.

(3) If the company proposes to rationalize placement of orders on quarterly basis, what percentage of discount in the prices of raw material should be negotiated.

[CA Inter Nov. 2001]

Solution:

$$\text{Economic Order Quantity} = \sqrt{\frac{2AB}{CS}}$$

A = Annual Consumption

B = Buying Cost per order

S = Storage and carrying cost

$$\text{A (Annual requirement of Raw Material in kgs)} = \frac{1\text{ kg} \times 1,00,000 \text{ units}}{2.5 \text{ units}}$$

$$= 40,000 \text{ kg.}$$

S Carrying Cost and Storage Expenses $= (0.5 \times 12) + \text{Rs. } 9$

$= \text{Rs. } 15$ per unit

B Buying Cost per order = Rs. 360 = Rs. 390 = Rs. 750

$$EOQ = \sqrt{\frac{2{,}40{,}00 \times 750}{15}}$$

= 2,000 kgs.

(2) Annual Consumption = 40,000 kgs.

Quantity per order = 2,000 kgs.

No. of orders = $\frac{40{,}000}{2{,}000}$ = 20 orders in 12 months

Frequency = $\frac{12 \text{ months}}{20 \text{ orders}}$ = 0.6 months

(or) = $\frac{365 \text{ months}}{20 \text{ orders}}$ = 18 days (approx)

(3) Quarterly Orders = $\frac{40{,}000 \text{ kgs.}}{4 \text{ orders}}$ = 10,000 kgs per order

No. of orders = $\frac{40{,}000}{10{,}000}$ = 4 orders

Total Cost : Rs.

Order Placing Cost (4 × 750) = 3,000

Carrying Cost = $\frac{10{,}000}{0.5 \times 4} \times 15$ = 75,000

78,000

Total Cost of EOQ : Rs.

No. of orders = 20

Order Placing Cost (20 × 750) = 15,000

Carrying Cost = $\frac{2{,}000}{0.5 \times 4} \times 15$ = 15,000

30,000

Increase in cost to be compensated by discount

Total Cost = Rs. 78,000

Less : Total Cost E O Q = Rs. 30,000

Increase in Cost 48,000

Price of discount per unit = $\frac{48{,}000}{40{,}000 \text{ kg}}$ = Rs. 1.20 per unit

Percentage of discount in the price of raw materials = $\frac{\text{Rs. } 1.20}{60} \times 100$

= 2% discount

Illustration: 5

Calculate the economic order quantity from the following particulars :

Annual requirements per year 6,000 units

Cost of materials per unit Rs. 5

Carrying cost per item for one year Re. 1

Cost of placing and receiving one order Rs. 60

Alternative order size in units 6,000, 3,000, 2,000, 1,200, 1,000, 600 and 200

Solution:

Tabular Model

Determination of Economic Order Quantity

(Schedule of costs for number of orders)

Cost of items Purchased each year 6000 unit × Rs. 5	30,000	30,000	30,000	30,000	30,000	30,000	30,000
Order size units	6,000	3,000	2,000	1,200	1,000	600	200
No. of orders per year	1	2	3	5	6	10	30
Average inventory in units	3,000	1,500	1,000	600	500	300	100
Total carrying cost Rs.	3,000	1,500	1,000	600	500	300	100
Total ordering cost Rs.	60	120	180	300	360	600	1800
Total carrying and ordering costs Rs.	3,060	1,620	1,180	900	860	900	1900
Total Cost Rs.	33,060	31,620	31,180	30,900	30,860	30,900	31,900

Ans : EOQ is 1000 units of 6 orders per year at a minimum total cost Rs. 30,860.

Working Notes :

(1) Number of orders $= \dfrac{\text{Annual consumption per year}}{\text{Order size}}$

(2) Average Inventory $= \dfrac{\text{Order size}}{2}$

(3) Total Carrying costs = Average inventory × Carrying cost per unit

(4) Total ordering costs = No of orders × Cost per order

(5) Total Cost = Cost of item purchased + Total carrying and ordering costs

Illustration: 6

Find out economic ordering quantity from the following particulars :

Annual usage 1200 units

Cost of materials per unit Rs. 50

Cost of placing and receiving one order is Rs. 30

Annual carrying cost of one unit is Re. 1

Alternative order size in units 1,200, 600, 400, 300, 240, 200, 100.

Solution:

Tabular Model

Calculation of Economic Order Quantity

(Schedule of costs of various orders)

Cost of items Purchased each year 1200 unit × Rs. 50	60,000	60,000	60,000	60,000	60,000	60,000	60,000
Order size units	1,200	600	400	300	240	200	100
No. of orders per year	1	2	3	4	5	6	12
Average inventory in units	600	300	200	150	120	100	50
Total carrying cost Rs.	600	300	200	150	120	100	50
Total ordering cost Rs.	30	60	90	120	150	180	360
Total carrying and ordering costs Rs.	630	360	290	270	270	280	410
Total Cost Rs.	60,630	60,360	60,290	60,270	60,270	60,280	60,410

Ans : Total cost of Rs. 60,270 is minimum when the ordering quantity is 300 units or 240 units of 6 or 5 orders, Thus, this is economic ordering quantity.

Illustration: 7

A firm is able to obtain quantity discount on its order of material as follows :

Price per tonne Rs.	Tonnes
6.00	Less then 250
5.90	250 and less than 800
5.80	800 and less than 2,000
5.70	2,000 and less than 4,000
5.60	4,000 and over

The annual demand for the material is 4,000 tonnes. Stock holding costs are 20% o material cost per annum. The delivery cost per order is Rs.6. You are required to calculat the best quantity to order.

Solution:

Tabular Model

Computation of Economic Order Quantity

Ordering Quantity (Q) tonnes	*Price per tonne (P) Rs.*	*Cost of Purchase (4,000 × P) Rs.*	*Ordering Cost* $\frac{(4000 \times 6)}{Q}$	*Cost of stock holding* $\left(\frac{Q}{2} \times P \times 20\%\right)$ *Rs.*	*Total Cost Rs.*
200	6.00	4,000 × 6 = Rs. 24,000	$\frac{4,000}{200} \times 6$ = 120	$\frac{200 \times 6 \times 20\%}{2}$ = 120	24,240
250	5.90	4,000 × 5.90 = Rs. 23,600	$\frac{4,000}{250} \times 6$ = 96	$\frac{250 \times 5.90 \times 20\%}{2}$ = 147.50	23,843.50
800	5.80	4,000 × 5.80 = Rs. 23,200	$\frac{4,000}{800} \times 6$ = 30	$\frac{800 \times 5.80 \times 20\%}{2}$ = 464	23,694
2,000	5.70	4,000 × 5.70 = Rs. 22,800	$\frac{4,000}{2,000} \times 6$ = 12	$\frac{2,000 \times 5.70 \times 20\%}{2}$ = 1140	23,952

Conclusion : The best quantity to order is 800 tonnes because at this quantity, total cost is lowest *i.e.*, Rs. 23,694.

Illustration: 8

The following details are available in respect of a firm:

(a) Annual consumption during the year is 3,000 units

(b) Cost of materials per unit Rs.5

(c) Cost of storage per unit is 10% of unit cost

(d) Cost of placing each order is Rs.30. you are required to find out EOQ

Using :

(1) Formula Method

(2) Tabulation Method

(3) Graphic Method

Solution:

Determination of EOQ :

(1) Formula Method

$$EOQ = \sqrt{\frac{2AB}{CS}}$$

Where :

A = Annual Consumption 3000 units

B = Buying cost per order Rs.30

C = Cost per unit Rs.5

S = Storage and Carrying cost 10% of per unit cost

$$EOQ = \sqrt{\frac{2AB}{CS}}$$

$$= \sqrt{\frac{2 \times 3{,}000 \times 30}{5 \times 10\%}}$$

= = 600 units

Thus, EOQ is 600 units or 5 orders (3,000 ÷ 600) per year.

(3) Graphic Method

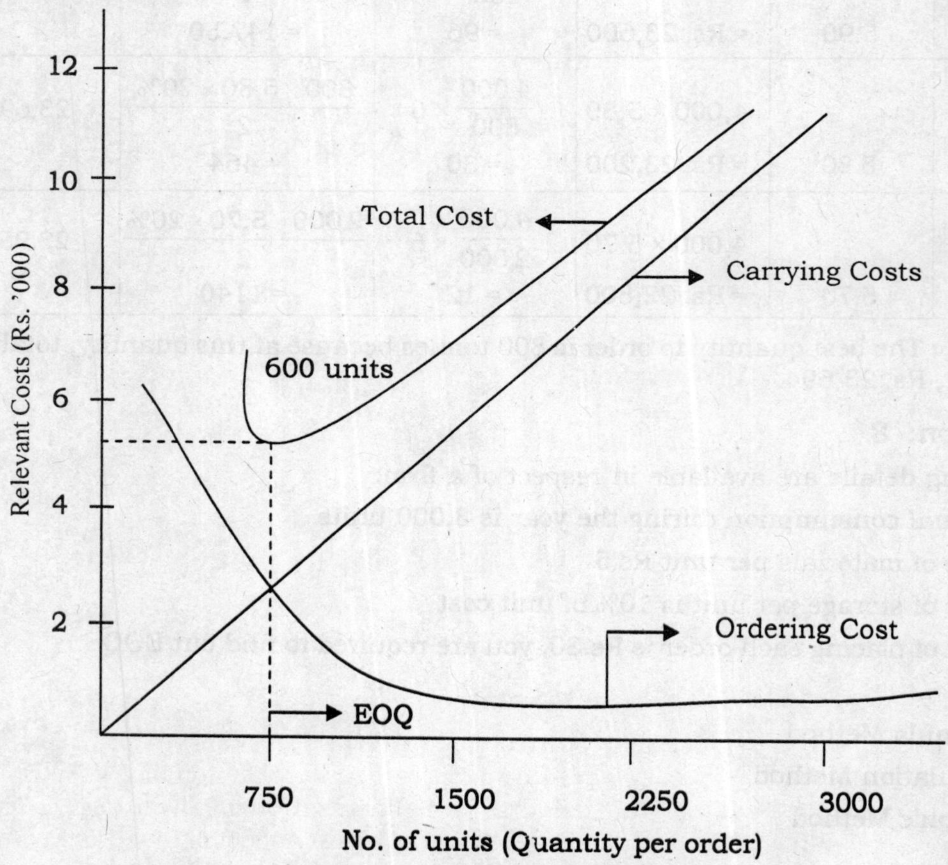

Fig 5.2 : Economic Order Quantity.

From the above Graph, it is clearly shows that the figure, costs—carrying ordering and total are plotted on vertical axis and horizontal axis is used to represent the order size. The carrying cost varies directly with the order size (since the average level of inventory is one half of the order size), whereas the ordering cost varies inversely with the order size. The economic order quantity occurs at the point where the total cost is minimum.

(2) Tabular Model

Determination of Economic Order Quantity

(Schedule of costs of various orders)

Annual Consumption demand in units	3,000	3,000	3,000	3,000	3,000	3,000	3,000
No. of orders per year	1	2	3	4	5	6	7
Order size units	3,000	1,500	1,000	750	600	500	428
Value per order (Rs. 5 per unit × Order size unit)	15,000	7,500	5,000	3,750	3,000	2,500	2,140
Average Inventory Value Rs.	7,500	3,750	2,500	1,875	1,500	1,250	1,070
Carrying Cost 10% of Average inventory value	750	375	250	187	150	125	107
Cost per order	30	60	90	120	150	180	210
Total Cost (Carrying Cost + Cost Per Order)	780	435	340	307	300	305	317

Ans : EOQ is 600 units of 5 orders per year at a minimum total cost of Rs.300

Working Notes :

(1) Number of Orders $= \dfrac{\text{Annual Consumption per year}}{\text{Order Size}}$

(2) Average Inventory Value (Rs) $= \dfrac{\text{Annual Consumption per year}}{\text{Order Size}}$

(3) Total Carrying Costs = Average inventory value x Carrying cost 10% of average inventory value

(4) Total Ordering Cost = Cost per order × No. of orders per year

(5) Total Cost = Total Carrying Cost + Total Ordering Cost

Fixation or Determination of Stock Level

Materials control involves physical control of materials, preservation of stores, minimization of obsolescence and damages through timely disposal and efficient handling. Effective stock control system should ensure the minimization of inventory carrying cost and materials holding cost. Level of stock is the important aspect of inventory control. Stock level may be over stocking or under stocking. Over stocking which leads to require large capital with high cost of holding. In the case of under stocking will affect the production and overall performance of the concern as a whole. Thus, fixation of stock level is essential to maintain sufficient and optimum stock for the smooth flow of production and sales. The following are the important technique usually adopted in different industries.

(1) Re-Order Level

(2) Minimum Stock Level

(3) Maximum Stock Level

(4) Danger Level

(5) Average Stock Level

(1) Re-Order Level : Re-Order is also termed as ordering level. It indicates when to order *i.e.*, order for its fresh supplies for procuring additional inventory equal to the economic order quantity. The re-order stock level is determined on the basis of economic order quantity, lead time and average rate of consumption. Calculation of re-order level is adopted by the following formula is

Re-Order Level = Lead Time × Average Usage

(or)

= Maximum Consumption × Maximum re-order period

= Minimum Stock Level + Consumption during the time to get fresh delivery

The term lead time refers to the time normally taken in receiving the delivery of inventory after placing orders with the suppliers. It covers the time span from the point when a decision to place an order for the procurement of materials is made to the actual reception of the material by the firm. It is also known as procurement time or re-order period.

(2) Minimum Stock Level : Minimum stock level indicates the minimum quantity of materials to be maintained in stock. Accordingly, the minimum quantity of an item should not allowed to fall. The minimum stock is also know as Safety stock or Buffer stock. In fixing this level, the following factors are to be considered.

(a) Lead time

(b) Average rate of consumption of materials

(c) Nature of materials

(d) Conditions of supply

The minimum stock level can be determined by the following formula;

(a) Minimum Stock Level = Re-order Level – (Normal Consumption × Normal Re-order period)

(3) Maximum Stock Level : The maximum stock level indicates the maximum quantity of an item should not allowed to increase. The maximum quantity of an item which can be held in stock at any time. The following factors can be considered while fixing the maximum stock levels.

(a) Availability of Capital

(b) Availability of floor space

(c) Cost of storage

(d) Possibility of fluctuation of prices in raw materials

(e) Cost of insurance

(f) Economic-order quantity

(g) Average rate of consumption

(h) Re-order level and lead time

(i) Seasonal nature of supply

(j) Risk of obsolescence, depletion, evaporation etc.

The formula for the determination of Maximum Stock Level is given below :

Maximum Stock Level = Re-order Level + Re-order quantity – (Minimum Consumption × Minimum Re-ordering Period)

(or)

= Economic Order Quantity + Safety Stock

(4) Danger Level : It is the stock level below the minimum level. This level indicates the danger point to affect the normal production. When materials reaches danger level, necessary steps should be taken for restock the materials. If any emergency, special arrangements should be made for fresh issue. Generally this level is fixed above the minimum level but below the re-ordering level. The formula for calculation of danger level is :

Danger Level = Average Rate of Consumption × Emergency Supply Time

(5) Average Stock Level : Average stock level is determined on the basis of minimum stock level and re-order level. This is calculated with the help of the following formula :

Average Stock Level = Minimum Stock Level + ½ of Re-order quantity

(or)

$$\frac{\text{Minimum Level} + \text{Maximum Level}}{2}$$

Illustration: 9

From the following particulars calculate the

(a) Maximum Stock Level

(b) Minimum Stock Level

(c) Re-ordering Level

(d) Average Stock Level

(1) Normal consumption = 600 units per week

(2) Maximum consumption = 840 units per week

(3) Minimum consumption = 480 unit per week

(4) Re-order quantity = 7200 units

(5) Re-order Period = 10 to 15 weeks

(6) Normal re-order period = 12 weeks

Solution:

Re-order Level

= Maximum Consumption × Maximum Re-order Period

= 840 × 15 = 12,600 units

Minimum Stock Level :

= Re-order Level—(Normal Consumption × Normal Re-order Period)

= 12,600 – (600 × 12)

= 12,600 – 7,200 = 5,400 units

Maximum Stock Level :

= Re-order Level + Re-Order Quantity – (Minimum Consumption × Minimum Re-order Period)

= 12,600 + 7,200 – (480 × 10)

= 19,800 – 4,800 = 15,000 units.

Average Stock Level :

$$= \frac{\text{Minimum Stock Level + Maximum Stock Level}}{2}$$

$$= \frac{5,400 + 15,000}{2}$$

$$= \frac{20,400}{2} = 10,200 \text{ units}$$

Illustration: 10

The following informations are available in respect of a material X :

Re-order Quantity	=	1800 units
Maximum Consumption	=	450 units per week
Minimum Consumption	=	150 units per week
Normal Consumption	=	300 units per week
Re-order Period	=	3 to 5 weeks

Calculate the following :

(a) Re-order Level

(b) Minimum Stock Level

(c) Maximum Stock Level

Solution:

(a) Re-order Level :

= Maximum Consumption × Maximum Re-order Period

= 450 × 5 = 2,250 units

(b) Minimum Stock Level :

= Re-order Level – (Normal Consumption × Normal Re-order Period)

= 2,250 – (300 × 4)

= 2,250 – 1,200 = 1,050 units.

(c) Maximum Stock Level :

= Re-order Level + Re-order Quantity – (Minimum Consumption × Minimum Re-order Period)

= 2,250 + 1,800 – (150 × 3)

= 4,050 – 450 = 3600 units

(d) Normal Re-order Period :

$$= \frac{\text{Minimum Re - order Level} + \text{Maximum Re - order Level}}{2}$$

$$= \frac{3 \text{ weeks} + 5 \text{ weeks}}{2}$$

$$= \frac{8}{2} = 4 \text{ weeks}$$

Illustration: 11

IPL Limited uses a small casting in one of its finished products. The castings are purchased from a foundry. IPL Limited purchases 54,000 castings per year at a cost of Rs. 800 per casting.

The castings are used evenly throughout the year in the production process on a 360-day-per-year basis. The company estimates that it costs Rs. 9,000 to place a single purchase order and about Rs. 300 to carry one casting in inventory for a year. The high carrying costs result from the need to keep the castings in carefully controlled temperature and humidity conditions, and from the high cost of insurance.

Delivery from the foundry generally takes 6 days, but it can take as much as 10 days. The days of delivery time and percentage of their occurrence are shown in the following tabulation :

Delivery time (days)	:	6	7	8	9	10
Percentage of Occurrence	:	75	10	5	5	5

Required :

(i) Compute the Economic Order Quantity (EOQ).

(ii) Assume the company is willing to assume a 15% risk of being out of stock. What would be the safety stock? The re-order point?

(iii) Assume the company is willing to assume a 5% risk of being out of stock. What would be the safety stock? The re-order point?

(iv) Assume 5% stock-out risk. What would be the total cost of ordering and carrying inventory for one year.

(v) Refer to the original data. Assume that using process re-engineering the company reduces its cost of placing a purchase order to only Rs. 600. In addition, company estimates that when the waste and inefficiency caused by inventories are considered, the true cost of carrying a unit in stock is Rs. 720 per year.

(a) Compute the new EOQ

(b) How frequently would the company be placing an order, as compared to the old purchasing policy?

Solution:

(1) Calculation of Economic Order Quantity :

$$EOQ = \sqrt{\frac{2AQ}{C \times I}}$$

Where :

A = Annual requirement 54,000 castings

C = Cost per Casting Rs. 800

O = Ordering Cost Rs. 9,000 per order

C × i = Carrying cost per casting P.a. Rs. 300

$$EOQ = \sqrt{\frac{2AQ}{C \times I}} = \sqrt{\frac{2 \times 54{,}000 \times 9{,}000}{300}}$$

= 1,800 castings.

(2) Calculation of Safety stock and Re-order Point :

(A) Safety Stock = Safety stock for one day 54,000/360

= 150 castings.

Re-order point = Minimum Stock Level + Average Lead Time × Average Consumption

= 150 + 6 × 150 = 1050 castings.

(B) Safety Stock for 3 days = 150 × 3 = 450 castings

Re-order Point = 450 + 900 = 1350 castings

(3) Calculation of costing and Cost of ordering :

$$\text{Cost of Carrying} = \frac{450 + 1800}{2} \times \text{Rs. } 300$$

$$= \frac{2250}{2} \times 300 = \text{Rs. } 3{,}37{,}500$$

Cost of Ordering = No. of orders × Cost per order

$$\text{No. of orders} = \frac{54{,}000}{1{,}800} = 30 \text{ orders}$$

Cost per orders = Rs. 9,000

Cost of ordering = 30 × Rs. 9,000 = Rs. 2,70,000

(4) Calculation of New EOQ :

$$EOQ = \sqrt{\frac{2AQ}{C \times I}}$$

$$= \sqrt{\frac{2 \times 54{,}000 \times 600}{720}}$$

300 castings

$$\text{No. of orders during the year} = \frac{\text{Annual Consumption}}{\text{Economic Order Quantity}}$$

$$= \frac{54,000}{300}$$

= 180 orders as against

$$= \frac{54,000}{1,800} = 30 \text{ orders earlier.}$$

Illustration: 12

A fire occurred in the factory premises on October 31, 2003. The accounting records have been destroyed. Certain accounting records were kept in another building. The reveal the following for the period September 1,2003 to October 31, 2003 :

(i) Direct materials purchased	Rs. 2,50,000
(ii) Work in process inventory , 1.9.2003	Rs. 40,000
(iii) Direct materials inventory, 1.9.2003	Rs. 20,000
(iv) Finished goods inventory, 1.9.2003	Rs. 37,750
(v) Indirect manufacturing costs	40% of conversion cost
(vi) Sales revenues	Rs. 7,50,000
(vii) Direct manufacturing labour	Rs. 2,22,250
(viii) Prime costs	Rs. 3,97,750
(ix) Gross margin percentage based on revenues	30%
(x) Cost of Goods available for sale	Rs. 5,55,750

The loss is fully covered by insurance. The insurance company wants to know the historical cost of the inventories as a basis for negotiating a settlement, although the settlement is actually to be based on replacement cost, not historical cost.

Required :

(i) Finished goods inventory, 31.10.2003

(ii) Work-in-process inventory, 31.10.2003

(iii) Direct materials inventory, 31.10.2003

Solution:

Prime Cost (Given) = Rs. 3,97,750

Direct Material used = Prime Cost – Direct Manufacturing Labour Cost

= 3,97,750 – 2,22,250

= Rs. 1,75,500

$$\text{Conversion Cost} = \frac{\text{Direct Manufacturing Labour Cost}}{0.6}$$

$$= \frac{2,22,250}{0.6} = \text{Rs. } 3,70,416.67$$

Indirect Manufacturing Cost = Conversion Cost—Direct Manufacturing Labour Cost

= Rs. 3,70,416.67 – Rs. 2,22,250

= Rs. 1,48,166.67

Schedule of Computations :

		Rs.
	Direct materials 1.9.2003	20,000
	Direct materials purchased	2,50,000
	Direct materials available for use	2,70,000
Less :	Direct material 31.10.2003 (Balancing figure)	94,500
	Direct materials used	1,75,500
Add :	Direct manufacturing labour cost	2,22,250
	Prime costs	3,97,750
Add :	Indirect manufacturing cost	1,48,166.67
	Manufacturing cost incurred during current period	5,45,916.67
Add :	Work-in-progress 31.10.2003	40,000
	Manufacturing cost to account for	5,85,916.67
Less :	Work in progress 31.10.2003	67,891.67
	Cost of goods manufactured	5,18,025
Add :	Finished goods 1.9.2003	37,750
	Cost of goods available for sale 31.10.2003	5,55,775
Less :	Finished goods 31.10.2003	30,775
	Cost of goods sold (70% of Rs. 7,50,000)	5,25,000

Ans : Finished Goods Inventory 31.10.2003 Rs. 30,775

WIP Inventory 31.10.2003 Rs. 67,891.67

Raw Material Inventory 31.10.2003 Rs. 94,500

Illustration: 13

Two components P, Q are used as follows Normal usage 1000 units per week each Re ordering quantity P – 20,000; Q – 8,000; Re ordering period P – 4 to 6 weeks : Q 2 to 4 minimum usage 2000 units per week each maximum usage 3,000 units per week each.

You are required to calculate the following each of the components

(1) Minimum Stock Level

(2) Maximum Stock Level

(3) Average Stock Level

(4) Re-ordering Level

Solution:

(1) Re-ordering Level = Maximum Consumption × Maximum Re-order period

Product P = 3000 × 6 = 18,000 units

Product Q = 3000 × 4 = 12,000 units

(2) Minimum Level = Re-order Level – (Normal Consumption × Normal Re-order Period)

Product P = 18,000 – (1,000 × 5)

= 18,000 – 5,000 = 13,000 units

Product Q = 12,000 – (1,000 × 3)

= 12,000 – 3,000 = 9,000 units

(3) Maximum Level = Re-order Level + Re-order Quantity – (Minimum Consumption × Minimum Re-order Period)

Product P = 18,000 + 20,000 – (2,000 × 4)

= 38,000 – 8,000 = 30,000 units

Product Q = 12,000 + 8,000 – (2,000 × 2)

= 20,000 – 4,000 = 16,000 units

(4) Average Stock Level = Minimum Level + ½ of Re order Quantity

Product P = 13,000 + ½ (20,000)

= 13,000 + 10,000 = 23,000 units

Product Q = 9,000 + ½ (8,000)

= 9,000 + 4,000 = 13,000 units

Illustration: 14

From the following information for last twelve months, compute the

(1) Re-Order Level

(2) Minimum Level

(3) Maximum Level

(4) Average Stock Level for the components of X and Y

	Components	
	X	Y
Maximum Consumption in a Month	3,000	3,000
Minimum Consumption in a Month	2,000	2,000
Average Consumption in a Month	1,000	1,000
Re-order Period in a Month	8 to 12	4 to 8
Re-order Quantity in units	8,000	12,000

Solution:

(1) Re-order Level = Maximum Consumption × Maximum Re-order Period

Product X = 3,000 × 12 = 36,000 units

Product Y = 3,000 × 8 = 24,000 units

(2) Minimum Level = Re-order Level—(Average Consumption × Average Re-order Period)

Product X = 36,000 – (1,000 × 10)

= 36,000 – 10,000 = 26,000 units

Product Y = 24,000 – (1,000 × 6)

= 24,000—6,000 = 18,000 units

(3) Maximum Level = Re-order Level + Re-order Quantity – (Minimum Consumption × Minimum Re-order Period)

Product X = 36,000 + 8,000 – (2,000 × 8)

= 44,000 – 16,000 = 28,000 units

Product Y = 24,000 + 12,000 – (2,000 × 4)

= 36,000 – 8,000 = 28,000 units

(4) Average Stock Level = Minimum Level + ½ of Re-order Quantity

Product X = 28,000 + ½ (8,000)

= 28,000 + 4,000 = 32,000 units

Product Y = 28,000 + ½ (12,000)

= 28,000 + 6,000 = 34,000 units

Normal Re-order Period :

$$\text{Product X} = \frac{8 \text{ Months} + 12 \text{ Months}}{2}$$

$$= \frac{20}{2} = 10 \text{ Months}$$

$$\text{Product Y} = \frac{4 \text{ Months} + 8 \text{ Months}}{2}$$

$$= \frac{12}{2} = 6 \text{ Months}$$

ABC Analysis : ABC Analysis is one of the important techniques which is based on grading the items to the importance of materials. This method is popularly known as Always Better Control. This is also termed as Proportional Value Analysis. In inventory control, this technique is helps to analyse the distribution of any characteristic by money value of importance of any characteristic by money value of importance in order to determine its importance. Accordingly materials are grouped into three categories on the basis of the money into three categories on the basis of the money value of importance of materials.

(1) A—High Value Materials

(2) B—Medium Value Materials

(3) C—Low Value Materials

The items which are high value and less than 10 percent of the total consumption of inventory can be called as 'A' grouped materials. It is required to exercise selective control and focus more attention because of high value items. Similarly 70 per cent of materials in total consumption of inventory which lies 10 per cent of the inventory value can be grouped under 'C' categories. The materials which have moderate value that lies between the high value materials and low value materials are grouped under 'B' category. The following table shows the example of ABC Analysis.

Category	*Percentage to Total Inventory (%)*	*Percentage to Total Inventory cost (%)*
A	Less than 10	70 to 80
B	10 to 20	15 to 25
C	70 to 80	Less than 10

The given below graph illustrates a typical classification of this type

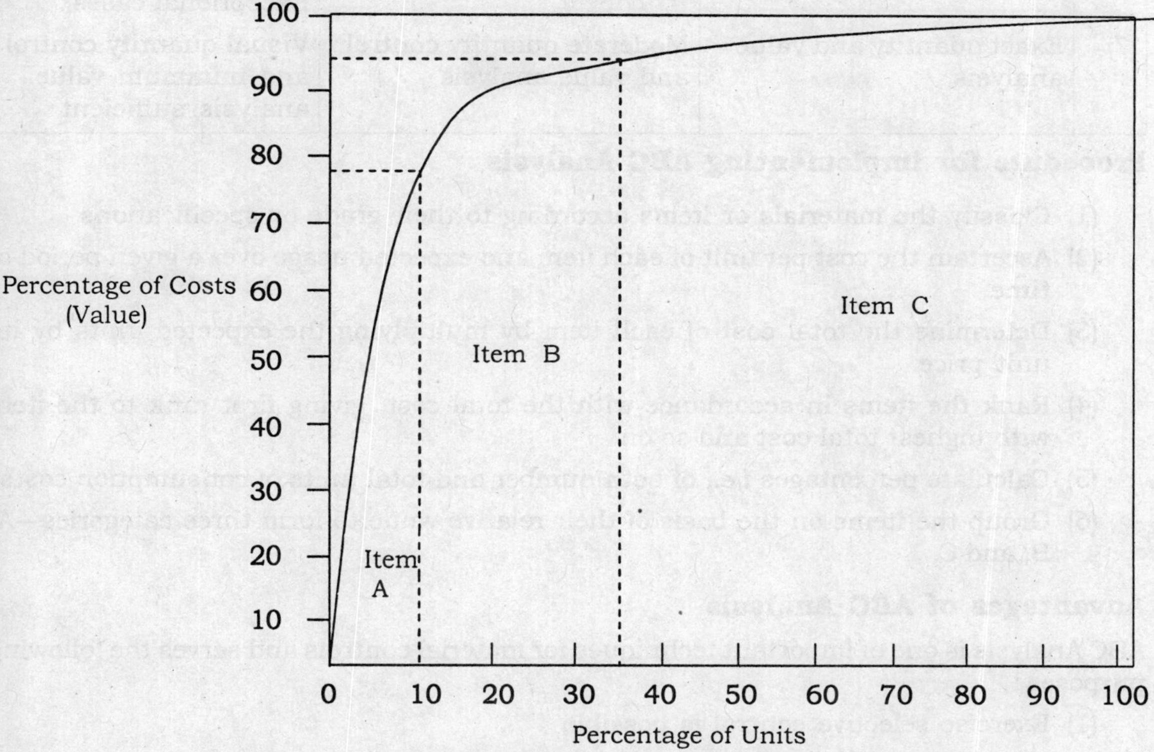

Fig 5.3 : Graphic Presentation of ABC Analysis.

From the graphical analysis, it is observed that about 10% of the items account for more than 70% of the cost of inventory. This is groped as A items which from the most important items from the control point of view. B components 25% of total items, account for 20% of the total cost of the inventory. These are of secondary importance. On the other hand, more than half to the total units are item C representing merely 10% of the total cost of the inventory. In the case of item 'C' need less attention and control will be sufficient.

In brief the selective inventory control should follow the given below patterns :

S.No.	*'A' Items*	*'B' Items*	*'C' Items*
(1)	High Consumption Value	Moderate Consumption Value	Low Consumption Value
(2)	Tight Control and focus more attention	Moderate Control	Loose Control and less attention required.
(3)	Frequent ordering based ordering on requirements	Ordering on the basis of exact requirements	Ordering on the basis of estimated consumption
(4)	Low safety stocks	Moderate safety stocks	Large safety stock
(5)	Maximum efforts and close check to reduce lead time lead time	Moderate efforts and some check to reduce lead time	Little efforts sufficient to reduce lead time

(6)	Required regular follow up	Required periodic follow up	Fellow up only in Exceptional cases
(7)	Exact quantity and value analysis	Moderate quantity control and value analysis	Visual quantity control and minimum value analysis sufficient

Procedure for implementing ABC Analysis

(1) Classify the materials or items according to their grade or specifications

(2) Ascertain the cost per unit of each item and expected usage over a given period of time.

(3) Determine the total cost of each item by multiplying the expected units by its unit price.

(4) Rank the items in accordance with the total cost, giving first rank to the item with highest total cost and so on.

(5) Calculate percentages *i.e.*, of both number and total units of consumption costs.

(6) Group the items on the basis of their relative value to form three categories—A, B, and C.

Advantages of ABC Analysis

ABC Analysis is one of important techniques for material controls and serves the following purposes :

(1) Exercise selective control is possible

(2) Focus high attention on high value item is possible

(3) It helps to reduce the clerical efforts and costs

(4) It facilitates better planning and improved inventory turnover

(5) It ensures good store keeping and effective materials handling

(6) It assists optimum working capital investment in inventories

(7) It facilitates determination of stock level to ensure continuous flow of production

Classification and Codification of Materials

In order to ensure the effective inventory control, it should be carried out with the classification and codification of materials. Codification is the process of representing each item by a number, the digits of which indicate the group, the sub group the type and the size and shape of the items. The codification process could be obtained by the nature of materials in grouping all items of the same metal content say ferrous and non ferrous etc. The system of codification could be built by the end use of items, that is items grouped according to maintenance, spinning, weaving, packing, foundry, machine shop etc.

Advantage of Codification

(1) Codes ensure the secrecy of materials

(2) It is essential for mechanical accounting

(3) Easy identification of material is possible

(4) It ensures effective materials control

(5) It minimizes length in description of materials

(6) Effective materials handling is possible

(7) It helps in avoiding duplication of materials

(8) Codification facilitates less clerical work

(9) Cost reduction is possible

Methods of Coding

The following are the three important Methods of Codification :

(1) Numerical Method

(2) Alphabetical Method

(3) Numerical Cum Alphabetical Method

(1) Numerical Method : Under this method, each number or numerical digits are allotted to each item or material. Accordingly, each code should uniquely indicate one item. For example, in printing press following codes may be assigned :

Paper	145
Ink	155
Gum	165

There are various universal decimal classification of codification used in libraries may be indicated for identification of items.

(2) Alphabetical Method : In this method alphabets or letter are used for codification of each category of materials. Accordingly. Each letter or alphabet is allotted for each item or material. For example, 'C' for copper. 'S' for steel and so on.

(3) Numerical Cum Alphabetical Method : This method is done by a combination of numerical and alphabetical method. Under this method, both numerical along with alphabet is allotted for each item. For example, IR 5 may indicate Ink Red of Grade 5, Steel Wire 6 may be denoted by SW 6 etc.

ventory System

The chief aims of inventory control is as follows :

(1) To maintains a balanced inventory

(2) To ensures the smooth flow of production

(3) To keep the investment in inventory as low as possible

Accordingly stock verification is an important aspect to ensure the maintain a balanced inventory. The following are the two systems of stock verification adopted in different industries :

(1) Periodic Inventory System

(2) Perpetual Inventory System

(3) Continuous Stock Taking

(1) Periodic Inventory System : Under this system, quantity and value of materials are checked and verified at the end of the accounting period after having a physical verification of the units in hand.

(2) Perpetual Inventory System : The Perpetual Inventory System is also known as

Automatic Inventory System. This is one of the important method adopted for verification inventories to know the physical balances. According to I C M A London defines Perpetual Inventory System as "a method of recording stores balances after every receipt and issue to facilitate regular checking and to obviate closing down for stock taking.

Advantages of Perpetual Inventory System

(1) It facilitates rigid control over stock of materials

(2) It gives upto date details about materials in stock

(3) Not necessary to stop production for stock talking

(4) It assists to minimize pilferage and fraudulent practices

(5) It enables to reconcile the stock records and document for accuracy

(6) It helps to take the important decisions for corrective actions

Perpetual Inventory Records

Perpetual Inventory represents a system of records maintained by the organization. The records are of two types viz :

(1) Bin Cards

(2) Stores Ledger

A constant comparison of the quantity balances of these two set of records is made and the balances are reconciled.

(1) Bin Cards : Bin Card is only quantitative record of stores receipt, issue and balance and is kept by the Store Keeper for each item of stores.

(2) Stores Ledger : Stores ledger is both quantitative and monetary value record of stores receipt, issue and balance and is prepared by the Cost Accounting Department.

Bin Card Vs Stores Ledger

The Difference between Bin Card and the Stores Ledger can be summarized as follows

Bin Card	*Stores Ledger*
(1) Bin Cards are maintained at the stores.	(1) Stores Ledger is maintained in the Accounts Department.
(2) It is posted by Issue Clerk.	(2) It is posted by Ledger Clerk.
(3) Bin Cards meant for recording of quantity only.	(3) It is as a record of quantity and value.
(4) Transactions posted individually.	(4) Transactions can be posted periodically.
(5) Posting can be made at the time of issue.	(5) In stores ledger posting can be made after issue.

(3) Continuous Stock Verification : Stock Verification of physical inventory is an essential feature of a sound system of material control, a system of continuous stock taking is introduced. Continuous stock taking ensures that the balances of all items of stocks are checked at least three to four times in a year by physical verification. It avoids long and costly procedure of closing down the stores for stock taking on periodical basis. Stock discrepancies are detected on timely basis and preventive measures can be taken. The correctness of the physical stocks as reflected in the books is ensured and thus the monthly accounts represent a true and fair view of the business. Continuous Stock Verification not only serves as an essential tool of material control but also will help in proper presentation of accounting information to the management.

Continuous Stock Taking Vs Periodic Stock Taking

The differences between Continuous Stock Taking and Periodic Stock Taking can be summarized as follows :

Continuous Stock Taking	*Periodic Stock Taking*
(1) Continuous tock taking is held throughout the year.	(1) It is held once in a year.
(2) Stock discrepancies are detected and prevented without delay.	(2) Under this system preventive measures is the delayed process.
(3) Under this system normal work will not be disrupted.	(3) Under this system there is closing down the stores for stock taking.
(4) Permanent personnels are required.	(4) Temporary personnel are required.
(5) Long and costly procedure on continuous tock verification.	(5) It is a cheaper and shorter period is required.
(6) Physical verification of materials are on random basis.	(6) All materials are thoroughly checked.

Material Storage Losses

The investment in materials constitute a major portion of current assets, so it is essential to exercise effective stores control. Stores control helps to avoid losses from misappropriation, damage, deterioration etc. Generally material storage losses arising during storage may be classified as :

(1) Normal Loss

(2) Abnormal Loss

Normal Loss : Normal Loses arise during the storage of materials due to the avoidable reasons of pilferage, theft, careless of materials handling, clerical errors, improper storage wrong entries etc.

Abnormal Loss : Abnormal losses arise during the storage of materials due to unavoidable causes of evaporation, shrinkage, bulk losses due to accident fire etc.

Accounting treatment of Normal Loss and Abnormal Loss :

The following are the accounting treatment of normal and abnormal loss of materials arising during storage :

(1) Normal Loss :

(a) Inflate the issue price.

(b) Charge to stores overheads.

(c) Treat it as a separate item of overheads to be recovered as a percentage of materials consumed.

(2) Abnormal Loss : Abnormal Losses are directly changed to Costing Profit and Loss Account .

(3) If the loss is due to error in documentation it should be corrected through adjustment entries

Inventory Turnover Ratio

This ratio is also called as 'Stock Turnover Ratio' or 'Stock Velocity'. Inventory Turnover Ratio may be defined as a ratio which measures the number of items a firm's average inventory is sold during the year. It establishes the relationship between the cost of goods sold during a given period and the average of the cost of opening and closing stock. This ratio indicates the investment in stock is effectively utilized or not. High rate of inventory turnover ratio denotes that materials are fast moving stock. It is reflector of good management. On the other hand, low turnover rate indicates the locking up of working capital in undesirable items. It is an indicator of the existence of poor quality goods which the company is unable to push through.

Calculation of Inventory Turnover Ratio

As the computations procedure of the ratio differs from trading concerns to manufacturing concern.

I. Trading Concern : Trading concern are those concerns which are engaged in the sale of goods and services purchased from other manufacturer. As a result, there are no raw materials and no work-in-progress. In this situation, the inventory turnover ratio can be calculated as given below :

$$\text{Inventory Turnover Ratio} = \frac{\text{Cost of goods sold}}{\text{Average Inventory}} \text{ (or) } \frac{\text{Sales Revenue}}{\text{Average Inventory}}$$

Where,

Cost of goods sold = opening stock + Purchases + Direct Expenses – Closing Stock

$$\text{Average Inventory} = \frac{\text{Opening Inventory + Closing Inventory}}{2}$$

II. Manufacturing Concern : Manufacturing concerns acquire raw materials and use them for the purpose of producing goods and services. As a result, the manufacturing company require to maintain a stock of raw materials, work-in-progress and finished goods. The ratio can be used as:

$$\text{(i) Inventory Turnover Ratio (Raw Materials)} = \frac{\text{Cost of raw materials consumed}}{\text{Average value of raw materials in stock}}$$

Where ,

Cost raw materials consumed during the year = Opening stock of raw materials + Purchase of raw materials – Closing stock of raw materials

$$\text{Average Stock of Raw Materials} = \frac{\text{Opening stock of Raw materials} + \text{Closing stock of Raw materials}}{2}$$

$$\text{(ii) Inventory Turnover Ratio (work-in-progress)} = \frac{\text{Cost Completed Works}}{\text{Average Stock of Work - in - Progress}}$$

Where ,

Cost of Competed Works = Opening Stock of work-in-progress + Manufacturing cost incurred during the period – closing stock of work in progress

$$\text{Average Work in Progress} = \frac{\text{Opening stock of Work - in - Progress} - \text{Closing stock of Work in Progress}}{2}$$

(iii) Inventory Turnover Ratio (Finished goods) $= \dfrac{\text{Cost of goods sold}}{\text{Average Stock of Finished goods}}$

Where,

Cost of goods sold = Opening stock of finished goods + Cost of Production – Closing stock of finished goods

$$\text{Average stock of finished goods} = \frac{\text{Opening stock of Finished goods} - \text{Closing stock of Finished goods}}{2}$$

vantages

(1) This ratio indicates whether investment on stock in trade is efficiently used or not.

(2) This ratio is widely used as a measure of investment in stock is with in proper limit or not.

(3) It highlights the operational efficiency of the business concern.

(4) It helpful in evaluating the stock utilization.

(5) It measures the relationship between the sale and the stock in trade.

(6) This ratio indicates the number of times the inventories has been turned over in business during a particular period.

ustration: 15

lculate the Inventory Turnover Ratio for the year 2003 from the following details :

	Material X *Rs.*	*Material Y* *Rs.*
Opening Stock	50,000	1,75,000
Closing Stock	30,000	1,25,000
Purchases	3,80,000	2,50,000

Determine fast moving materials

lution:

	X	*Y*
Opening Stock	50,000	1,75,000
Add : Purchases	3,80,000	2,50,000
	4,30,000	4,25,000
Less : Closing Stock	30,000	1,25,000
Material Consumed	4,00,000	3,00,000

$$\text{Average Inventory} = \frac{\text{Opening Stocking} + \text{Closing Stock}}{2}$$

$$= \frac{50,000 + 30,000}{2} \quad \frac{1,75,000 + 1,25,000}{2}$$

$$= \frac{80,000}{2} \quad \frac{3,00,000}{2}$$

$$= 40,000 \quad = 1,50,000$$

$$\text{Material Turnover Ratio} = \frac{\text{Material Consumed}}{\text{Average Inventory}}$$

$$\text{Material X} = \frac{4,00,000}{40,000} = 10 \text{ times}$$

$$\text{Material Y} = \frac{3,00,000}{1,50,000} = 2 \text{ times}$$

The turnover ratio of Material X being higher than that of Material Y, the former i faster moving material.

Illustration: 16

From the following particulars calculate Stock Turnover Ratio

Gross Sales	Rs. 5,00,000
Sales Return	Rs. 25,000
Opening Stock	Rs. 70,000
Closing Stock at Cost	Rs. 85,000
Purchases	Rs. 3,00,000
Direct Expenses	Rs. 1,00,000

Solution:

$$\text{Inventory Turnover Ratio} = \frac{\text{Cost of goods sold}}{\text{Average Inventory at Cost}}$$

Cost of goods sold = Opening Stock + Purchases + Direct Expenses – Closing Stock

$$= \text{Rs. } 70,000 + 3,00,000 + 1,00,000 - 85,000$$

$$= \text{Rs. } 3,85,000$$

$$\text{Average Stock} = \frac{\text{Opening Stock} + \text{Closing Stock}}{2}$$

$$= \frac{70,000 + 85,000}{2} = \text{Rs. } 77,500$$

$$\text{Inventory Turnover Ratio} = \frac{3,85,000}{77,500} = 4.97 \text{ times}$$

ustration: 17

e following figures are extract from the Trading Account of X A/c you are required to culate Stock Turnover Ratio :

Opening Stock Rs. 30,000; Purchases Rs. 1,10,000; Direct Expenses Rs. 10,000; Gross fit Rs. 75,000; Gross Sales Rs. 2,20,000; Sales Return Rs. 10,000; Closing Stock at st Rs. 15,000.

lution:

$$\text{Stock Turnover Ratio} = \frac{\text{Cost of goods sold}}{\text{Average Inventory at Cost}}$$

Cost of goods sold = Opening Stock + Purchases + Direct Expenses – Closing Stock

= Rs. 30,000 + Rs. 1,10,000 + Rs. 10,000 – Rs. 15,000

= Rs. 1,35,000

$$\text{Average Inventory} = \frac{\text{Opening Stock} + \text{Closing Stock}}{2}$$

$$= \frac{30{,}000 + 15{,}000}{2} \quad \frac{\text{Rs. } 45{,}000}{2}$$

= Rs. 22,500

$$\text{Stock Turnover Ratio} = \frac{1{,}35{,}000}{22{,}500} = 6 \text{ times}$$

Valuation of Material Issues

roduction

receipts and issues of materials are the important aspects to continuous flow of duction. A systematic procedure should be adopted for movement of materials from place to another place. Materials received and stored are issued on the basis of res requisition, bills of materials, stock in balance, proper authorization and pricing terial issues etc. It is clear that ascertainment of accurate material cost, fixing of terial issue and effective cost control are the primary objective in order to fulfil the ds of management. For this reasons the following aspects consider to be the subject tter of valuation of materials issues.

(1) Valuation of total cost of materials purchased

(2) Material Issue Procedure

(3) Important methods of pricing of materials issued

(1) Valuation of Total Cost of Materials Purchased : Material costing is very ortant in terms of the valuation of the cost of materials consumed by the production artment as well as in terms of the estimation of the value of materials in stock. For ting purposes, the material cost is work out the actual cost incurred by taking price ted by supplier as the basis subtracting the discounts and adding any other expenses covered. In practice discounts may be allowed by the supplier in the following ways h as (a) Trade Discount, (b) Quantity Discount and (c) Cash Discount.

(a) Trade Discount : Trade Discount is allowed by the seller to the buyer who has resell the goods. This allowance is to compensate the buyer for the cost of storage, breaki bulk, selling repacking the goods etc.

(b) Quantity Discount : This discount refers to the allowance which is allowed by t supplier to the buyer to encourage large orders. Placing the large orders from the buye gives savings in costs which arise from large scale production to the supplier. Part of t savings allowed by supplier to the buyer by means of a quantity discount.

(c) Cash Discount : Cash Discount is allowed by the supplier to a buyer to encoura prompt payment of cash with in the stipulated period.

(2) Materials Issue Procedure : Issues of materials are based on producti programme. Based on this and the bill of materials work orders are printed, listing each material quantity to be issued against each component requiring that materi The store keeper is very much concerned with the material control, as he is responsi for the issue of materials based on the proper authorization of material requisition a bills of materials.

Materials Requisition

Purchase or Material Requisition is also known as Intent for Materials. This is a docum prepared by the production department for requisition of materials is known as Materi Requisition. The store keeper is authorized to issue the materials based on the pro authority to avoid the misappropriation of material. The store keeper is responsible maintained a record of serial number on requisition, issues and stock balances are to date are must be posted in stores ledger.

Bill of Materials

Bill of materials is a document which shows a complete listing for each material, quan to be issued against each component requiring that materials for a particular job or or process. Bill of Materials is prepared by the production department before the quan of the components to be manufactured. This is helpful for the purpose of initiate mate requisition and estimation of cost materials to collect quotations.

(3) Method of Pricing of Materials Issues : In the relation to the estimation of cost of the product for pricing decisions, material issues assures a key role. Mate price usually refers to the price quoted and accepted in the purchase orders. Mater are issued from the stores to work orders based on the material requisition. But stoc materials consists of different consignment received at different dates and prices. Th are different methods used for pricing the materials issues may be summarized in following categories.

(A) Actual Price Method (or) Cost Price Method

(1) First In First Out (FIFO)

(2) Last In First Out (LIFO)

(3) Specific Price Method

(4) Base Stock Method

(5) Highest In First Out (HIFO)

(B) Average Cost Method

(1) Simple Average Method

(2) Weighted Average Method

(3) Periodic Simple Average Method

(4) Periodic Weighted Average Method

(C) Standard Price Method

(D) Inflated Price Method

(E) Market Price Method (or) Replacement Price Method

(A) Actual Price Method : In this method, the materials issued are priced at their actual cost and this involves identification of each lot purchased. This method is suitable only in the case of materials purchased for a specific job. There are several methods frequently used under actual cost price method will be discussed in details:

(1) First In First Out (FIFO) : First In First Out is also known as FIFO. Under this method, the pricing of issue is based on a assumption made that the oldest stock is issued first. Therefore at the time of issue, the rate pertaining to that will be applied until the whole lots is exhausted.

Advantages

(1) It is simple and easy to adaptability

(2) It is beneficial when the prices are falling

(3) As actual prices are issued, it reflecting no profit no loss in the pricing

(4) This method is very useful for slow moving materials.

Disadvantages

(1) Calculation becomes complicated due to fluctuation of material prices.

(2) More chances of clerical errors due to complicated calculations.

(3) Under fluctuating prices, one requisition involves more than one price

(4) In times of raising prices this method tends to show the production at low cost since the cost of replacing the material will be higher.

Illustration: 18

From the following particulars, prepare the Stores Ledger Account showing how the value of the issues would be recorded under FIFO methods.

01.12.2003 Opening Stock 1000 Units at Rs.26 each

05.12.2003 Purchased 500 Units at Rs.24.50 each

07.12.2003 Issued 750 Units

10.12.2003 Purchased 1500 Units at Rs.24 each

12.12.2003 Issued 1100 Units

15.12.2003 Purchased 1000 Units at Rs.25 each

17.12.2003 Issued 500 Units

18.12.2003 Issued 300 Units

25.12.2003 Purchased 1500 Units at Rs.26 each

29.12.2003 Issued 1500 Units

Solution:

Stores Ledger Account (FIFO)

Date	Receipts			Issues			Balance		
	Qty.	Rate Rs.	Amt. Rs.	Qty.	Rate Rs.	Amt. Rs.	Qty.	Rate Rs.	Amt. Rs.
01.12.2003	—	—	—	—	—	—	1,000	26	26,000
05.12.2003	500	24.50	12,250				1,000	26	26,000
							500	24.50	12,250
07.12.2003				750	26	19500	250	26	6,500
							500	24.50	12,250
10.12.2003	1500	24	36,000				250	26	6,500
							500	24.50	12,250
							1,500	24	36,000
12.12.2003				250	26	6,500			
				500	24.50	12,250			
				350	24	8,400	1,150	24	27,600
				1,100					
15.12.2003	1000	25	25,000				1,150	24	27,600
							1,000	25	25,000
17.12.2003				500	24	12,000	650	24	15,600
							1,000	25	25,000
18.12.2003				300	24	7,200	350	24	8,400
							1,000	25	25,000
25.12.2003	1500	26	39,000				350	24	8,400
							1,000	25	25,000
							1,500	26	39,000
29.12.2003				350	24	8400			
				1,000	25	25,000			
				150	26	3,900	1,350	26	35,100
				1,500					

(2) Last In First Out (L I F O) : This method is just opposite to First In First Out method. The basic assumption here is that the most recent receipts are issued first. The price of the materials to be issued would be the cost price of the last lots of materials purchased.

Advantages

(1) It is beneficial when the period of raising prices.

(2) Under this method, latest prices are issued there by leading to lower reported profits hence savings in taxes.

(3) When there are wide fluctuations in price levels this methods tends to minimize unrealized gains or losses in inventory.

Disadvantages

(1) This method involves more clerical work which leads to complicated calculations.

(2) Under this method more than one price is to be adopted for the same issue lot of material.

(3) Due to wide fluctuation of prices, comparison of cost of similar jobs is very difficult.

Illustration: 19

By Solving the illustration No.18, under LIFO method.

Solution:

Stores Ledger Account (LIFO)

Date	Receipts			Issues			Balance		
	Qty.	*Rate Rs.*	*Amt. Rs.*	*Qty.*	*Rate Rs.*	*Amt. Rs.*	*Qty.*	*Rate Rs.*	*Amt. Rs.*
01.12.2003	—	—	—	—	—	—	1,000	26	26,000
05.12.2003	500	24.50	12,250				1,000	26	26,000
							500	24.50	12,250
07.12.2003				500	24.50	12,250			
				250	26	6,500	750	26	19,500
				750					
10.12.2003	1,500	24	36,000				750	26	19,500
							1,500	24	36,000
12.12.2003				1,100	24	26,400	750	26	19,500
							400	24	9,600
15.12.2003	1,000	25	25,000				750	26	19,500
							400	24	9,600
							1,000	25	25,000
17.12.2003				500	25	12,500	750	26	19,500
							400	24	9,600
							500	25	25,000
18.12.2003				300	25	7,500	750	26	19,500
							400	24	9,600
							200	25	5,000
25.12.2003	1,500	26	39,000				750	26	19,500
							400	24	9,600
							200	25	5,000
							1,500	26	39,000
29.12.2003				1,500	26	39,000	750	26	19,500
							400	24	9,600
							200	25	5,000

(3) Specific Price Method : Specific Price Method is one of the methods of actual price method. In this method adopted where the materials are purchased for particular job or operation and the issue is charged with the actual cost price. This method is suitable only in the case of special purpose materials are purchased for a particular job. This method has been widely used in job order industries which carryout individual jobs or contract against specific orders.

Advantages

(1) This method is simple and easy to operate.

(2) This method is useful where the job costing is in operation.

(3) Under this method, the actual material cost can be easily identified.

(4) This method is desirable because actual cost of materials is charged to production and therefore no profit no loses.

Disadvantages

(1) This method involves considerable amount of clerical work.

(2) If the purchases and issues are numerous, it is difficult to identification of issues for a particular job.

(4) Base Stock Method : Under this method pricing is determined on the basis of assumption made here is that a certain minimum quantity of materials maintained in stock. This minimum quantity is known as Base Stock or Safety Stock. This quantity can not be used unless an emergency arises. The minimum stock is in the nature of fixed assets because it is created out of the first lot of the material purchased. Therefore it always valued at the actual cost price of the first lot and is carried forward as a fixed assets. This method is usually applied with FIFO or LIFO.

Illustration: 20

From the following details of stores receipts and issues of materials in a manufacturing unit, prepare the stores ledger using Base Stock Method of valuing the issues; Assume base stock is 200 tonnes.

1.1.2003 Purchased 500 tones at Rs. 2 per tone

10.1.2003 Purchased 300 tones at Rs. 2.10 per tone

15.1.2003 Issued 600 tones

20.1.2003 Purchased 400 tones at Rs. 2.20 per tone

25.1.2003 Issued 300 tones

27.1.2003 Purchased 500 tones at Rs. 2.10 per tone

31.1.2003 Issued 200 tones

Solution :

Stores Ledger Account (Base Stock - FIFO)

Date	Receipts			Issues			Balance		
	Qty.	Rate Rs.	Amt. Rs.	Qty.	Rate Rs.	Amt. Rs.	Qty.	Rate Rs.	Amt. Rs.
01.01.2003	500	2	1,000				500	2	1,000
10.01.2003	300	2.10	630				500	2	1,000
							300	2.10	630
15.01.2003				300	2	600			
				300	2.10	630	200	2	400
20.01.2003	400	2.20	880				200	2	400
							400	2.20	880
25.01.2003				300	2.20	660	200	2	400
							100	2.20	220
27.01.2003	500	2.10	1,050				200	2	400
							100	2.20	220
							500	2.10	1,050
31.01.2003				100	2.20	220	200	2	400
				100	2.10	210	400	2.10	840

Closing Stock = 600 tons (200 × Rs. 2 + 400 × Rs. 2.10) = R. 1,240.

Illustration: 21

By solving illustration No. 20 Under Base Stock—LIFO method

Solution:

Stores Ledger Account (Base Stock - LIFO)

Date	Receipts			Issues			Balance		
	Qty.	Rate Rs.	Amt. Rs.	Qty.	Rate Rs.	Amt. Rs.	Qty.	Rate Rs.	Amt. Rs.
01.01.2003	500	2	1,000				500	2	1,000
10.01.2003	300	2.10	630				500	2	1,000
							300	2.10	630
15.01.2003				300	2	600			
				300	2.10	630	200	2	400
20.01.2003	400	2.20	880				200	2	400
							400	2.20	880
25.01.2003				300	2.20	660	200	2	400
							100	2.20	220
27.01.2003	500	2.10	1,050				200	2	400
							100	2.20	220
							500	2.10	1,050
31.01.2003				200	2.10	420	200	2	400
							100	2.20	220
							300	2.10	330

Closing stock = 600 tons (200 × Rs. 2 + 100 × Rs. 2.20 + 300 × Rs. 2.10) = Rs. 1,250.

(5) Highest In First Out - (HIFO) : This method is based on the assumption that the stock of materials should always be valued at the lowest possible price. Accordingly materials purchased at the highest price should be used for making the issue. This method is useful because issues are based on actual cost. It aims at recovering the highest cost of materials when the market is constantly fluctuating. But at the same time this method involve too many complicated calculations. And also this method has not been adopted widely.

Illustration: 22

From the following details of stores receipts and issues of material "XYZ" in a manufacturing unit prepare the Stores Ledger Using Highest In First Out Method (HIFO) :

2003	January 1 Opening stock 4000 units at Rs.5
"4	Purchased 1000 units at Rs.7 per unit
"8	Purchased 1200 units at Rs.8 per unit
"12	Issued 1000 units
"15	Purchased 700 units at Rs.10 per units
"19	Purchased 300 units at Rs.8 per unit
"23	Issued 800 units
"25	Purchased 500 units at Rs.10 per unit
"31	Issued 400 units.

Solution:

Stores Ledger Account (Base Stock - LIFO)

Date	Receipts			Issues			Balance		
	Qty.	*Rate Rs.*	*Amt. Rs.*	*Qty.*	*Rate Rs.*	*Amt. Rs.*	*Qty.*	*Rate Rs.*	*Amt. Rs.*
01.01.2003							4,000	5	20,000
04.01.2003	1,000	7	7,000				4,000	5	20,000
							1,000	7	7,000
08.01.2003	1,200	8	9,600				4,000	5	20,000
							1,000	7	7,000
							1,200	8	96,000
12.01.2003				1,000	8	8,000	4,000	5	20,000
							1,000	7	7,000
							200	8	1,600
15.01.2003	700	10	7,000				4,000	5	20,000
							1,000	7	7,000
							200	8	1,600
							700	10	7,000
19.01.2003	300	9	2,700				4,000	5	20,000
							1,000	7	7,000

							200	8	1,600
							700	10	7,000
							300	9	2,700
23.01.2003				700	10	7,000	4,000	5	20,000
				100	9	900	1,000	7	7,000
				800			200	8	1,600
							200	9	1,800
25.01.2003	500	10	5,000				4,000	5	20,000
							1,000	7	7,000
							200	8	1,600
							200	9	1,800
							500	10	5,000
31.01.2003				400	10	4,000	4,000	5	20,000
							1,000	7	7,000
							200	8	1,600
							200	9	1,800
							100	10	1,000

B. Average Cost Method : In this method, the issues to the production department are split into equal batches from each shipment at stock. It is a realistic method reflecting the price levels and stabilizing the cost price. The following various methods of averaging issue prices may be used :

(1) Simple Average Method

(2) Weighted Average Method

(3) Periodic Simple Average Method

(4) Periodic Weighted Average Method

(1) Simple Average Method : Under this method, price of issue materials is determined by dividing the total of the prices of the materials in stock *i.e.*, adding of different prices by the number of different prices. Then, this average price is applied to the issues to production. This method is simple and easy to operate. The value of closing stock becomes unrealistic. The following formula is applied for calculation of material issue price under simple average method :

$$\text{Issue Price} = \frac{\text{Total of Unit Prices of Materials in Stock}}{\text{Number of Prices}}$$

Illustration: 23

From the following prepare stores ledger account using Simple Average Method for the month of January 2003.

January 1 opening balance 500 units at Rs.2 per unit

3 Issued 100 units

4 Issued 100 units

8 Issued 100 units
13 Purchased 400 units at Rs. 3 per unit
14 Purchased 200 units at Rs. 1 per unit
16 Issued 150 units
20 Purchased 400 units at Rs. 4 Per unit
24 Issued 250 units
25 Purchased 500 units at Rs. 5 per unit
26 Issued 300 units
28 Purchased 200 units at Rs. 2 per unit
31 Purchased 200 units at Rs. 4 per unit

Solution:

Stores Ledger Account (Simple Average Method)

Date	*Receipts*			*Issues*			*Balance*		
	Qty.	*Rate Rs.*	*Amt. Rs.*	*Qty.*	*Rate Rs.*	*Amt. Rs.*	*Qty.*	*Rate Rs.*	*Amt. Rs.*
01.01.2003	500	2	1,000				500	2	1,000
03.01.2003				100	2	200	400	2	800
04.01.2003				100	2	200	300	2	600
08.01.2003				100	2	200	200	2	400
13.01.2003	400	3	1,200				200	2	400
							400	3	1,200
14.1.2003	200	1	200				200	2	400
							400	3	1,200
							200	1	200
16.01.2003				150	2	300	650		1,500
20.01.2003	400	4	1,600				1,050		3,100
24.01.2003				250	2.5	625	,800		2,475
25.01.2003	500	5	2,500				1,300		4,975
26.01.2003				300	3.25	975	1,000		4,000
28.01.2003	200	2	400				1,200		4,400
31.01.2003	200	4	800				1,400		5,200

Working Notes :

Issue rate on 3rd, 4th and 8th at Rs. 2 per unit

$$\text{Issue rate on } 16^{th} = \frac{\text{Rs. }2 + \text{Rs. }3 + \text{Rs. }1}{3} = \frac{\text{Rs. }6}{3} = \text{Rs. }2$$

$$\text{Issue rate on } 24^{th} = \frac{\text{Rs. }2 + \text{Rs. }3 + \text{Rs. }1 + \text{Rs. }4}{4} = \frac{10}{4} = \text{Rs. }2.5$$

Issue rate on 26th $= \dfrac{\text{Rs. } 3 + \text{Rs. } 1 + \text{Rs. } 4 + \text{Rs. } 5}{4} = \dfrac{13}{4} = \text{Rs. } 3.25$

Simple Average Rate $= \dfrac{\text{Total Unit Prices of Materials in Stock}}{\text{Number of Prices}}$

(2) Weighted Average Method : Under this method, the price of materials issue is determined by dividing the total cost of materials in stock by the total quantity of material in stock. Here weighted average rate is calculated based on both quantity and price of the materials in stock. As more issues are made, a new average rate is computed and this average rate is applied to the subsequent issues. The material issue price is calculated by the formula given below :

Weighted Average Price $= \dfrac{\text{Value of Materials in Stock}}{\text{Quantity in Stock}}$

Illustration: 24

From the following particulars, prepare stores Ledger Account on weight Average basis :

2003 March 1 Opening balance 200 units at Rs. 2 per unit
10 Purchased 300 units at Rs. 2.40 per unit
15 Issued 250 units
18 Purchased 250 units at Rs. 2.60 per unit
20 Issued 200 units.
25 Purchased 300 units at Rs. 2.50 per unit
31 Purchased 100 units at Rs. 2 per unit

Solution:

Stores Ledger Account (Weighted Average Method)

Date	Receipts			Issues			Balance		
	Qty.	*Rate Rs.*	*Amt. Rs.*	*Qty.*	*Rate Rs.*	*Amt. Rs.*	*Qty.*	*Rate Rs.*	*Amt. Rs.*
01.03.2003	200	2	400				200	2	400
10.03.2003	300	2.40	720				200	2	400 }
							300	2.40	720 }
15.03.2003				250	2.24	560	250		560
18.03.2003	250	2.60	650				500		1,210
20.03.2003				200	2.42	484	300		726
25.03.2003	300	2.50	750				600		1,476
31.03.2003	100	2	200				700		1,676

Working Notes:

Issue Price $= \dfrac{\text{Value of Materials in Stock}}{\text{Quantity in Stock}}$

Issue Rate on 15th $= \frac{400 + 720}{200 + 300} = \frac{1120}{500} = $ Rs. 2.24

Issue Rate on 20th $= \frac{560 + 650}{250 + 250} = \frac{1210}{500} = $ Rs. 2.42

(3) Periodic Simple Average Method : Under this method, the simple average rat is calculated for a particular period ignoring the rate of opening stock. The issue price i calculated by totaling the unit price of all materials purchased during a particular perio by the total number of prices during that period. Thus, this rate is applied to the issue t production for a particular period say a month and not at the occasion of each issue c materials.

Illustration: 25

From the following detail of stores receipts and issues of material "EXE" in a manufacturin unit, prepare the Stores Ledger using Periodic Simple Average Method.

2003 January Jan. 1 Opening Stock 200 units at Rs. 2 per unit
Jan. 5 Purchased 400 units at Rs. 3 per unit
Jan. 10 Issued 250 units
Jan. 16 Purchased 500 units at Rs. 3 per unit
Jan. 20 Issued 300 units
Jan. 31 Purchased 200 units at Rs. 4 per unit
Feb. 10 Issued 500 units
Feb. 15 Purchased 400 units at Rs. 4.50 per unit
Feb. 20 Issued 300 units
Feb. 25 Purchased 200 units at Rs. 6 per unit

Solution:

Stores Ledger Account (Periodic Simple Average Method)

Date	*Receipts*			*Issues*			*Balance*		
	Qty.	*Rate Rs.*	*Amt. Rs.*	*Qty.*	*Rate Rs.*	*Amt. Rs.*	*Qty.*	*Rate Rs.*	*Amt. Rs.*
01.01.2003	200	2	400				200	2	400
05.01.2003	400	3	1,200				400		
10.01.2003				250			350		
16.01.2003	500	3	1,500				850		
20.01.2003				300			550		
31.01.2003	200	4	800				750		
	1,300		3,900	550	4.66	2,563	750	4.66	3,495
Feb.1 Balance	750	4.66	3,495				750	4.66	3,495
10.02.2003				500			250		
15.02.2003	400	4.50	1,800				650		
20.02.2003				300			350		
25.02.2003	200	6	1,200				550		
	1,350		6,495	800	5.25	4,200	550	5.25	2,888

Working Notes:

Issue rate on Jan. = $\frac{3+3+4}{3} = \frac{14}{3}$ = Rs. 4.66

Issue rate on Feb. = $\frac{4.50+6}{2} = \frac{10.50}{2}$ = Rs. 5.25

(4) Periodic Weighted Average Method : This method is similar to the periodic simple average method. In this method issue rate is calculated by total cost of materials purchased during a period by the total quantity of materials purchased during that period. Here both quantity and prices of materials in stock during a particular period are taken into account for calculation of periodic weighted average rate. Under this method the issue rate is determined for a particular period ignoring the rate and quantity of opening stock. A new average rate is computed at the end of each period say a month and this average rate is applied to subsequent issues.

Illustration: 26

By solving the illustration No.25, under Periodic Weighted Average Method.

Solution:

Stores Ledger Account (Periodic Simple Average Method)

Date	*Receipts*			*Issues*			*Balance*		
	Qty.	*Rate Rs.*	*Amt. Rs.*	*Qty.*	*Rate Rs.*	*Amt. Rs.*	*Qty.*	*Rate Rs.*	*Amt. Rs.*
01.01.2003	200	2	400				200		
05.01.2003	400	3	1,200				400		
10.01.2003				250			350		
16.01.2003	500	3	1,500				850		
20.01.2003				300			550		
31.01.2003	200	4	800				750		
	1,300		3,900	550	3.18	1,749	750	3.18	2,385
Feb.1 Balance	750	3.18	2,385				750		
10.02.2003				500			250		
15.02.2003	400	4.50	1,800				650		
20.02.2003				300			350		
25.02.2003	200	6	1,200				550		
	1,350		5,385	800	5	4,000	550	5	2,750

Working Notes:

ssue rate on Jan. = $\frac{1200+1500+800}{400+500+200} = \frac{3500}{1100}$ = Rs. 3.18

ssue rate on Feb. = $\frac{1800+1200}{400+200} = \frac{3000}{600}$ = Rs. 5

gnoring Opening Stock of Jan. & Feb.

C. Standard Price Method : Under this method, standard price of material issues are calculated on the basis of detailed analysis of market prices and trends. The standard price also referred to as predetermined price is fixed for a definite period of six months or more. Accordingly the material issue is done on the basis of standard price irrespective of actual rate. The difference between actual price and standard price is treated as material variance. At the end of the period, new standard price is fixed for a further period.

Illustration: 27

From the following particulars prepare a stores Ledger Account by Standard Price Method of issue of materials. The standard price of a material is fixed at Rs.10 per unit.

2003

Mar. 1	Opening stock of materials 1,000 units at Rs. 15 per unit
" 3	Purchased 500 units at Rs. 10 per unit
" 7	Issued 500 units
" 12	Purchased 1,000 units at Rs. 15
" 15	Purchased 800 units at Rs. 10
" 19	Issued 700 units
" 22	Issued 500 units
" 27	Purchased 600 units at Rs. 12
" 29	Issued 300 units
" 30	Purchased 100 units at Rs. 14
" 31	Issued 400 units

Date	*Receipts*			*Issues*			*Balance*		
	Qty.	*Rate Rs.*	*Amt. Rs.*	*Qty.*	*Rate Rs.*	*Amt. Rs.*	*Qty.*	*Rate Rs.*	*Amt. Rs.*
01.03.2003							1,000	15	15,000
							1,500		20,000
03.03.2003	500	10	5,000						
07.03.2003				500	10	5,000	1,000		15,000
12.03.2003	1,000	15	15,000				2,000		30,000
15.03.2003	800	10	8,000				2,800		38,000
19.03.2003				700	10	7,000	2,100		31,000
22.03.2003				500	10	5,000	1,600		26,000
27.03.2003	600	12	7,200				2,200		33,200
29.03.2003				300	10	3,000	1,900		30,200
30.03.2003	100	14	1,400				2,000		31,600
				400	10	4,000	1,600		27,600

D. Inflated Price Method : This method is used to cover material losses on account of obsolescence, deterioration, and materials handling expenses. Under this method st of materials issue, such losses and expenses are directly charged to material cost. erefore, when the issue of materials is made, the price is to inflated to cover all the sses and expenses.

E. Market Price Method : This method is also known as Replacement Rate Method. der this method issue materials that are valued at the market rate prevailing at the ne issue. It therefore follows that when prices increase the stock on hand is ntinuously under estimated because receipts are cost at actual and issued at higher tes. Conversely hand grossly over estimated. This method is most suitable when otations or tenders have to be made because they are to be quoted at competitive ices. Besides this system requires continuous monitoring of market price for all aterials and hence it is very unwieldy.

CHOOSE THE CORRECT ANSWER

———— refers to the scientific way of determining the requirement of raw materials, components spares and other items that go into meeting production needs.

(a) Materials Planning (b) Production Planning

(c) Sales Planning (d) Both a and b

———— refers to the process of systematically defining and describing all items in stock

(a) Identification (b) Classification (c) Codification (d) Grading

———— refers to assigning or giving a code number or symbol to a store item

(a) Classification (b) Codification (c) Grading (d) Identification

Material Handling is the ————

(a) Art (b) Science (c) Both a and b (d) Profession

Safety stock is also called as ————

(a) Minimum Inventory (b) Buffer Stock

(c) Reserve Stock (d) All the above

Inventory Control is the function relating to

(a) Production Management (b) Material Management

(c) Marketing Management (d) Production and Material Management

Cost of receiving and inspecting the materials relates to

(a) Ordering Cost (b) Carrying Costs

(c) Storage Space Cost (d) Inventory Service Cost

A B C Analysis stands for ————

(a) Always Better Control (b) Always Best Control

(c) Accurate Better Control (d) Always Before Control

According to ABC Classification 'C' indicates ————

(a) High in value and low in quantity

(b) High in quantity and low in value

(c) More or less equal in quantity and in value

(d) None of these

Answer : (1) d—Both a and b (2) a—Identification (3) b—Codification (4) c—Both a and
(5) d—All the above (6) d—Production and material Management
(7) a—Ordering Cost (8) a—Always Better Control
(9) b—High in quantity and low in value

QUESTIONS

(1) What do you meant by store and store keeping?

(2) Explain the purpose of store keeping.

(3) What are the important function of store keeper?

(4) What do you mean by stores layout?

(5) Explain briefly the different types of stores.

(6) What do you understand by Maximum Stock, Minimum Stock and Re order Level?

(7) What is Economic Order Quantity? Explain its significance.

(8) Explain the concept of A B C Analysis.

(9) Explain briefly the Classification and Codification of materials.

(10) What are the advantages of Codification?

(11) Explain briefly the Methods of Coding.

(12) What is Perpetual Inventory System? Explain its advantages.

(13) What do you understand by Bin Card and Stores Ledger?

(14) What are the differences between Bin Card and Stores Ledger?

(15) What is Continuous Stock Verification? What are the differences between continuou Stock Taking and Periodic Stock Taking?

(16) Explain briefly the material storage losses.

(17) What is Inventory Turnover Ratio? Explain its importance.

(18) Discuss the various methods of pricing materials issues to production.

(19) Which of the issuing methods would you recommend under conditions of raisin prices and why?

(20) What do you understand by FIFO? What are its merits and demerits?

(21) What do you understand by LIFO? What are its merits and demerits?

(22) What is Specific Price Method? Explain its significance.

(23) Write short notes on :

(a) Base Stock Method

(b) Market Price Method

(c) Inflated Price Method

(d) Standard Price Method

(24) From the following particulars calculate

(a) Re-order Level

(b) Minimum Level

(c) Maximum Level

(d) Average Level

Normal usage 100 units per day

Maximum usage 130 units per day

Minimum usage 60 units per day

Economic Order Quantity 5,000 units

Re order Period 25 to 30 days

ns : (a) Reorder Level = 3,900 units

(b) Minimum Level = 1,150 units

(c) Maximum Level = 7,400 units

(d) Average Level = 4,275 units]

5) Calculate E O Q from the following:

Annual Consumption = 600 units

Ordering Cost Rs. 12 per order

Carrying Cost 20%

Price per unit Rs. 20

ns : E O Q = 60 units]

5) Calculate (a) Maximum Level (b) Minimum Level and (c) Re order Level

Re order Quantity = 1,500 units

Re order Period = 4 to 6 weeks

Maximum Consumption = 400 units per week

Normal Consumption = 300 units per week

Maximum Consumption = 250 units per week

ns : Re order Level = 2,400 units

Maximum Level = 2,900 units

Minimum Level = 900 units

Normal Re order Period = 5 weeks]

) A manufacturing company purchases 2000 units of a particular material per year at a unit cost of Rs. 20, the ordering cost per order is Rs. 50 and the inventory carrying cost is 25%. Find out the Economic Order Quantity and number of orders to be placed in a year.

s : E O Q 200 units each in 10 orders]

) Calculate Economic Order Quantity from the following particulars:

Annual Consumption = 20,000 units

Buying Cost per order Rs. 10

Cost per unit Rs. 100

Inventory Carrying Cost 10% of cost

s : E O Q = 200 units]

) The following information is available in respect of Material X

Re order Quantity = 3,000 units

Re order Period = 4 to 6 weeks

Maximum Consumption = 800 units per week

Normal Consumption = 600 units per week

Minimum Consumption = 500 units per week

Calculate : (a) Re order Level (b) Minimum Level

(c) Maximum Level (d) Average Stock Level

[Ans : (a) Re order Level = 4,800 units; Minimum Level = 1,800 units

Maximum Level 5,800 units; Average Stock Level : 3,800]

(30) The following information is available in respect of Component Y

Maximum Stock Level 84,000 units

Maximum Consumption 1,500 units per month

Minimum Consumption 800 units per month

Re-order period 2 to 4 months

You are required to calculate

(1) Re-order Level

(2) Re-order Quantity

(Ans : 6,000 units; 4,000 units)

(31) Two Components of X and Y are used as follows :

Normal usage 50 units per week each

Minimum usage 25 units per week each

Maximum usage 75 units per week each

Re-order Quantity X : 400 units, Y : 600 units

Re-order Period X : 4 weeks, Y : 2 to 4 weeks

Calculate for each components

(a) Re-order Level

(b) Minimum Level

(c) Maximum Level

(d) Average Stock Level

[Ans : (a) 300 units (b) 150 units (c) 850 units (d) 500 units.]

32. Calculate the economic order quantity from the following particulars

Annual requirement 1,600 units

Cost of materials per units Rs. 40

Cost of placing and receiving one order Rs. 50

Annual carrying cost of inventory 10% of inventory value

(33) Calculate economic order quantity from the following

Annual consumption 600 units

Ordering cost Rs. 12 per unit

Carrying cost 20%

Price per unit Rs. 20

[Ans : 60 units]

(34) Find out the economic order quantity and the number of orders per year from the following information.

Annual consumption 36,000 units

Cost per units Rs. 54

Ordering cost Rs. 150 per order

Inventory carrying cost 20% of the average inventory

[Ans : EOQ—1,000 units, No. of orders 36]

(35) The following information relating material Q.75 is available,

Annual consumption 2,400 units

Cost per unit Rs. 2.40

Ordering Cost per order Rs. 4

Storage cost 2% per annum

Interest rate 10% per annum

Calculate EOQ and No. of orders to be placed in a year

(Ans : EOQ-258 units : No. of orders 10)

(36) 2003 Jan 2 Purchased 4,000 units at Rs. 4.40 per unit

Jan 20 Purchased 500 units at Rs. 5 per unit

Feb. 5 Issued 2,000 units

Feb.10 Purchased 6,000 units at Rs. 6 per unit

Feb.12 Issued 4,000 units

March 2 Issued 1,000 units

March 5 Issued 2,000 units

March 15 Purchased 4,500 units at Rs. 5.50 per unit

March 20 Issued 3,000 units

From the above, prepare the stores ledger account in two ways (a) by adopting FIFO (b) by adopting LIFO method.

(Ans : (1) FIFO Closing Stock = 3,000 units at Rs. 5.50 = Rs. 16,500

(2) LIFO Closing Stock = 3,000 units

1,500 units at Rs. 4	=	6,000
1,500 units at Rs. 5.50	=	8,250
Total 3,000 units	=	14,250

)

(37) From the following receipts and payments of a material X prepare a stores ledger account showing under Simple Average Method and Weighted Average Method.

2003 Jan 1 Opening stock 200 units at Rs. 3.50 per unit

3 Purchased 300 units at Rs. 4 per unit

5 Issued 400 units

13 Purchased 900 units at Rs. 4.30 per unit

15 Issued 600 units

23 Purchased 600 units at Rs. 3.80 per unit

25 Issued 600 units.

(Ans : Issued price rate 5th, 15th, 25th, closing stock

(a) Simple Average Rs. 3.75, 4.15, 4. 400 units Rs. 1,630

(b) Weighted Average Rs. 3.80, 4.25, 3.98, 400 units Rs. 1,592)

(38) From the following receipts and payments of a material X prepare stores ledger account under Base Stock Method with FIFO. Assume base stock of 400 units out of opening stock

2003 Jan. 1 Opening stock 1,000 units at Rs. 2 each

3 Purchased 800 units at Rs. 2.10 per unit

5 Issued 800 units

12 Purchased 1,600 units at Rs. 2.10 per unit

17 Issued 1,500 units

20 Purchased 900 units at Rs. 2.50 per unit

25 Issued 600 units

(Ans : Closing stock : Base Stock 400 units at Rs. 2 per unit = Rs. 800

Closing Balance 100 units at Rs. 2.10 = Rs. 210

900 units at Rs. 2.50 = Rs. 2,250)

MANAGEMENT OF ACCOUNTS RECEIVABLE (SUNDRY DEBTORS)

Meaning & Definition

trader very often buy and sells goods on credit. Credit is a very powerful instrument to romote sales. In working capital management Sundry Debtors are one of the significant nd major components. In a business concern next to inventories and cash, the accounts ceivable is considered to be an important aspect of financial planning and control. The orld 'Account Receivable' otherwise termed as 'Sundry Debtors' or 'Trade Debtors' or ook Debts'. Sundry Debtors may be define as "money due from a customer for sale of oods or services in the ordinary course of business".

According to Receivable Management, the term Accounts Receivable is defined as ebt owned to the firm by customers arising from sale of goods or services". Accordingly, hen a purchaser makes the purchases on credit, he undertakes to make the payment the goods purchased to the seller at a future date. In other words, when goods or rvices sold on credit finished goods get converted into accounts receivable in the books the seller. On the other hand, debt due to the seller or any goods or services purchases credit is termed as Accounts Payable or Sundry Creditors or Trade Creditors.

A firm's total volume of business in accounts receivable at any one time depends on sell on credit and collection policies. These policies significantly influence working pital requirements. In order to achieve efficient accounts receivable management, it essential to consider the following aspects of credit management.

1. Objectives of Accounts Receivable Management
2. Advantages or Benefits of Trade Debtors Management
3. Costs of Maintaining Accounts Receivable
4. Formulation of Credit Policies :
   (a) Credit Standard
   (b) Credit Analysis (or) Credit Evaluation
   (c) Credit Terms or Terms of Credit

(d) Cash Discount

(e) Cash Discount Period

(f) Credit Period

5. Execution of Credit Policies :

(i) Determination of Size of Receivables

(ii) Control or Forecasting of Accounts Receivables

Objectives of Receivable Management

The following are the objectives of receivable management :

(1) To increase the volume of sales.

(2) To ensure the adequate flow of cash from trade debtors to meet curren obligations.

(3) To facilitate liberal credit transactions.

(4) To settle trade debts without loss.

(5) To promote international trade transactions.

(6) To achieve the target return on investments.

(7) To create an essential part of competitive business.

(8) To create a written proof about debt obligations.

(9) To achieve the objectives or goals of the organization.

(10) To minimize the cost and risk involved in trade credit planning and control.

(11) To create additional source of finance through accounts receivable.

(12) To maintain adequate liquid capital of the firm.

(13) To ensure credit worthiness or financial soundness of the concern.

(14) To measure the effective handling of accounts receivables.

(15) To take the maximum advantages of trade discount and cash discount facilitie

(16) To aim at a weigh the benefit against risk or cost.

Advantages or Benefits of Receivable Management

The main benefits of receivable management can be enumerated as follows :

(1) Liberalized credit policy helps to increase the growth of sales.

(2) It helps to increase the operating profits because of more credit sales.

(3) Credit policy helps to meet the competition.

(4) Credit sales helps to attract the existing customer but also to new customers i the ordinary course of business.

(5) It ensure higher investment in trade debtors will produce larger sales.

(6) It helps to minimize bad debts without taking stringent measures.

(7) It facilitates adequate working capital to meet its current obligations.

(8) It gives the guidance to the management for effective financial planning an control.

(9) It helps to make effective co-ordination between finance, production, sales, prof and cost.

Cost of Maintaining Accounts Receivables

The following specific costs are identified while extension of credit and maintaining accounts receivables :

(1) Capital Costs

(2) Administration Costs

(3) Collection Costs

(4) Delinquency Costs

(5) Default Cost

(1) Capital Costs : The increased level of accounts receivable is an investment in current assets results in blocking of the firm's capital. There is a time lag between the sale of goods to and the payments by them. Meanwhile, the firm has to arrange for additional funds eitner from outside or out of retained profits or share capital to pay employees and suppliers of raw materials etc. while waiting for payment for its customers. The firm incurs a cost on account of arising additional capital to support credit sales, the capital which alternatively could be earned profitably employed else where.

(2) Administration Costs : Another costs comes from an enlarged credit department. This cost involved in the form of clerical working involved in checking additional accounts serving the added volume of receivables, maintaining accounting records, cost of conducting investigation to assess the credit worthiness of the customers.

(3) Collection Costs : Some costs are to be incurred by a firm for collecting the amount from the customers on account of credit sales. Sometimes, additional expenses involves sending frequent follow up letters, cost of collection of exchange or cost of discounting bills and expenses of stringent action against default customers etc.

(4) Delinquency Cost : These cost are those which are to be incurred by a firm when extending credit to the defaulting customers. The delinquency costs includes the:

(a) Committing funds to the investments additional receivables for extended credit period.

(b) Cost involved in putting extra effort to recover the over dues from the customers.

(c) Cost associated with frequent reminders.

(d) Cost incurred on account of legal charges.

(5) Default Costs : Another cost comes from the probability of bad debt losses. The cost of bad debts which arises due to firm may not able to recover from defaulting customers.

(4) Formulation of Credit Policies : Economic Conditions, product pricing, product quality and the firm's credit policies are the chief influences on the level of a firm's account receivable credit policy can have a significant boosting on sales. Thus, credit is one of the many factors that stimulate the demand for a firm's product. The term credit policy refers to a firm contains guidelines for determining quality of trade accounts to be accepted, the length of the credit period, the cash discount, any special term given, such as seasonal dating, the collection programme and policy as to discounting of bills.

Determination of credit policy involves a trade-off between the profit on additional sales that arise due to credit being extended on the one hand and the cost of carrying those debtors and losses suffered on account of bad debts on the other hand.

The important dimensions of a firm's credit policies are :

(a) Credit Standard

(b) Credit Analysis

(c) Credit Terms

(d) Cash Discount

(e) Cash Discount Period

(f) Credit Period

(a) Credit Standard : The credit standard refers to the minimum quality of credit worthiness of a credit applicant that is acceptable to the firm. In other words, the quality of the trade accounts to be accepted is called as credit standard.

Types of Credit Standard

Credit Standards that adopted by a firm may be broadly classified into two categories :

I. Lenient or Liberal Credit Standard

II. Strict or Restrictive Credit Standard

(I) Liberal Credit Standard indicates : The following effects are the indicate on liberal credit standard :

(1) The firm can stimulate sales and attracting more customers.

(2) Increased sales may be accompanied by added costs, the Gross Profit may be high due to growth of sales.

(3) It involves larger working capital investment in receivables.

(4) Higher rate of bad debt losses resulting from extension of credit facilities to less credit worthy customers.

(5) Average collection period may be slower.

(6) High cost of establishment charges due to enlarged credit department.

(7) Additional cost incurs due to clerical expenses involved in investigating additional accounts.

(8) Cost of servicing involved in added volume of receivables.

(9) Collection cost may be higher.

(10) Higher rate of default because of the inability of the customer.

(11) It incurs higher costs for capital tied in accounts receivables.

(12) Expected rate of return or gross margin is likely to be affected by the added costs.

(II) Strict or Restrictive Credit Standard Indicate : In the firm adopting stricter credit policy the effect may be represented as follows :

(1) Decrease in sales as few customers are attracted.

(2) Reduce the incidence of bad debt loss.

(3) Decrease the amount of working capital to finance receivables.

(4) Credit standards of the firm are normally high.

(5) Strict credit policy is difficult to attract or satisfy the customers.

(6) Low collection cost is possible.

(7) Low cost carrying the debtors.

(8) It facilitates discounting bills from banks without risk or loss.

(9) Extension of credit facilities available to more credit worthy customers only.

(10) Decrease in profit due to decrease in sales.

Effect of Liberalizing Credit Standards on Profit

To assess the profitability of a more liberal extension of credit, we must assess the following dimensions:

(1) Profitability of increased volume of sales

(2) Increased demand for products arising from the liberalized credit standards

(3) Increased length of average collection period

(4) Increased in receivable investments

(5) Bad Debt loss ratio on additional sales

(6) Required return on investment

From the above dimension, it is observed that if credit standard are relaxed, the volume of sales are expected to increase. On the other hand, if credit standard are tightened, the expected volume of sales will be decline.

The effect of liberalizing the credit standard on profit may be estimated on the basis of matching between the profits or incremental earnings resulting from increased sales and the costs to be incurred or associated with relaxation of credit terms. Accordingly, with the help of analysis of profitability versus required return in evaluating a credit standard change the financial manager should strive to determine credit standard for the firm.

Simply, it can be expressed that, if it additional profit on sales exceeds the cost of incremental investment in accounts receivable, the said proposal may be accepted and the same should be rejected in the opposite case.

The effect on profit resulting from the liberalizing the credit standard may be estimated as follows :

(1) Additional or Increased Profit on Sales : It can be ascertained in the following ways:

(a) By Shorter Approach

(b) By Longer Approach

(ii) Cost of Investment Increment in Accounts Receivable

I. Additional or Increased Profit on Sales :

(a) By Short Cut Method : According to this method, the formulas are used to measure the following :

$$\text{Profitability of Additional Sales} = \text{Contribution Margin Per Unit} \times \text{Additional Units Sold}$$

$$\text{Additional Receivables} = \frac{\text{Additional Sales Revenue}}{\text{Receivable Turnover for New Customers}}$$

$$\text{Investment in Additional Receivable} = \frac{\text{Variable Cost Per Unit}}{\text{Sales Price Per Unit}} \times \text{Additional Receivables}$$

Required before – tax return on additional investment } = Opportunity Cost × Investment in Additional Receivable

(b) Longer Approach : Under this method, the costs and profits on existing sales and proposed sales will be determined and the difference in profit will be treated as incremental profit. Accordingly, the incremental earnings resulting from increased sales must be matched with incremental costs associated with relaxation of credit terms before taking the final decisions.

Illustration: 1

The following are the details regarding the operation of a firm during a period 12 months.

Sales	Rs. 24,00,000
Selling Price Per Unit	Rs. 20
Variable Cost Price Per Unit	Rs. 14
Total Cost Per Unit	Rs. 18

Credit Period allowed to customers one month

The firm is considering a proposal for a more liberal extension of credit which will result in increasing the average collection period from one month to two months. This relaxation is expected to increase the sales by 25% from its existing level.

You are required to advise the firm regarding adoption of the new credit policy. Presuming that it firm's required return on investment 25%.

Solution:

Relaxing Credit Standards : Profit Vs Retired Return :

Computation of New Sales = Present Sales + Additional Sales

Present Sales = 1,20,000 units × Rs. 20 = Rs. 24,00,000

Additional Sales in Units = 25% of Present Sales

Additional Sales in Value = 30,000 units × Rs. 20 per unit = Rs. 6,00,000

∴ Total of New Sales = Rs. 24,00,000 + Rs. 6,00,000 = Rs. 30,00,000

Computation of New Total Cost :

New Total Cost = Present Total Cost + Cost of Additional Sales

Present Total Cost of Sales = 1,20,000 units × Rs. 18 = Rs. 21,60,000

Cost of Additional Sales (only variable cost) = 30,000 units × Rs. 14 = Rs. 4,20,000

Total Cost of New Sales of 1,50,000 units (1,20,000 units + 30,000 units) } = Rs. 25,80,000

$$\text{New average cost per unit} = \frac{\text{New Total Cost of Sales}}{\text{New Total Sales in Units}}$$

$$= \frac{\text{Rs. } 25{,}80{,}000}{1{,}50{,}000 \text{ units}} = \text{Rs. } 17.2 \text{ per unit}$$

Average Investment in Receivables after Credit Standard Relaxation (Cost) :

Total of annual new sales in units = $\frac{\text{New Total Sales}}{\text{Selling Price Per Unit}}$

$= \frac{\text{Rs. } 30,00,000}{\text{Rs. } 20} = 1,50,000$ units

Cost of Sales (1,50,000 units × Rs. 17.2 per unit) = Rs. 25,80,000

Average Collection Period = 2 months

Amount invested in Receivable = Rs. 25,80,000 × $\frac{2}{12}$ = Rs. 4,30,000

(New Investments)

Additional investment in receivables = New Investment – Existing Investment

New Investments = Rs. 4,30,000

Existing Investment = $\frac{\text{Rs. } 21,60,000}{12}$ = Rs. 1,80,000

∴ Additional Investment in receivable = Rs. 4,30,000 – Rs. 1,80,000 = Rs. 2,50,000

Profitability of Additional Sales = Additional Unit Sold × Contribution Per Unit

Additional Unit Sold = 30,000 units

Contribution Per Unit = Selling Price Per Unit – Variable Cost Per Unit

= Rs.20 – Rs.14

= Rs. 6

Profitability of Addition Sales = 30,000 units × Rs. 6

= Rs. 1,80,000

Return on Additional Investment in Receivable = $\frac{\text{Profitability of Additional Sales}}{\text{Additional Investment in Receivable}} \times 100$

$= \frac{\text{Rs. } 1,80,000}{\text{Rs. } 2,50,000} \times 100$

= 72%

Command : The required return on investment is only 25% While the actual return on additional investment in receivables come to 72%. The proposal should, therefore be accepted.

Illustration: 2

A firm's current credit sales are Rs. 36,00,000. The firm is considering of lowering its credit standards, which will result in a slowing in the average collection period from one to two months. This relaxation is expected to increase sales by 20 percent. The firm's required return to investment is 20 percent. At the existing level of sales, the production and selling cost is 90 percent of sales. The variable production and selling cost of increased volume of sales will be 70 percent of sales. Should the credit standards be relaxed?

Solution:

The decision to relax credit standard will depends upon :

(1) Additional Profit on Sales and

(2) Required return on incremental investment in account receivables.

Matching Profit and Required Return of Liberalizing Credit Standards.

		Rs.
Profit on additional sales (Rs. 7,20,000 × 30%)	=	2,16,000
Current average investment in receivables (cost) (Rs. 36,00,000 ÷ 12 × 90%)	=	2,70,000
Average investment in receivables after credit Standard relaxation (cost) (3,60,000 ÷ 6) × 90% + (7,20,000 ÷ 6)	=	6,24,000
Additional investment receivables (*i.e.*, Rs. 6,24,000 – 2,70,000)	=	3,54,000
Required return on additional investment Rs. 3,54,000 × 20%	=	70,800

The profit on additional sales is Rs. 2,16,000 while the required return on additional investment is only Rs. 70,800. It is, therefore desirable to relax the credit standard.

Working Notes:

(1) Calculation of Addition Sales :

$$\text{Addition Sales 20\% of Existing Sales} = \text{Rs. } 36{,}00{,}000 \times \frac{20}{100} = \text{Rs. } 7{,}20{,}000$$

(2) Calculation of Profit on Additional Sales :

Additional Sales = Rs. 7,20,000

Profit on Additional Sales = 30% of Additional Sales

$$= \text{Rs. } 7{,}20{,}000 \times \frac{30}{100}$$

= Rs. 2,16,000

(3) Calculation of Additional Investment in Sales :

= New Investment – Existing Investment (or)

= Average investment in receivable after credit standard relaxed – Current Average Investment in Receivable

= Rs. 6,24,000 – Rs. 2,70,000

= Rs. 3,54,000

Illustration: 3

A firm's current credit terms are "net 30". It is considering to change them to "3/15 net 45" credit terms in order to push sales. The proposed change is expected to have the following implications :

	Rs.
Current Sales	50,00,000
Add : Estimated Additional Sales	5,00,000
Total Sales	55,00,000
Estimated total sales that will avail discount offer	15,00,000
Estimated increased receivables	4,00,000

Estimated increased costs :

Bed debt losses	1% of increased sales
Production and selling	70% of increased sales
Administrative expenses	47% of increased sales
Opportunity cost	10% of increased investment in receivables
Cash discount	3% of total sales that avail discount

Is it desirable to produce the changes in credit terms?

Solution:

Comparing cost and Benefits of Liberal Credit Terms

Particulars	*Rs.*	*Rs.*
Increased Sales		5,00,000
Less : Increased Costs :		
Bad Debts	5,000	
Production and Selling Costs	3,50,000	
Administrative Expenses	20,000	
Opportunity Cost	29,600	
Cash Discount	45,000	4,49,600
Increased Profits		50,400

Working Notes:

(1) Calculation of Bad Debt losses :

1% of increased Sales $= 5,00,000 \times \frac{1}{100}$

$= \text{Rs. } 5,000$

(2) Calculation of Production and Selling Expenses :

70% of increased Sales $= \text{Rs. } 5,00,000 \times \frac{70}{100}$

$= \text{Rs. } 3,50,000$

(3) Calculation of Administrative Expenses :

4% of increased Sales $= \text{Rs. } 5,00,000 \times \frac{4}{100}$

$= \text{Rs } 20,000$

(4) Calculation of opportunity cost :

Opportunity Cost :

= 10% of increased investment × (70% of production and selling expense of cost of increased investment + 4% of Administrative expenses of cost of increase investment)

$$10\% \text{ of increased investment} = \text{Rs. } 4,00,000 \times \frac{10}{100} \text{ Rs. } 40,000$$

$$70\% \text{ of production and selling cost of increased investment} = \text{Rs. } 40,000 \times \frac{70}{100}$$

$$= \text{Rs. } 28,000$$

$$4\% \text{ of administrative expenses of increased investment} = \text{Rs. } 40,000 \times \frac{4}{100} = \text{Rs. } 1,60$$

∴ Total opportunity cost = Rs. 28,000 + Rs. 1,600 = Rs. 29,600

Calculation Cash Discount :

3% of Estimated Total Sales of Rs. 15,00,000

$$= \text{Rs. } 15,00,000 \times \frac{3}{100} = \text{Rs. } 45,000$$

Comment : In this case, the relaxation in the credit term is desirable because th profits generated by increased sales are greater than the cost of increased sale.

Illustration: 4

ABC Ltd is considering relaxing its credit policy and evaluating two proposed pla Currently the firm has credit sales amounting to Rs. 50,00,000 and accounts receivabl of Rs. 12,50,000. The current level of loss due to bad debts is Rs. 1,50,000. The firm required to give a return of 20% on investment in the new (additional) accounts receivab The company's variable costs are 70% of the selling price. The following for the informati is given below:

Particulars	*Present Plan*	*Proposed Plan I*	*Proposed Plan II*
Annual Credit Sales	50,00,000	60,00,000	67,50,000
Accounts Receivable	12,50,000	20,00,000	28,12,500
Bad Debt Losses	1,50,000	3,00,000	4,50,000

What will be the most rewarding credit plan in the cash ABC Ltd under the abo circumstances?

Solution:

Statement of Evaluation of Credit Policies

Particulars	*Present Plan*	*Proposed Plan I*	*Proposed Plan II*
Annual Credit Sales	50,00,000	60,00,000	67,50,000
Increase in Sales over Present Sales	—	10,00,000	17,50,000
Contribution on increase in Sales @ 30%	—	3,00,000	5,25,000
Increase in bad debt losses over present bad debt losses	—	1,50,000	3,00,000
Net Contribution	—	1,50,000	2,25,000
Required return on investment in additional account receivable	—	1,50,000	3,12,500
Surplus/Deficit	—	Nil	(-) 87,500

Comment : It is advised that proposed plan I should be exercised as it meets the required return of 20% on investment in the new (additional) accounts receivable.

Working Notes:

(1) Calculation of Additional Sales :

Additional Sales of Plan I = Rs. 6,00,00,000 – Rs. 50,00,000
= Rs. 10,00,000

Additional Sales of Plan II = Rs. 67,50,000 – 50,00,000
= Rs. 17,50,000

(2) Contribution on Increase in Sales :

Plan I @ 30% of Rs. 10,00,000 = Rs. 10,00,000 × $\frac{30}{100}$
= Rs. 3,00,000

Plan II @ 30% of Rs. 17,50,000 = Rs. 17,50,000 × $\frac{30}{100}$
= Rs. 5,25,000

(3) Calculation of Additional Investment in Receivables :

Additional Investment in receivables = New Investment – Existing Investment

Plan I = Rs. 20,00,000 – Rs. 12,50,000
= Rs. 7,50,000

Plan II = Rs. 28,12,500 – Rs. 12,50,000
= Rs. 15,62,500

(4) Required return on investment on Additional Investment on Receivables :

Plan I, 20% of Rs. 7,50,000 additional receivables = Rs. 7,50,000 × $\frac{20}{100}$

= Rs. 1,50,000

Plan II, 20% of Rs. 15,62,500 additional receivables = $15,62,500 \times \frac{20}{100}$

= Rs. 3,12,500

Illustration: 5

XYZ Ltd is examining the question of relaxing its credit policy. It sells at present 60000 units at a price of Rs. 20 per unit, the variable cost per unit is Rs. 12 and average cost per unit at the current sales volume is Rs.16. All the sales are on credit, the average collection period being 30 days. The firm desire to relax the credit standard for which sales are expected to the credit standard for which sales are expected to increase by 15% and the average age of receivables increased by 15 days. Assuming 15% return on investment should the firm relax its credit policy?

Solution:

Incremental Analysis (Relaxation in Credit Terms or Not)

Particulars	*Existing Plant 60,000 units*	*Proposed Plan 69,000 units*	*Differential Cost and Revenue*
Sales Revenue @ Rs. 20 per unit	12,00,000	13,80,000	(+) 1,80,000
Less : Cost :			
(1) Variable cost @ Rs. 12 per unit	7,20,000	8,28,000	(+) 1,08,000
(2) Fixed Cost @ Rs. 4 Per unit	2,40,000	2,40,000	—
(3) Investment Cost	12,000	20,025	(+) 8,025
Incremental Profit	2,28,000	2,91,975	(+) 63,975

The firm should relax its credit policy as it increases profit by Rs. 63,975.

Working Notes:

(1) Calculation of Variable Cost :

Variable Cost of Present Plan = 60,000 units × Rs. 12 per unit

= Rs. 7,20,000

Proposed Plant = 69,000 units × Rs. 12 per unit

= Rs. 8,28,000

(2) Calculation of Fixed Cost :

Contribution = Average cost of Sales Volume Per Unit—Variable Cost Per Unit

= Rs. 16 – Rs. 12 = Rs. 4

Thus, Rs. 4 represent the contribution of each of the 60,000 units towards the fixed cost.

Total fixed cost of present plan = 60,000 units × Rs. 4 per unit

= Rs. 2,40,000

Proposed Plan = Rs. 2,40,000 (remain constant)

(3) Calculation of investment in accounts receivable :

$$= \frac{\text{Total Variable Cost + Total Fixed Cost}}{\text{Average age of accounts receivable in a year}}$$

Average age of accounts receivable in a year :

$$\text{Present Plan} = \frac{360 \text{ days}}{30 \text{ days}} = 12 \text{ times}$$

$$\text{Proposed Plan} = \frac{360 \text{ days}}{45 \text{ days}} = 8 \text{ times}$$

$$\therefore \text{Investment in accounts receivable for present plan} = \frac{\text{Rs. } 7{,}20{,}000 + \text{Rs. } 2{,}40{,}000}{12}$$

$$= \frac{\text{Rs. } 9{,}60{,}000}{12} = \text{Rs. } 80{,}000$$

$$\text{Investment in accounts receivable for proposed plan} = \frac{\text{Rs. } 8{,}28{,}000 + \text{Rs. } 2{,}40{,}000}{2}$$

$$= \frac{\text{Rs. } 10{,}68{,}000}{8} = \text{Rs. } 1{,}33{,}500$$

(4) Cost of investment in receivable :

resent Plan (15% of investment in accounts receivable) = Rs. 80,000 × $\frac{15}{100}$ = Rs. 12,000

roposed plan (15% of investment in accounts receivable) = Rs. 1,33,500 × $\frac{15}{100}$ = Rs. 20,025

(5) Calculation of Incremental Profit = Profit on Existing Plan – Profit on Propose Plan

Profit = Total Sales Revenue – Total Cost

Profit on Present Plan = Rs. 12,00,000 – Rs. 9,72,000 = Rs. 2,28,000

Profit on Proposed Plan = Rs. 13,80,000 – Rs. 10,88,025 = Rs. 2,91,975

Incremental Profit = Rs. 2,28,000 – Rs. 2,91,975

= Rs. 63,975

(6) Calculation of required return on increased investment = 15% of Rs. 8,025

$$= \text{Rs. } 8{,}025 \times \frac{15}{100}$$

= Rs. 1,203. 75

From the above analysis, it is observed that the additional profit on increased rate e., Rs. 63,975) is more than this cost or such incremental investment is accounts ceivable (*i.e.*, Rs. 1,203.75) due to relaxing of credit standard. Hence it is justified.

Illustration: 6

Sivadasan & Co Ltd is currently selling 60,000 units at the rate of Rs. 20 per unit. The cost per unit is Rs. 16 at current level of production and variable cost per unit Rs. 12. The company's current credit policy is extension of credit for 30 days. The management is contemplating to extend credit for a two month period so as to boost sales by 30 percent The company's required rate of return on investments is 15 percent should the management liberalize credit standards?

Solution:

Incremental Analysis (Liberalizing Credit Standard or Not)

Particulars		*Present Plan 60,00 units*	*Proposed Plan 78,000 units*	*Differential Revenues and Costs*
Sales Revenue (Rs.) (60,000 units @ Rs. 20; 78,000 units @ Rs. 20)		12,00,000	15,60,000	+ 3,60,000
Less :				
Variable Cost @ Rs. 12 per unit	(Rs.)	7,20,000	9,36,000	+ 2,16,000
Fixed Cost	(Rs.)	2,40,000	2,40,000	—
Incremental Profit	(Rs.)	2,40,000	3,84,000	+ 1,44,000
Incremental cost of receivables	(Rs.)	12,000	31,200	+ 19,200
Surplus	(Rs.)	2,28,000	3,52,800	+ 1,24,800

Decision : Since incremental profits Rs. 1,44,000 considerably exceed incremental cost of Rs. 19,200 the management must liberalize credit standard.

Working Notes:

(1) Annual Credit Sales :

(a) Present Plan 60,000 units × Rs. 20 per unit = Rs. 12,00,000

(b) Proposed Plan 78,000 units × Rs. 20 per unit = Rs. 15,60,000

(2) Turnover of Receivable :

(a) Present Plan $= \frac{360 \text{ days}}{30 \text{ days}} = 12$ times

(b) Proposed Plan $= \frac{360 \text{ days}}{60 \text{ days}} = 6$ times

(3) Calculation of Average Accounts Receivable :

$$= \frac{\text{Annual Credit Sales}}{\text{Turnover of Receivables}}$$

(a) Present Plan $= \frac{\text{Rs. } 12{,}00{,}000}{12} = \text{Rs. } 1{,}00{,}000$

(b) Proposed Plan $= \frac{15,60,000}{6}$ = Rs. 2,60,000

(4) Average Investment in receivable :

$$= \frac{\text{Total Cost of Sales}}{\text{Turnover of Receivables}}$$

Total Cost of Sales :

(a) Present Plan = 78,000 units × Rs. 16 per unit

= Rs. 12,48,000

(b) Proposed Plan = 60,000 units × Rs. 16 per unit

= Rs. 9,60,000

∴ **Average Investment in Receivables :**

(a) Present Plan $= \frac{\text{Rs. } 9,60,000}{12 \text{ times}}$ = Rs. 80,000

(b) Proposed Plan $= \frac{12,48,000}{6 \text{ times}}$ = Rs. 2,08,000

Calculation of Incremental Investment in Receivables :

= Average Investment in Receivable of Proposed Plan – Average investment in Receivable of Present Plan

= Rs. 2,08,000 – Rs. 80,000 = Rs. 1,28,000

(6) Calculation of Incremental Cost of Receivables :

= Incremental Investment in Receivables × Rate of Return

= Rs. 1,28,000 × 15 percent

= Rs. 1,28,000 × $\frac{15}{100}$ = Rs. 19,200

llustration: 7

firm has credit sales amounting to Rs. 62,00,000. The sale price per unit is Rs. 40, the ariable cost is Rs.25 per unit while the average cost per unit is Rs. 32. The average age f accounts receivable of the firm is 72 days. The firm is considering to tighten the redit standards. It will result in a fall in the sales volume Rs. 56,00,000, and the average ge of accounts receivable to 45 days. Assume 20% rate of return. Is the proposal under onsideration feasible?

Solution:

Incremental Analysis (tightening credit standard or not)

Particulars	*Present Plan 1,60,000 units*	*Proposed Policy 1,40,000 units*	*Differential Revenues and Costs (decreases)*
Sales Revenue @ Rs. 40 (Rs.)	64,00,000	56,00,000	(-) 8,00,000
Less :			
Variable Cost @ Rs. 25 Per Unit (Rs.)	40,00,000	35,00,000	(–) 5,00,000
Fixed Cost (Rs.)	11,20,000	11,20,000	—
Investment Cost (Rs.)	2,04,800	1,15,500	(–) 89,300
Savings (Deficiency) (Rs.)	10,75,200	8,64,500	(–) 2,10,700

The firm should not adopt more strict credit collection policy, as it will decrease profits by Rs. 2,10,700.

Working Notes:

Investment in accounts receivable :

Present Plan = $\frac{\text{Total Variable Cost + Total Fixed Cost}}{\text{Average age of accounts receivable in a year}}$

Total Variable Cost = 1,60,000 units × Rs. 25 per unit

= Rs. 40,00,000

Total Fixed Cost = 1,60,000 units × Rs. 7 per unit (Rs. 32 – Rs. 25)

= Rs. 11,20,000

Average age of accounts receivable in a year = $\frac{360 \text{ days}}{72 \text{ days}}$ = 5 times

∴ Investment in accounts receivable for present plan = $\frac{\text{Rs. } 40{,}00{,}000 + \text{Rs. } 11{,}20{,}000}{5}$

= $\frac{\text{Rs. } 51{,}20{,}000}{5}$

= Rs. 10,24,000

Investment in accounts receivable for proposed plan = $\frac{\text{Total Variable Cost + Total Fixed Cost}}{360 \div 45 \text{ days}}$

Total Variable Cost = 1,40,000 units × Rs. 25 per unit

= Rs. 35,00,000

Total Fixed Cost = Rs. 11,20,000 (remain constant)

Average age of accounts receivable in a year = $\frac{360 \text{ days}}{45 \text{ days}}$ = 8 times

∴ Investment in accounts receivable for proposed plan = $\frac{\text{Rs. } 35{,}00{,}000 + \text{Rs. } 11{,}20{,}000}{8}$

$= \frac{\text{Rs. } 46{,}20{,}000}{8} = \text{Rs. } 5{,}77{,}500$

Cost Investment :

Present Plan = Rs. 10,24,000 × $\frac{20}{100}$
(20% of Investments in accounts receivable)

= Rs. 2,04,800

Proposed Plan = Rs. 5,77,500 × $\frac{20}{100}$
(20% of Investments in accounts receivable)

= Rs. 1,15,500

Credit Terms

The term credit terms refers to the stipulation under which the firm sells on credit is extended to a customer. Thus, the size of the accounts receivables is also affected by terms of credit. Three important components of the credit terms are : (1) Credit Period (2) Cash Discount, and (3) Cash Discount Period :

(1) Credit Period : The term credit period refers to the period of credit is extended to the customers. It is generally stated in terms of 'net date'. For example, if a firm's credit terms are "net 45", it is expected by the firm that payment will be made 35 days from the date credit sale. The period of credit is also depended on the industry norms and usual practices followed by the firm. The availability of funds and risk involved also determine the credit period. Change in the credit period is also affect the firm's profitability. If lengthening the credit period, the possibility of increasing sales associated with increase in both its collection costs and bad debt losses. In order to maintain the trade off between costs and profitability, the financial manager should formulate optimal credit period for the firm.

(2) Cash Discount : Cash discount is a powerful device to speed up the payment of receivables. Many firms offer cash discount to debtors, in order to encourage them to pay their dues early. It helps to reduction of investment in accounts receivables. The term cash discount indicate the rate of discount and the period for which discount has been offered. In other words, a percent (%) reduction in sales or purchase price allowed for early payment of invoices. It is an incentive for credit customers to pay invoices in a timely fashion. The rate of cash discount determined on the basis of cost of carrying the debtors.

3. Cash Discount Period : The cash discount period represents the period of time during which a cash discount can be taken for early payment. Thus, period of discount also influences average collection of receivables. For example, credit term may be expressed as 3/10, net 30. This implies that a concern may fix 10 days period for allowing a cash discount; all the debtors paying upto 10th day after credit sale will be required to pay after deducting cash discount. If cash discount allowed at 3%, then debtors paying up to 10 days will be required to pay Rs. 97% only out of every Rs. 100. If the period of credit allowed is 30 days then all debtors should pay with in that stipulated period but after 30 days they will not be allowed a cash discount.

(B) Evaluation of Credit : The chief aim of debtors management is to ensure the minimum or optimum investment in receivable and consider able reducing in bad debt losses. In order to achieve this, the financial manager should follow the clear cut principles and procedure to evaluate the credit worthiness of the applicants regarding to how much credit can be extended and how long. The evaluation of credit process consists of the following three important steps :

I. Gathering Credit Information : Credit information gathered about the credit applicant

II. Analysis of customer's Credit Worthiness : Collecting information about the Credit worthiness of the client, his requirement for credit.

III. Credit Decisions : Making decisions to grant credit facilities

I. Gathering Credit Information

Before granting credit facilities to a customer, a firm must identify the sources of information about the customer to assess clients credit worthiness. The amount of information collected needs to be considered in relation to the time and expenses required. The sources for such information are :

(1) Financial Statements (Trading, Profit and Loss Account and Balance Sheet)

(2) Bazar Reports

(3) Reports of Credit Rating Agencies

(4) Reports from Banks

(5) Firm's Own Records

(6) Trade References

(7) Other Sources

(1) Financial Statements : Financial Statement is one of the most desirable sources of information for credit analysis. Audited profit and loss account and Balance sheet shows the operational efficiency of the business of the customer. The study of the current ratio, Liquid ratio and Absolute Liquid ratio are good indicator to know the liquid or financial credit worthiness of the customer. It also indicates the productive ability of the business in order to meet its debts in time.

(2) Bazar Reports : Information about the customers can be obtained from various market particularly from businessmen carrying on the same trade. Such bazar reports are closely related and highly useful to asses the credit worthiness of the customer.

(3) Reports of Credit Rating Agencies : In additional to financial statements and bazaar reports, credit ratings are available from various credit reporting agencies. In recent years organization like National Association of Credit Management, National Credit Office, CRISIL and CARE have been developed for the purpose of credit rating of their customers. These organization provide useful and necessary authentic information about the credit worthiness of customers.

(4) Reports From Banks : Another sources of credit information can be obtained from different banks with which the customer deal. Accordingly, the banker of the customer may be requested to highlight the credit worthiness. The analysist can obtain information such as average cash balance carried, loan availed, financial solvency position and operational efficiency of a customer etc. Normally Indian commercial banks do not give detailed and unqualified credit reference.

(5) Firm's Own Records : Firm's own records highlight the accurate and specific information about the credit standing of the customers. It indicates promptness of past payments, reports from salesmen, seasonal pattern and past experiences with customers while provide useful information about credit worthiness of the customer.

(6) Trade Reference : This is one of the useful sources of information available without cost. Credit information is frequently exchanged among companies selling to the same customer. It may be collected by a firm contracting personally to obtain all relevant information.

(7) Other Sources : Other sources of credit information on business firms, especially the large ones, might be trade journals, periodicals, newspapers, trade directories public records such as income tax statements wealth tax returns, sales tax returns, reports about actions and decrees in government gazettes, registration, revenues and municipal records etc. Normally Indian commercial banks do not give detailed and unqualified credit reference.

II. Analysis of Customer's Credit Worthiness

After collection of credit information about the customer from identified sources, the firm must make analysis of customer's credit worthiness. Proper analysis of credit worthiness helps to establishing credit limits and determine the degree of risk associated with the account. To analysis the credit risk and customer's credit worthiness, the financial manager consider the following four important approaches which are :

(1) Traditional Credit Analysis

(2) Sequential Credit Analysis

(3) Numerical Credit Analysis

(4) Risk—Class Credit Analysis

(1) Traditional Credit Analysis : Traditional Approach to credit analysis which involves assessment of a customer interms of the "five 'C' of credit" will be

(a) Character

(b) Capacity

(c) Capital

(d) Conditions

(e) Collateral

(a) Character : Credit character of a customer refers to the moral trait of a customer which determine his willingness to pay off debts in time. It will reflect the reputation of the company and its management. This should be considered carefully by the credit manager to test of credit character.

(b) Capacity : It indicates the ability of the customer to pay his dues in time. It depends upon the customer's liquidity, ability to pay bills on time, profitability and operational efficiency of the concern.

(c) Capital : Capital represents the financial soundness of the concern during the particular period of time. It also indicates the company's financial resources with which the customer will meet his obligations in time. Customer's tangible net worth is the key factor to be consider to governs the amount of credit.

(d) Conditions : Conditions refer to prevailing economic conditions of the business environment. It includes business cycle, general credit trend and intensity of competition which will affect the conditions ability to meet their obligation .

(e) Collateral : The term collateral refer to the assets given by the firm as security against credit extension. Collateral, thus, serves as a cushion or shock absorber if one or several of the first three 'C's are insufficient to give reasonable assurance of repayment of the loan on maturity. Some time the company may obtaining third part guarantee due to insufficient collateral security.

(2) Sequential Credit Analysis : Under this method, credit analysis can be effectively carried out on the basis of the expected benefit from an order and the cost of investigation. Sequential credit analysis consists of three stages such as (a) review of previous stages of payment records (b) detailed internal analysis and (c) Credit investigation by eternal analysis. Accordingly, credit analysis can be proceeds from one stage to another stage. The first stage consists of simply consulting past experience to see the previous sales and payment records. Internal credit analysis should be undertaken when there is no past payment history of the applicant. Likewise, external credit analysis can be carried further if added cost associated with the previous stage of investigation would not be worthwhile and the customer poses a medium risk. This approach is treated as more efficient method while compare with traditional credit analysis.

(3) Numerical Credit Scoring Method : It is one of the quantitative approaches has been developed to estimate extending trade credit to the customer on the basis of available information. The numerical credit scoring system is more successful in determining the granting of credit which involves the following steps :

(1) Identify the socio-economic and demographic factors relevant for credit evaluation. Relevant factors includes age, education, employment, occupation, experience, annual income. Ownership etc.

(2) Weight allotted to each factors on the basis of their relative importance.

(3) Factors of a customer are quantitatively rated by using suitable rating scale (3 point scale or 5 point scale or 7 point scale).

(4) For each factor, multiply the factor rating with the factor weight to get the factor score.

(5) Add all the factors scores to get the overall customer rating index.

(6) Based on the numerical credit scoring index, identify clearly unacceptable and acceptable, as a credit customer.

(4) Risk—Class Credit Analysis : In credit analysis, Risk—Class Approach is one of the important technique established by Hamption. According to him, customers can be classified into various risk categories ranging from strongest to weakest. These risk class are classified on the basis of gathered information and analysis in the credit investigation process. In order to meet the firm's needs, a separate credit policy is developed in due course for each risk class of credit applicant. The given below table shows the risk classification scheme :

Risk Class	*Description*	*Credit Policy*
Risk Class I	Customer's financial position and past records indicates highly satisfied with no risk of default.	A line of credit is a maximum limit.
Risk Class II	Review of previous records indicates satisfactory with negligible risk exposure	A line of credit is a maximum limit with approval
Risk Class III	Analysis of past payment records and liquidity position indicates less satisfied with little risk of exposure	Streamlines the credit line upto specified limit
Risk Class IV	Less satisfied with moderate risk exposure *i.e.*, some risk of default	Limited credit line with revaluated or frequent check on regular basis
Risk Class V	Not satisfied with maximum risk exposure or default	No credit

It is observed from the above table that a firm placed in risk class I indicates its financial position and past payment records are highlighted highly satisfied with no risk of default. The credit policy of risk class I is that of customer is to be allowed open credit without approval for purchases in excess of maximum amount of specified limit. On the other hand, a firm placed in risk class V indicates maximum risk exposure or default, no credit facilities or limit offered to the customer.

Credit Decisions and Line of Credit

After analysis of customer's credit worthiness, the financial manager has to decide in an initial sale whether or not credit facilities extended to him. If repeat sales are likely, he line of credit procedure can be established in order to avoid the needs of investigate he extension of credit each time an investigate the extension of credit each time an order is received. The term line of credit refers to a limit to the amount of credit extended o an account. Purchaser can buy on credit up to that limit at a given period. Suppose ustomer's past payments records and liquidity position, indicates less satisfied with ttle risk of exposure, the firm should streamlines the credit line up to specified limit. ustomers not satisfied with maximum risk exposure, the firm has to decide instead of utright refusing to grant credit facilities, be offered cash on delivery terms. In practice, redit decision and line of credit can be fixed on the basis of customer's regular buying end, past payment records, liquidity position, streamline the operation and defining esponsibilities of concern executives.

nportant Function of a Credit Manager

he following are the important functions of a credit manager

(1) Establish appropriate credit policy.

(2) Maintaining credit card of a customer.

(3) Assess customer's credit worthiness.

(4) Formulation of clear cut credit procedure.

(5) Ensure effective administration of trade debtors.

(6) Ensure effective credit control system.

(7) Establish a policy on bad debts.

(8) Sent reminders to the slow payers.

(9) Systematic review should be carried on existing debtors.

(10) Make prompt decision about extending credit to customers.

(11) Encourage customers initiate payment sooner rather than letter.

(12) Arrange training facilities to credit department personnel's.

(13) Gathering reliable information from identified sources before allowing trade credit.

(14) Ensure no goods are despatched until it has been vouched.

(15) Give proper response on customer's complaints.

(16) Make co-ordination with other departments.

(17) Take legal actions in the case of default.

Collection Policy and Procedures

After giving credit, the next stage involved in planning of receivables is collection policies. An efficient management of receivables calls for designing clear cut collection policy of the firm and laid down collection procedure. These procedures include things such as remaining of customers letters, phone calls, personal visits and legal action. The purpose of every collection policy is to speed up the collection of from dues from slow—payers after expiry of the credit period. A concern to incur expenses on credit collection efforts. Efficient and timely collection of dues ensures that the bad debt losses are reduced to the minimum and the average collection period is short. Other things remaining the same, if the firm spends more amount on collection efforts, the lower the proportion of bad-debt losses and the shorter is the average collection period. On the other hand, lenient collection policy would be increase in bad debt losses increase in collection period and increase in collection cost. Thus, a firm must workout the optimum amount that it should spend on collection of debtors.

Steps in Debt Collection

The following effective steps to be taken for ensuring minimum bad debts and cost on collection efforts :

(1) Designing appropriate collection policy.

(2) Ensuring proper system collection of accounts receivable.

(3) Organizing a collection cell to keep the amount of outstanding in check.

(4) Send reminders including letters, phone calls, personal visits etc.

(5) Taking other necessary steps to collect the dues.

(6) Fixing specific responsibility for collection dues.

(7) Take legal actions be instituted against default.

(8) Obtaining third party guarantee for settlement in case of dispute.

(9) Organizing collection machinery to ensure the reduction of collection expenditure

(10) Insuring the accounts receivable.

Norms for Effective Collection System

The effectiveness of credit policy and collection system could be known through th following norms :

(1) The ratio of credit sales to total sales.

(2) The percentage, the outstanding bear to total credit sales.

(3) Percentage of accounts receivable outstanding beyond the sanctioned credit limits to total credit sales and accounts receivable.

(4) The percentage the accounts receivable bear to total resources.

(5) The quality of the account accepted.

(6) The length of the credit period.

(7) The size of the cash discount given.

(8) Any special terms such as seasonal dating.

(9) The level of collection expenditure.

(10) Better co-ordination between sales, production and finance departments.

(11) Well defined collection programme.

(1) Factors Influencing the Size of Receivables : The role which receivables play in the total fiancial picture directly or indirectly affected by the following important factors :

(1) Size of Credit Sales

(2) Credit Policies

(3) Terms of Trade

(4) Profits

(5) Credit Collection Policies

(6) Expansion Plans

(7) Habits of Customers

(8) Operating Efficiency

(9) Size of Market

(1) Size of Credit Sales : Size of credit sales is one of the important factor in determining the volume of receivables. With an increase in the size of credit sales, it may decide to bring about a proportionate increase in the magnitude of receivables. If a firm sells only on cash basis there will no increase or decrease in the size of receivables.

(2) Credit Policies : A firm may be adopt liberal credit policy or restrictive credit policy. The concern with a liberal credit policy will have a higher level receivables while a firm with strict credit policies, the size of the receivables will be high. Moreover, credit worthiness of the customers, extension of credit facilities incidence of bad debt loss, collection charges and terms of credit etc. are the important aspects of credit policies to affect the size of its receivables.

(3) Terms of Trade : The size of the receivables is closely associated with a firm's trade credit. The length of credit period and the rate of discount given also depends upon the size of receivables. The pressure of competitors always tends to constrain a firm to offer credit terms which are at least as generous as those offered by competitors. The terms of credit thus become almost customary.

(4) Profits : A firm's added expected profitability on the additional sales is one of the important aspect of determining size of receivables. As the level of receivable increases the cost of investment in receivable also goes up. However, the profitability of additional sales generated exceeds the added cost of the receivables.

(5) Credit Collection Policies : Size of the receivables depends upon the appropriate collection policy of the firm. Prompt collection of account tends to reduce investment required to carry receivables and the costs associated with it.

(6) Expansion of Credit Plan : Expansion of credit plan is usually stimulate the volume of credit sales and attracting more customers. Expansion of credit facilities is likely to increase the working capital investment in receivables.

(7) Habits of Customers : Paying habits of customers is one of the factor also influence the size of the receivables. There are certain type of customers who consistently pay their debts promptly. Some other customers may be delaying payments though they are financially sound. Thus, it ensures the earliest possible payment on receivables without customer losses though ill will.

(8) Operating Efficiency : Establishment of credit department and its functions of operating efficiency in billing, record keeping, inspecting the credit worthy of customers, reminder or follow up letters etc. are the important aspect of determinination of the size of the size of receivables.

(9) Size of Market : Size of receivables are closely associated with a firm to explore a new market for its product or services. More liberal extension of credit, a firm can easily enter in to a new market by attracting new customers. This factor will make the firms to arrange additional size of receivables.

Control of Accounts Receivable

The following are the important approaches undertaken for controlling the accounts receivable :

I. Traditional Approach :

(a) Ageing Schedule Technique

(b) Days Sales Outstanding (DSO)

II. Modern Approach :

(a) Control of Average Collection Period

(b) Determination of Cost of Goods Sold

(c) Control of Discount Facilities

(d) Control of Administrative Cost, collection cost and bad debts

I. Traditional Approach : Traditionally, two approaches has been developed for controlling accounts receivables such as:

(a) Ageing Schedule Technique and (b) Day's Sales—Outstanding (DSO) Method

(a) Ageing Schedule Technique : A firm has to control the level of sales with each alternative for the age of receivables. This technique classifies the outstanding debtors at a given point of time into different age groups. Usually the greater the age of the receivables, the greater is the level of credit sales. Many concerns prepare this schedule at periodic intervals for the purpose of controlling quality of individual account receivables. The given below illustration will clarify the same.

Age Classes (in Days)	% of Accounts Receivable (Debtors)
0—30	29%
31—60	48%
61—90	17%
91 and more	7%

The ageing schedule (actual) of a firm is compared with some standard ageing schedule to find out whether the debtors are in control or not.

(b) Day's Sales Outstanding (DSO) Approach : This technique refers to the ratio of the outstanding debtors at a given point of time to average daily sales figure during the preceding a month, 2 months or 3 months etc. Day's sales outstanding may be determined by using given below formula :

$$\text{Day's Sales Outstanding (DSO)} = \frac{\text{Debtors at a given time}}{\text{Average Daily Sales}}$$

It can be explained with following illustration :

Illustration: 7

ABC Ltd supplied you the following information relating to the first 3 months of the year 2004, from which you are requested to calculate Day's Sales Outstanding.

Month	*Sales* Rs.	*Debtors* Rs.
January	6,00,000	16,00,000
February	6,24,000	14,40,000
March	6,32,000	12,80,000

Solution:

$$\text{Day's Sales Outstanding (DSO)} = \frac{\text{Accounts Receivable at a given time}}{\text{Average Daily Sales}}$$

$$\text{Average Daily Sales} = \frac{\text{Rs. }6{,}00{,}000 + \text{Rs. }6{,}24{,}000 + \text{Rs. }6{,}32{,}000}{90 \text{ days}}$$

$$= \frac{\text{Rs. }18{,}56{,}000}{90 \text{ days}}$$

$$\text{Day's Sales Outstanding Ratio} = \frac{\text{Rs. }12{,}80{,}000}{20622.22}$$

$$= 62.06 \text{ days}$$

Days Sales Outstanding Ratio for the first quarter of 2004 of 62.06 days indicates that debt collection policy of ABC Ltd is not quiet satisfactory.

II. Modern Approach :

(a) Control of Average Collection Period : This approach involves preparation of statement which reflects the pattern of collection from account receivable associated with credit sales. It is necessary for a firm to control its average collection period. Many concerns now-a-days have adopted this method, to control the percentage of those likely to make late payments.

Computation of average age of receivable involves the computation of average collection period. Two ratios are used to judge firm's liquidity position on the basis of efficiency of credit collection and credit policy. They are (1) Debtor's Turnover Ratio and (2) Debt Collection Period. Debtors Turnover Ratio is also termed as Receivable Turnover Ratio or Debtors Velocity. Debtors velocity indicates the number of time the receivables are turned over in business during a particular period. In other words it indicates that how quickly the debtors are converted into cash. This ratio establishes the relationship between receivables and sales. This ratio may be computed as :

$$\text{Debtor's Turnover Ratio} = \frac{\text{Net Credit Sales}}{\text{Average Receivables (or) Average Accounts Receivables}}$$

$$\text{Net Credit Sales} = \text{Total Sales} - \text{Cash Sales}$$

$$\text{Accounts Receivables} = \text{Sundry Debtors or Trade Debtors} + \text{Bills Receivable}$$

$$\text{Average Accounts Receivable} = \frac{\text{Opening Receivable} + \text{Closing Receivable}}{2}$$

It is to be noted that opening and closing receivable and credit sales are not available, this ratio may be calculated as :

$$\text{Debtor's Turnover Ratio} = \frac{\text{Total Sales}}{\text{Accounts Receivable}}$$

Illustration: 8

Calculate Debtor's Turnover Ratio, from the following information.

	Rs.
Sundry Debtors as on 1.1.2004	7,00,000
Sundry Debtors as on 31.12.2004	9,00,000
Bills Receivable as on 1.1.2004	2,00,000
Bills Receivable as on 31.12.2004	3,00,000
Total Sales for the year 2004	70,00,000
Sales Return	2,00,000
Cash Sales for the year 2004	10.00,000

Solution:

$$\text{Debtors Turnover Ratio} = \frac{\text{Net Credit Sales}}{\text{Average Account Receivable}}$$

$$\text{Net Credit Sales} = \text{Total Sales} - (\text{Credit Sales} + \text{Sales Return})$$

$$= \text{Rs. } 70,00,000 - (\text{Rs. } 10,00,000 + \text{Rs. } 2,00,000)$$

$$= \text{Rs. } 58,00,000$$

$$\text{Average Accounts Receivable} = \frac{\text{Opening Receivable} + \text{Closing Receivable}}{2}$$

$$= \frac{(\text{Rs. } 7,00,000 + \text{Rs. } 2,00,000) + (\text{Rs. } 9,00,000 + \text{Rs. } 3,00,000)}{2}$$

$$= \frac{\text{Rs. } 9,00,000 + \text{Rs. } 12,00,000}{2}$$

$$= \frac{\text{Rs. } 21,00,000}{2} = \text{Rs. } 10,50,000$$

$$\text{Debtor's Turnover Ratio} = \frac{\text{Rs. } 10,50,000}{2} = 5.52 \text{ times}$$

alculation of Average Collection Period

erage Collection Period otherwise called as Debt Collection Period. This technique of mputation of average collection period indicates the efficiency of the debt collection riod and the extent to which the debt have been converted into cash. Both the chniques are used to measure the quality of accounts receivable. It point-out the uidity of trade debtors *i.e.*, higher turnover ratio and shorter debt collection period dicate that prompt payments by debtors. Similarly, low turnover ratio and higher llection period implies that payment by trade debtor are delayed. The Debt Collection riod can be determined as follows :

$$\text{Debt Collection Period} = \frac{\text{Month or Days in a Year}}{\text{Debtor's Turnover}}$$

(or)

$$\text{Debt Collection Period} = \frac{\text{Average Accounts Receivable} \times \text{Month or Days in a Year}}{\text{Net Credit Sales in a Year}}$$

ustration: 9

om the following information calculate (a) Debtor's Turnover Ratio and (b) Debt Collection riod

	Rs.
Total Sales	10,00,000
Cash Sales	2,50,000
Sales Return	50,000
Opening Accounts Receivable	1,00,000
Closing Accounts Receivable	1,50,000

lution:

Calculation of Debtor's Turnover Ratio :

$$\text{(a) Debtor's Turnover Ratio} = \frac{\text{Net Credit Sales}}{\text{Average Accounts Receivables}}$$

Net Credit Sales = Total Sales – (Cash Sales + Sales Return)

= Rs. 10,00,000 – (Rs. 2,50,000 + Rs. 50,000)

= Rs. 10,00,000 – Rs. 3,00,000

= Rs. 7,00,000

$$\text{Average Receivables} = \frac{\text{Opening Receivable} + \text{Closing Receivable}}{2}$$

$$= \frac{\text{Rs. 1,00,000} + \text{Rs. 1,50,000}}{2}$$

$$= \frac{\text{Rs. 2,50,000}}{2} = \text{Rs. 1,25,000}$$

$$\therefore \text{Debtor's Turnover Ratio} = \frac{\text{Rs. 7,00,000}}{\text{Rs. 1,25,000}} = 5.6 \text{ times}$$

Calculation of Debt Collection Period :

$$\text{Debt Collection Period} = \frac{\text{Average Accounts Receivable} \times \text{Month or Days in a Year}}{\text{Net Credit Sales for the Year}}$$

$$= \frac{\text{Rs. 1,25,000} \times 12 \text{ Months}}{\text{Rs. 7,00,000}} = 2.14 \text{ Months}$$

Alternatively :

$$\text{Debt Collection Period} = \frac{\text{Month or Days in a Year}}{\text{Debtor's Turnover Ratio}}$$

$$= \frac{12 \text{ Months}}{5.6 \text{ times}} = 2.14 \text{ Months}$$

(b) Determination of Cost of Good Sold : While the level of sales, it is essential for firm to determine the cost of goods sold which have been sold. Suppose, this cost is 60 of the sales, when sales level is Rs.17 lakhs. It may be reduced to 55% of the sales lev is increased to Rs.23 lakhs. It would be better for the firm to decide to keep the level sales Rs.23 lakhs in order to take fullest advantage of the efficient utilization of pla and machinery.

(c) Control of Discount Facilities : A firm estimates the number of customers wl might take advantages of its discount facilities. Past data and experience of other fir in the industry may be pressed into service for this purpose. It is, therefore, very importa for a firm to forecast the percentage of customers who would take advantage of speci discount terms.

(d) Control of Administration Costs, Collection Cost and Bad Debts : A fir maintains a detailed accounts and records of the cost of administration, collection ar bad debts losses for different credit policies. An increase in the size of receivables likely to setup administrative and collection costs, and bad debts losses. However, these expenses and losses are sufficiently compensated by an expenses and losses a sufficiently compensated by an increase in the gains emerging from an increase sales, a firm may decide infavour of increasing its sales levels.

Factoring of Receivables

Factoring is among the oldest of financial services for facilitating trade transactior The term factor refers to a person who buys trade receivables with or without resourc actoring is a method by which a businessman can pledged the trade receivables as llateral to obtain cash. This is called discounting of receivables or Invoice discounting. ommercial banks and financial companies are the leading institutions involves by rangement and servicing the receivables the factor receives a commission. The mmission varies according to the size of the individual accounts, the volume of ceivables sold and the quality of the account.

efinition

ctoring may be defined as a continuing arrangement between a financial institution .e factor) and a business concern (the client) selling goods or services to trade customers e customers) where by the factor purchases and clients book debts (accounts ceivable)either with or without resources to the client and in relating there to controls credit extended to the customers and administers the sales ledger.

nction of Factoring

actor perform the following important functions for his client :

(1) Administration of the seller's sales ledger.
(2) Provision of prepayment against the debt purchased.
(3) Undertakes the responsibility of collecting the receivables for his client.
(4) Covering the risk involved.
(5) Effective credit control and credit protection.
(6) Rendering useful advisory services.
(7) Supplying necessary information to the clients.
(8) Offers a distinct solution to the problems posed by working capital tied up in trade debts.

pes of Factoring

(1) Full Factoring
(2) Recourse Factoring
(3) Maturity Factoring
(4) Advance Factoring
5) Undisclosed Factoring
6) Invoice Discounting
7) Bulk Factoring

(1) Full Factoring : Under full factoring, a factor provides finance, maintains sales er, undertakes collection of receivables, offer credit control and risk bearing against debts. When a firm factors its receivable may be either with or without resources ending upon the type of arrangement negotiated. If the factor arrangement has been e as factoring with resource, the liability to repay the dues vests with the clients. he other hand, the liability of the factor is limited only to the defaults arising out of ts financial inability to pay.

2) Resource Factoring : It is otherwise termed factoring with recourse or with urse factoring. Under this method, the factor does not provide any protection against debts in case customers failure to pay debts. If the customers failure to pay debts. If the customer fails to pay his dues on maturity on any reason, the factor is entitled t recover from the client, the amount paid in advance.

(3) Maturing Factoring : It is also called as collection factoring. Under this methoc factor offer only services relating to maintaining clients sales ledger and renders deb collection services.

(4) Advance Factoring : Under this method of factoring, factor is provide finance i advance for clients debts. This is only a prepayment arrangement and not an advance

(5) Undisclosed Factoring : In this undisclosed factoring, instead of making a sal direct to the customer, on arrival of the time for delivery goods sold to a factor for cas who then appoints the business as its agent to collect the debt outstanding. The facto maintain the sales ledger on the basis of the copy of the invoice :

(6) Invoice Discounting : Under this method, factors offer financial services only t his selected customers invoice on the basis prescribed rate of discount.

(7) Bulk Factoring : Under this arrangement, the factor buy total agreed bunch c invoices of the customer. The responsibility of maintaining sales ledger and collectio of debts are vests with customer himself.

QUESTIONS

(1) What do you understand by accounts receivable?

(2) What are the objectives of receivable management?

(3) Explain the benefits of receivable management.

(4) Discuss the major costs involved in maintaining accounts receivables.

(5) What are the important dimensions of a firm's credit policy? Explain them in detail

(6) Define credit standard.

(7) Explain the types of credit standard.

(8) Discuss the effect of liberal credit standard.

(9) Discuss the effect of strict credit standard.

(10) What are the effect of liberalizing credit standard on profit?

(11) Write Short Notes On :

(a) Credit Period

(b) Cash Discount

(c) Cash Discount Period

(12) How would you judge the credit worthiness of a customer?

(13) Discuss the sources of credit information gathered about the credit applicant.

(14) Discuss the following methods of credit analysis :

(1) Traditional Credit Analysis

(2) Sequential Credit Analysis

(3) Numerical Credit Analysis

(4) Risk—Class Credit Analysis

(15) What are the important functions of a credit manager?

(16) Critically evaluate the collection policy and procedure.

(17) Explain the steps involved in debt collection.

(18) What are the norms for effective collection system?

(19) Discuss the factors influencing the size of receivables.

(20) Discuss the different approaches for controlling accounts receivable.

(21) What you understand by Factoring?

(22) Explain the functions of Factoring.

(23) Discuss in details in different kinds of factoring.

PRACTICAL PROBLEMS

(1) A firm has annual credit sales of Rs. 15,00,000 at "net 40". Management is wondering whether, they should increase by 15% or 25%. The reason is that it sales are increased by 15% , the average collection period will have to be raised to 60 days and the bad debts would also increase from 1.5% to 4%. If sales are increased by 25% , the firms average collection period will have to 90 days and bad debts would be increased to 6%. The selling price of the product is Rs.50 per unit and Rs.30 is per unit variable cost. The firm is required to pay taxes at 40% on profit before tax. Would you advise the firm to relax its credit policy? Which plan is better?

(Ans : Plan II (–) Rs. 2,900 and Plan III (–) Rs. 12,000 Both Plans are not considered as satisfactory)

(2) ABC Ltd currently provides 45 days of credit to its customers. Its present level of sales is Rs. 1.5. crores. The firm's cost of capital is 15 percent and the ratio of variable costs to sales is 0.80. The firm is considering extending its credit period to 60 days. Such an extension is likely to bush sales up by Rs. 15 lakhs. The bad debt proportion on additional sales would be 5 percent. What will be the effect of lengthening the credit period on the gross profit of the firm?

(3) A firm has credit sales amounting Rs. 32,00,000. This sales price per unit is Rs. 40; the variable cost is Rs. 25 per unit while the average cost per unit is Rs. 32. The average age of accounts receivable of the firm is 72 days. The firm is planning to tighten credit standards. It will result in a fall in the sales volume to Rs. 28,00,000 and the average age of accounts receivable to 45 days.

Assume a 20% rate of return. Is the proposal under consideration feasible?

(4) A firm has sales of Rs. 5,00,000 and desires 15% return on investment. It is thinking of relaxing its credit policy by increasing the average collection period from 45 days to 90 days, where by sales are estimated to increase by Rs. 50,000. The price of the product per unit is Rs. 200. The variable cost and the average total cost per unit are Rs. 150 and Rs. 175 respectively.

You are required to advise the firm whether it should relax its credit policy.

(5) XYZ Ltd's credit sales amount to Rs. 60 lakhs with variable cost to sales ratio of 60% and annual fixed cost of Rs. 12 lakhs. Its present credit policy is 60 days. It proposes to introduce 2% discount if payment is received before the 10th day after the date of invoice. Payment is ordinarily due to the 60th day. It is also estimated that 50% of debtors will take advantage of the discount scheme. As a result, the average of debtors would be reduced to 1 month. The required rate of return on investment in debtors may be taken at 20% before tax. Evaluate the proposal.

(6) The management of Gupta & Co Ltd is contemplating a increase in credit period from

30 days to 50 days. The average collection period, which is at present 40 days, is likely to increase to 60 days. It is further expected that bad debts expenses will increase from the current level of 1 percent to 2 percent sales. Total credit sales are expected to increase from the level of 25,000 unit to 40,000 units. The present average cost per unit is Rs. 16 the variable cost per unit Rs.12 and sales per unit Rs. 20. The management expects 20 percent rate of return.

Should the management lengthen the credit period?

(Ans : Incremental benefits of Rs. 60,000 considerably exceed incremental costs of Rs. 20,667, the management should decide to lengthen credit period)

GLOSSARY OF TERMS

solute Liquid Ration :

It establishes the relationship between the absolute liquid assets and current bilities.

solute Liquid Assets :

It includes cash in hand, cash at bank and marketable securities.

gressive Policy :

Lower level of current asset to fixed assets. It indicates higher risk and poor liquidity ition.

crued Expenses :

A firm can postpone the payment of expenses for shorter period is referred to as standing expenses.

C Analysis :

Always Better Control (ABC) which is based on grading the items to the importance of erials.

normal Loss :

Arise during the storage of materials due to unavoidable causes of evaporation, nkage, bluk losses due to accident, fire etc.

ual Price Method :

Materials issued are priced at their actual cost and this involves identification of lot purchased.

ounts Receivable :

Debt owned to the firm by customers arising from sale of goods or services.

ance Sheet Working Capital :

Balance Sheet Working Capital is one which is calculated from the items appearing e Balance Sheet.

Bank Credit :

Important external source of medium and short-term source of working capital.

Banker's Acceptance :

It is an instrument that are accepted by banks, and they are used in financing international trade.

William J. Baumol Model :

The optimum cash level is that level of cash where the carrying costs and transaction cost and the minimum.

Bin Cards :

Quantitative record of stores receipt, issue and balance and it kept by the store keeper for each item of stores.

Bill of Materials :

A document which shows a complete listing for each material, quantity to be issued against each component requiring that materials for a particular job order or process.

Concentration Banking :

A system of decentralized collection of accounts receivable.

Cash Forecast :

A Summary of expected cash inflows and outflows over a period of time.

Cash Budget :

A budget is planned for a shorter period to anticipate short term financing.

Cash Flow Statement :

A statement is prepared to movement of cash inclusive of inflow of cash and outflow of cash.

Codification of Materials :

Codification is the process of representing each item by a number, the digits of which indicate the group, the sub group the type and the size and shape of the items.

Continuous Stock Verification :

It ensures that the balances of items of stocks are checked atleast three to four times in a year by physical verification.

Cash Discount :

Allowed by the supplier to a buyer to encourage prompt payment of cash within the stipulated period.

Credit Standard :

The minimum quality of credit worthiness of a credit applicant that is acceptable to the firm.

Credit Terms :

The stipulation under which the firm sells on credit is extended to a customer.

Credit Period :

The period of credit is extended to the customers.

Cash Discount Period :

The period of time during which a cash discount can be taken for early payment.

Current Assets :

Those assets which in the ordinary course of business can be, or will be, turned in to cash with in one year.

Current Liabilities :

Those liabilities which are interned at their inception to be paid in the ordinary course of business with in a year.

Cash Working Capital :

A firm's cash working capital is required to make payments to its suppliers, to incur day to day expenses.

Current Ratio :

It establishes the relationship between current assets and current liabilities.

Current Assets to Fixed Assets Ratio :

It establishes the relationship between current assets and fixed assets on the basis of liquidity, risk, level of output and returns.

Conservative Policies :

Assuming a constant level of fixed assets a higher current assets to fixed assets ratio.

Customer Credit :

Installment credit as it is usually allowed by retailers for selling consumer durable goods.

Cash :

Near cash assets. It includes coins, currency notes, bank draft, with draws by cheques on demand and bank balances in bank accounts.

Commercial Paper :

A commercial paper is a short term usance promissory note issued by a company, negotiable by endorsement and delivery, issued at such a discount on face value as any be determined by the issuing company.

Depreciation :

Decrease in the value of asset due to wear and tear, lapse of tie obsolescence, exhaustion and accident.

Discounting Bills :

Companies can get the medium and short term working capital assistance by discounting their bill of exchange, promissory notes and hundies from banks.

Danger Level :

The stock level below the minimum level which indicates the danger point to affect the normal production.

Excessive Working Capital :

Idle funds which earn no profits for the firm.

Factoring :

It involves provision of specialized services relating to credit investigation, sales ledger management, purchase collection of debts, credit protection as well as provision of finance against receivables and risk bearing.

Economic Order Quantity (EOQ) :

A technique used to determine the optimum quantity or number of orders to be placed from the suppliers.

Float :

The period that affect cash as it moves through the different stages of the collection process.

Fund :

Refers to cash, to cash equivalent or to working capital and all financial resources which are used in business.

Flow of Fund :

Refers to changes or movement of funds or changes in working capita in the normal course of business transactions takes place.

Fund Flow Statement :

A Statement summarizing the significant financial changes in items of financial position which have occurred between the two different balance sheet dates.

First In First Out (FIFO) :

Pricing of materials issued is based on a assumption made that the oldest stock is issued first.

Five 'C' of Credit :

Character, Capacity, Capital, Conditions, Collateral.

Gross Working Capital :

Firm's investments in total current or circulating assets.

Global Depository Receipts :

Depository Receipts issued by a company any where in the global other than USA.

Highest In First Out (HIFO) :

Materials purchased at the highest price should be used for making the issue.

Inadequate Working Capital :

Impairs firm's profitability and liquidity.

Inventories :

Includes all requirements in raw materials, work in progress and consumable items.

Inventory Control :

Concerned with the control of quantities or monetary value of these items at predetermined level or with in safe limits.

Inventory Turnover Ratio :

It establishes the relationship between the cost of goods sold during a given period and the average of the cost of opening and closing stock.

Inflated Price Method :

When the issue of materials is made, the price is to inflated to cover all the loses and expenses.

Liquidity :

The ability of a firm to meet its obligations in the short run usually one year (or) The extent of quick convertibility of short term nature.

Liquid Assets :

Those assets which can be immediately converted into cash.

Long Term Loans :

Important sources of permanent working capital.

Lock-box System :

Another means of accelerating the flow of funs is a lock-box arrangement.

Last In First Out (LIFO) :

The price of the materials to be issued would be the cost price of the last lots of materials purchased.

Moderate Policies :

It occurs between higher and lower ratio of current assets to fixed assets ratio.

Millor-Orr Cash Management Model :

According to their model, when cash balance reaches the upper limit the transfer of cash equal to "h—z" is invested in marketable securities account.

Minimum Stock Level :

Minimum quantity of materials to be maintained in stock.

Maximum Stock Level :

Maximum quantity of an item should not allowed to increase.

Material Requisition :

Intent for materials which is prepared by the production department for requisition of materials.

Market Price Method :

Issue of materials valued at the market rate prevailing at the time of issue.

Net Working Capital :

The portion of a firm's current assets which is financed with long term funds.

Net Working Capital Turnover Ratio :

It establishes the relationship between cost of sales and net working capital.

Negotiable Certificate of Deposits :

Certificate of deposits are negotiable instruments evidencing of the deposits of funds at a commercial bank for a specified period of time at a specified rate of interest.

Non-Current Liabilities :

Any Amount owing by the business which are payable over a longer period time.

Normal Loss :

Normal loss arise during the storage of materials due to the avoidable reasons of pilferage, theft, careless of materials handling clerical errors, improper storage, wrong entries etc.

Operating Cycle :

The time—lag between the sale of a product and the realization of cash.

Ordering Costs :

The variable cost associated with placing an order for the materials.

Overstock Cost :

Cost associated with carrying inventory result when there is a stock left on hand after the demand for the item has terminated.

Positive Net Working Capital :

Will arise when the excess of current assets over the current liabilities.

Permanent Working Capital :

The minimum amount of current assets which are kept by a firm over the entire year to ensure uninterrupted course of operation.

Percentage Sales Method :

The requirement of working capital can be determined on the basis of sales, amount of working capital required and prior year's experiences.

Periodic Inventory System :

Quantity and value of materials are checked and verified at the end of the accounting period after having physical verification of the units in hand.

Perpetual Inventory System :

A method of recording stores balances after every receipts and issue to facilitate regular checking and to obviate closing down for stock taking.

erpetual Inventory Records :

A system of record maintained by the organization.

eriodic Simple Average Method :

The issue price is calculated by totaling the unit price of all materials purchased ıring a particular period by the total number of prices during the period.

eriodic Weighted Average Method :

Under this method issue rate is calculated by total cost of materials purchased during eriod by the total quantity of materials purchased during that period.

uick Ratio :

It establishes the relationship between the liquid assets and current liabilities.

uick Assets :

It includes all current assets except inventories and prepaid expenses.

uantity Discount :

The allowance which is allowed by the supplier to the buyer to encourage large orders.

w Materials :

All commodities or components which are consumed in the process of manufacture.

-Order Level :

It indicates when to order *i.e.* order for its fresh supplies for procuring additional entory equal to the economic order quantity.

are :

Share in the capital of a company and includes stock except where a distinction ween stock and share is expressed or implied.

ort Costs :

The expenses incurred as a result of short fall of cash.

tement of changes in Working Capital :

This statement helps to measure the movement or changes of working capital during ırticular period.

ck-Out Costs :

Cost incurred when an item is out of stock.

res Ledger :

Both quantitative and monetary value record of stores receipt, issue and balance and repared by cost accounting department.

ple Average Method :

Price of issue materials is determined by dividing the total of the prices of the erials in stock *i.e.* adding of different prices by the number of different prices.

Standard Price Method :

Standard price of material issues are calculated on the basis of detailed analysis o market prices and trends.

Temporary Working Capital :

Extra Working Capital needed changing production and sales activities (or) Additiona current assets required to meet fluctuations during the operating year.

Trade Credit :

Form of medium and short term finance granted by the seller of raw materials an goods to manufacturer.

Treasury Securities :

Type of marketable securities.

Trade Discount :

Allowed by the seller to the buyer who has to recall the goods.

Working Capital :

Excess of current assets over current liabilities and provisions.

Work-in-Progress :

These are processed or semi-finished products manufactured at various stages durir the production cycles.

Weighted Average Method :

The price of materials issue is determined by dividing the total cost of materials stock by the total quantity of material in stock.